Achieving

QTS

meeting the **professional standards framework**

Learning and
Teaching

in Primary Schools

Achieving QTS

meeting the **professional standards framework**

Learning and Teaching

in Primary Schools

Denis Hayes

LearningMatters

First published in 2009 by Learning Matters Ltd

British Library Cataloguing in Publication Data
A CIP record for this book is available from the British Library

ISBN 978 1 84445 202 6

Cover design by Topics – The Creative Partnership
Project Management by Deer Park Productions, Tavistock, Devon
Typesetting by PDQ Typesetting Ltd, Newcastle-under-Lyme
Printed and bound in Great Britain by Bell & Bain Ltd, Glasgow

Learning Matters Ltd
33 Southernhay East
Exeter EX1 1NX
Tel: 01392 215560
info@learningmatters.co.uk
www.learningmatters.co.uk

Contents

The author

After spending 17 years in a variety of primary schools, including two deputy headships, a headship, as well as being a former Professor of Education at the University of Plymouth, Denis Hayes is now an education writer and consultant. His principal interests relate to classroom practice, the teacher's role and the emotions of teaching. Denis is widely published and has written numerous books, all with relevance to primary teaching. He believes that the vast majority of primary teachers are motivated by altruism and the opportunity to influence young minds positively, such that teaching is as much a 'calling' as a career. Denis has researched many aspects of motivation for teaching and trainee teacher experiences on school placement.

1
Teachers and teaching today

Learning outcomes

To understand:

- **recent trends in primary education;**
- **constituents of classroom interaction;**
- **the relationship between teaching skills and strategies;**
- **how creative teaching can be recognised and promoted;**
- **the part relationships play in effective teaching.**

Introduction

Learning and Teaching in Primary Schools aims to inform, challenge and offer you, the reader, opportunities to grapple with the complexities that attend regular systematic teaching and innovative, creative teaching. Throughout the book there is an emphasis on human interactions in classrooms, taking close account of the realities facing new and inexperienced teachers. Threaded throughout the book are questions and dilemmas intended to stir, stimulate and cut deep to the heart of the educational enterprise. If you are looking for formulaic, conventional, 'ready-made meal' approaches to teaching, look elsewhere!

Chapter 1 sets the scene by introducing key terminology used throughout the book and offering some insight into the educational issues that face teachers. Chapter 2 looks in depth at the concept of an 'effective' or 'good' teacher and probes ways in which effectiveness can be achieved. Chapter 3 engages with the fundamental issues associated with organising and managing a group or class of pupils. Chapter 4 explores the knowledge and techniques required to master the single most important interactive teaching skill, that of *questioning*. Chapter 5 deals with the area of teaching that is often of greatest concern to student teachers and newly qualified teachers, namely, maintaining discipline without endangering a purposeful learning environment. Chapter 6 contains a lot of practical advice about enhancing classroom communication and Chapter 7 interrogates creativity and its twin cousins, imagination and spirituality. Chapters 8 and 9 deal specifically with exploring and meeting the QTS Standards, which are simply referred to as Q Standards throughout the book; thus: Q1, Q2, and so on. Chapter 10 concludes by asking whether the job of teacher is truly worthwhile.

An essential part of being a teacher is to develop the habit of reflecting on what has taken place in the classroom and consider helpful modifications to classroom practice. To develop these skills *Learning and Teaching in Primary Schools* includes practical task boxes as well as a number of Reflective task boxes, with statements and questions to challenge and extend thinking. The statements are designed to be sufficiently provocative to stimulate the reader to consider the related issues in depth and contemplate their implications for classroom practice. In addition, Research summaries are offered throughout the book to provide a window on recent education research and scholarship.

The suggestions, descriptions and advice given throughout the book are principally concerned with the work of teachers but also have considerable relevance for the army of teaching assistants (TAs) that support pupil learning. Education has always been a collaborative effort between parents, teachers and ancillary staff; this principle has gained credence over the years and is now enshrined in legislation and education practice.

Recent trends in primary education (Q3a)

The rate of change in school policy and practice during the late twentieth and early twenty-first centuries has been and remains extremely rapid. In recent years primary teachers have had to implement a revised version of the National Curriculum, a structured approach to teaching mathematics and literacy and an inclusive policy to accommodate emotionally vulnerable pupils and those with disabilities. Schools have also had to increase substantially the number of teaching assistants, provide ever more detailed reports to parents about their children's progress, play a greater role in training new teachers and demonstrate a commitment to employing creative approaches to teaching and learning. New initiatives include expanded opportunities for regular physical exercise, healthy eating, breakfast clubs, extension classes in literacy, homework clubs and facilities for children requiring pre- and post-school supervision (extended schools initiative or 'wrap-around' provision).

The government has also stated its intentions to create 'joined up' provision for children and young people up to the age of 19 years through its initiative, *Every Child Matters: Change for Children* (DfES, 2005). The aim is for all children, regardless of their background or circumstances, to be supported in staying healthy and safe, achieving success, making a positive contribution to society and learning how to handle their finances. As a result, the organisations involved with providing services to children (schools, police, voluntary groups and so on) share information and work together to protect and empower children and young people. The first Children's Commissioner for England was appointed in March 2005 to pay particular attention to gathering and promoting the views of those considered most vulnerable. As part of the strategy, the under-19s are consulted about issues that affect them individually and collectively.

Testing and assessment (Q11, 12, 13)

The present education system obliges schools to exploit all available means to ensure that pupils attain the highest possible scores on national tests, for example through intensive one-to-one coaching, rooted in the concept of 'individualised learning'. In late 2005 the Department for Education and Skills (DfES) introduced a new system called 'Pupil Achievement Tracker' (PAT) that allows schools and local authorities (LAs) to import and analyse their own pupil performance data against national data. There are four areas of analysis available: school level analysis; pupil level value added; target setting; and question level analysis. (The term 'value added' refers to the formally assessed improvement in pupil national test scores.) As a result of these powerful external requirements dominating the educational agenda, the prospect of failing to meet the necessary standards in mathematics and English (specifically, in numeracy and literacy) has assumed such significance that it has permeated school life, sometimes at the expense of more creative and spontaneous practice. Head teachers and governors anxiously examine the latest results. How has this year group fared? Is there some year-upon-year improvement? Can dips in achievement be explained to parents and the community? Yet all teachers know that groups of children differ markedly from one year to the next; some classes contain a wealth of talented, highly academic pupils and the sure prospect of good results; others have more than their fair share of unexceptional or unmotivated pupils, with the inevitable impact on results.

The received wisdom about placing pupils in ability groups to facilitate targeted teaching, tight monitoring and close assessment as a means of raising standards is now well established in primary schools. This trend has led to a large amount of 'setting' in mathematics and English, a procedure by which all the pupils in a cohort (or sometimes several year groups) are divided into groups based on their achievement in the subject. However, there a number of other factors that need to be taken into account when making judgements about competence, such as the amount of effort they make and the extent to which pupils are liberated to take greater responsibility in charting their way through the curriculum rather than following a predetermined route. MacGilchrist (2003) argues that teachers *need to ensure that the classroom climate they create fosters a learning orientation in which it is acceptable to take risks and make mistakes* so that pupils *develop a positive view of themselves as learners* (p63).

Loosening the stranglehold on what is taught in school, the way it is carried out and the assessments used to monitor pupils' progress also has its pitfalls. Dadds (1999), for instance, defines her view of a modern professionalism as lying somewhere between an *unstructured do-as-you-like individualism ... and the centralist do-as-you-are-told approach of today* (p43).

Schools, in the meantime, continue to be judged on the basis of their ability to respond to government priorities, as resistance invites scrutiny and monitoring by OFSTED (Office for Standards in Education) inspectors. If inspection results are considered to be unsatisfactory a school can be placed in 'special measures'; if an improvement in standards is not noted within a year or two, the school can be closed. Understandably, head teachers and governors are not willing to risk such sanctions and continue to comply with the government's wishes. Under such circumstances it requires high levels of self-confidence and a great deal of personal commitment and energy for school leaders to sustain their personal values and educational priorities.

Standardised teaching (Q5, 25)

Some education policy-makers assert that if the right teaching methods are used in conjunction with an appropriate curriculum, pupils will *all* prosper, regardless of their background and disposition. Thus pupils in a mixed-age class in a small rural primary school, those in a city centre school surrounded by high-rise flats, those in very large and small classes, those containing large and small numbers of pupils with challenging behaviour, those in single-sex classes and all other combinations have been brought under the edict of national expectations. The 'one fit' maxim has dominated the education system and brought consistency to teaching methods and curriculum coverage, but it has also threatened the spontaneity and innovation that was once held to be the province of primary teachers in England. Squires (2004) argues that, while it is true that teaching methods are bound to include a substantial procedural element, *teaching is not methods but what we* do *with methods* (p348). In other words, even the plainest, least inspiring teaching method can, with a little imagination, be transformed into something special. In 2006 the concept of national primary strategy networks was launched, the purpose of which is to ensure that every primary teacher has the opportunity to work with teachers from other local schools to strengthen pupil learning and implement professional development programmes.

REFLECTIVE TASK
REFLECTIVE TASK

Balancing enjoyment with academic progress

Consider the following statement: *'Although teachers may aspire to offer children a diverse and exciting curriculum, supported by imaginative teaching and learning, such an approach is only justifiable if test results are improved as a result.'*

How might you explain to parents that although their children were highly motivated, creative thinkers and enjoyed coming to school, their formal test scores were lower than hoped for?

Classroom implementation (Q1, 8, 15, 25)

Policy decisions, whether national, local authority or school-initiated, have to be interpreted in the context of each classroom situation. Practitioners have to implement new initiatives, guided by advice from government and attendance at training courses. For example, a decision about using 'synthetic phonics' as the core strategy in teaching reading to be employed in schools was made by the government early in 2006. Synthetic phonics is a system based on teaching pupils letter sounds so that they recognise the different components within a word. Training establishments have had to adjust their programmes rapidly; teachers of younger pupils are obliged to attend relevant courses and answer questions from parents who are anxious to ensure that their children benefit from the changes. It is important to note that this process has taken place, regardless of whether teachers approve of the new direction for teaching reading or not. The extent to which teachers wholeheartedly employ the newly configured method will depend on several factors, including pressure from the head teacher and local authority, but teachers' commitment to the efficacy of (in this case) synthetic phonics is assumed, not invited. Teachers have no choice but to accept externally imposed decisions and implement them professionally.

Advice offered to trainee teachers about demonstrating their competence in behaviour management (Q2, 10, 31) provides another example of how external forms of guidance, while useful for formulating principles, requires careful scrutiny if adoption of the new strategy is to be anything more than formulaic. Trainees are said to be meeting the standard if they are seen to be teaching assertively, maintaining a brisk pace to their lessons, setting and maintaining high expectations, using their voice effectively, using praise and encouragement, asking carefully formulated questions and intervening in a timely way to maintain or refocus pupils on task.

At first sight these suggested indicators of competence seem entirely reasonable. After all, what teacher would object to the principle of high expectations, using the voice effectively and intervening appropriately? On the other hand these 'common-sense' statements benefit from close interrogation.

- Do teachers always need to teach assertively?
- Is a brisk pace necessarily conducive to a thoughtful, well-considered response from pupils?
- Where does encouragement end and praise begin?
- Should every question be carefully formulated?
- Does intervention always have to relate specifically to the task?

It could be argued that *assertive teaching* sometimes fails to take sufficient account of sensitive pupils' needs because they become alarmed by the adult's forceful manner.

High expectations assume that the teacher is always the final arbiter of acceptable achievement, whereas there is considerable merit in promoting pupil self- and peer-assessment. The requirement to maintain a *brisk pace* can turn into a gallop unless it is moderated by pauses, time to reflect and probing questions. Many practitioners reserve their *praise* for pupils' genuine effort and perseverance rather than for mere engagement with the work. Again, many *questions* arise spontaneously out of the work as opposed to being pre-designed. Finally, it is sometimes the case that *adult intervention* should be withheld to allow a pupil to grapple with problems and try out different approaches rather than relying on the teacher for immediate answers. So whereas the broad thrust of the advice offered in the guidance is uncontroversial, its interpretation relies on a thoughtful consideration of each point and its implementation has to take account of prevailing classroom priorities.

There have been encouraging signs that central policy-makers are now aware that flexibility of teaching approach is not only acceptable but also highly desirable if teachers are to use the full scope of their talents and initiative. The government's strategic document for primary schools, *Excellence and Enjoyment* (DfES, 2003) advocates greater creativity in primary education and insists that teachers should have a considerable degree of latitude in lesson planning and implementation. The creativity website established through the DfES (www.naction.org.uk/creativity) asserts that an increased emphasis placed on critical thinking skills in schools will enable pupils to focus more on their creative talents.

RESEARCH SUMMARY RESEARCH SUMMARY **RESEARCH SUMMARY** RESEARCH SUMMARY

Critical thinking

Fisher (2003) argues that clarity about what is involved in critical thinking is important. She concludes that it includes the ability to:

- articulate a contextual awareness of one's own position through identifying the impact of one's own influences and background;
- identify one's own values, beliefs and assumptions;
- consider other perspectives or alternative ways of viewing the world;
- identify how one's views can have a particular bias that privileges one view over another;
- perceive contradictions and inconsistencies in one's own story or account of events;
- imagine other possibilities and envision alternatives.

Despite the assertion that creativity is the route to higher standards and the government's legitimisation of creative approaches in teaching and learning, some teachers are tentative about employing innovative practice for fear of jeopardising national test results by deviating from 'teaching to the test'. Instead, they adopt a more tactical approach by expending considerable effort in teaching set lessons in numeracy and literacy, using highly structured teaching with predetermined tasks and activities that are locked into the stated learning objectives. Pupils are given numerous practice examples to ensure that they have (say) grasped the correct procedures for working out a mathematical problem or employing the correct vocabulary in scientific writing. Assessment tends to be rigorous, based firmly on the principle of 'correct equals acceptable; incorrect equals unacceptable'. Failure to achieve the anticipated standard of work results in 'booster' strategies such as additional adult one-to-one support, extra tuition and the reinforcement of previous work by repeated practice.

It is not difficult to see that focusing on a 'mastery of content and revision of concepts' approach sits somewhat uneasily with an enquiry-based, investigative approach where pupils are encouraged to explore, innovate and collaborate to find solutions (plural) rather than *the* solution (singular). Learning outcomes and assessment of pupils' understanding and competence in such a problem-solving environment are, of course, far less predictable than in a strictly objectives-driven one. There appears to be something of a divide between, on the one hand, the encouragement for teachers to be adventurous and, on the other hand, the use of an assessment system that relies on systematic forms of teaching to prepare pupils for success in tests. As Campbell (2005) cannily notes, it is ironic that *when our future may be dependent upon adults who are creative, original and able to use their own initiative – as well as being literate and numerate – that primary schooling may be restricting the development of those [very] qualities* (p6, my addition). These tensions and opportunities exist in every primary school for every teacher.

Initial teacher education and training (Q7a, 16)

Teacher training has not been immune from the criteria-driven agenda and trainee teachers ('trainees') are assessed on the basis of performance criteria under the umbrella term, *Standards*. The Standards for the award of qualified teacher status are outcome statements that set out what an aspiring teacher should know, understand and be capable of doing, with particular regard to their classroom practice. The Standards fall under three main headings: (1) *Professional attributes* (2) *Professional knowledge and understanding* and (3) *Professional skills*. The *professional attributes* standards incorporate relationships with children and adults; communicating and working with others; personal professional development. The *professional knowledge and understanding* standards incorporate teaching and learning; assessing and monitoring; subjects and curriculum; literacy, numeracy (maths) and ICT; achievement and diversity; health and wellbeing. The final section, *professional skills*, incorporate planning; teaching; assessing, monitoring and giving feedback; reviewing teaching and learning; learning environment; team-working and collaboration. Class management requires an ability to exercise appropriate discipline, and mentors and tutors responsible for initial teacher training have been given guidance about the characteristics of good practice (TDA, 2007).

There are many Standards covering the key areas of professional attributes, some of which are simply expressed, others of which contain several strands. Chapters 8 and 9 provide a Standards lexicon, plus a comprehensive analysis of their content and how to successfully meet the requirements. Attention to the Standards offers insights in respect of the ability to:

- be a positive adult influence in the classroom;
- understand what has to be taught and why;
- plan sessions systematically but not inflexibly;
- teach in a way that motivates the pupils and maintains control;
- assess pupil progress and offer them constructive feedback;
- deal effectively with pupils who need special provision;
- liaise with teachers and assistants as a useful team member;
- relate formally and informally to parents;
- make a contribution to wider school life;
- listen, learn, evaluate and implement advice from colleagues.

Any trainee considered satisfactory or better in these ten areas should have no fear about failing to match the criteria for success, though there may be minor points to address. On the very rare occasions that a trainee has severe problems on school placement, it is most commonly associated with poor class management, inadequate paperwork or failure to respond to advice.

Evidence and confirmation that Standards have been met (Q14, 15, 16)

Evidence that teaching Standards have been satisfactorily met is gained through a process of (a) the student teacher demonstrating competence, together with (b) a tutor or teacher confirming that the evidence is valid. It is important to note that evidence is not the same as proof. Whereas evidence allows for professional judgement, discussion and flexibility, proof is absolute, with no room for manoeuvre.

Demonstrating each of the Standards can be found in a variety of forms and many of them are interdependent. Furthermore, as every teacher is constantly striving to improve practice, it is hardly surprising if identifying a single piece of evidence that demonstrates compliance turns out to be a shallow and unrealistic exercise. For instance, it would be ridiculous for a student to claim that s/he had 'met' the Standard Q1 about high expectations of pupils by producing a tutor's commending written feedback after a particular lesson if, on most other occasions, low expectations prevailed. Again, it would make a mockery of the Standards if a student's solitary attendance at an after-school club were advanced as evidence of meeting Standard Q32 about contributing to corporate life. It is easy for trainees to become hooked on the notion that they must find a single piece of confirmatory evidence that a particular Standard is, so to speak, 'in the bag'. In practice, accumulating evidence of meeting the majority of Standards has, necessarily, to be based on the most recent events to show that competence or acquiring specific knowledge has not only been reached at some point in the past, but is presently active. See Chapters 8 and 9 for further details.

There are several significant people that every trainee needs to impress on school placement and employing a number of seminal strategies ensures that the relationship is fruitful.

- Smile and make regular eye contact.
- Learn classroom routines and pupils' names quickly.
- Listen carefully to advice and act on it.
- Volunteer to assist at every opportunity.
- Be positive and enthusiastic.
- Give the teacher 'space' to do her/his job.
- Express gratitude when the teacher sacrifices time.
- Try hard to implement the teacher's suggestions.
- Help with organising the room and tidying.
- Look and sound as if teaching is a joy.

The purpose of learning (Q10, 14, 17)

The commitment of the teacher to the pupil rather than merely to the subject that is taught is important, but the commitment of the pupil to the process of learning is vital. Some teachers are uneasy that a culture of competition and formal testing might have had an adverse effect upon pupils' morale and enthusiasm for learning. In addition, though instances of challenging pupil behaviour in schools may simply reflect a breakdown in commonly held societal norms, it might be due in part to an education system that rewards pupils (and teachers) who meet designated arbitrary targets, with less emphasis on the need for pupils to feel valued and accepted as individuals. Educational progress is formally measured in terms of pupils' ability to gain examination success, but the sheer joy of learning should be a source of inspiration that eclipses any single measure of achievement.

Learning is most effective when it is supported through careful listening, the employment of tactile senses, enquiry-based activities, peer discussion, practising skills and reinforcing knowledge. While the oft-repeated claim that each pupil only learns in one particular mode (cerebral, practical, visual or tactile) is over-simplistic, it is true that some pupils employ one mode more effectively than another. Thus innovative and imaginative learners learn well if they use the full range of their senses and are able to clarify their thinking by asking questions. Analytical learners process information by examining a range of possibilities, thinking deeply and reflecting carefully on the issues to develop and shape their own ideas. Pragmatic learners speculate and make tentative suggestions before discovering if their ideas work in practice. Dynamic learners learn best by experimenting with ways in which they can use their present knowledge and offering insights about new possibilities. Teachers have to be aware of these learning preferences when they plan lessons, including the needs of pupils with special educational needs (SEN) and those for whom English is an additional language.

Classroom experience should give pupils a unique viewpoint from which to make connections between the subject taught and the rest of the world. Teachers engender a vibrant learning climate if they read as widely as possible in fields other than their own, talk about their own experiences to pupils and encourage them to do the same. In turn this desire to discover and construct meaning leads to depth of understanding. Teachers must also be sensitive to the fact that the construction of meaning is context-dependent and individual to each pupil; as a result, on occasions pupils may not be learning precisely what teachers intended them to learn.

A curriculum based on the principle that learning is for living, not merely for knowing, reflects a conviction that education is not only for the purpose of producing future workers and compliant citizens, but for developing thinking, reasoning and cooperative people, sensitive to their own and others' needs. Despite advances in technology, government interventions, policy decisions and discussions about teaching methods that have saturated educational debate over the past decade, the essence of primary education remains unchanged. Its heart lies in providing learning opportunities that motivate pupils from all backgrounds, such that they are stimulated and sustained by a powerful sense of purpose and individual and corporate fulfilment. The maxim 'All for one and one for all' may sound a little quaint but it still characterises the best form of learning found in primary schools.

RESEARCH SUMMARY RESEARCH SUMMARY **RESEARCH SUMMARY** RESEARCH SUMMARY

Learner-centred education

White (2002) argues that in a genuinely learner-centred education system pupils are encouraged to explore, discover and develop an understanding of the things that amaze and mystify them, guided by well informed and sensitive teachers, liberated to pursue ideas, grapple with uncertainties and explore possibilities. Teachers then have reason to be confident that: *In equipping their charges with different kinds of understanding, with aesthetic sensitivity, with dispositions towards self-directedness and accomplishment they were enriching their [pupils'] lives.* (p444)

Interactive teaching (Q1, 17, 25a, 25c, 31)

For anyone who works in a school it is impossible *not* to interact with pupils and colleagues throughout almost every moment of the day (Burns and Myhill, 2004). It is, however, the quality and effectiveness of the interactions that is important, whether in a teaching situation, a casual encounter in the corridor or talking to a parent in the playground. One important aspect of interaction that receives only brief mention in this book is the role that information technology plays in learning, which, though significant, is the subject of specialist texts (e.g. Gage, 2005).

A general definition of interaction is that it consists of an encounter in which both the instigator and the receiver of an action share an experience, with the emphasis on 'action' and 'share'. The experience may be practical (such as completing a task), emotional (such as offering reassurance) or physical (such as a pat on the back). As used in this book the expression 'classroom interaction' is broadly synonymous with *communication* and refers in the main to a range of person-to-person verbal encounters, formal and informal (see Chapter 6). A lot of communication is non-verbal (such as a wave, a nod or a scowl) suggesting that teachers can increase their effectiveness with careful attention to the unspoken as well as spoken messages that they convey to pupils. Non-verbal communication is frequently used in conjunction with speech; for example, a teacher might verbally approve a pupil's behaviour and reinforce it with a bright smile.

Interaction that has an *educational* purpose tends to take place at two levels. First, *ordinal* interaction is unidirectional, usually from adult to child, for example where the teacher gives an explanation about procedures. Second, *reciprocal* interaction is bidirectional, where an adult initiates talk then invites and acknowledges pupils' comments, for example during a class debate about the rights and wrongs of an ethically sensitive situation. Interaction also takes place when a group of pupils collaborate (with minimal adult intervention) to solve problems or exchange information, ideas and opinions. Interaction sometimes necessitates or is enhanced by the use of technology, for example use of electronic mail to contact pupils in another part of the world. Experience suggests, however, that in the minds of some teachers interactivity has become inextricably tangled with the technique of asking pupils large numbers of superficial questions and then making a rapid evaluation of their answers (sometimes in an unimaginative way), rather than encouraging them to think, interrogate issues and offer creative insights and solutions.

Interactive teaching is a term that was originally designed for the first version of the national literacy strategy in 1999 and recommended as an example of a good teaching method. It has also been employed in mathematics with reference to the opening question and answer phase (often referred to by the odd expression 'mental–oral session'). A lot has been written about the relevance of interactive teaching in literacy and numeracy teaching (e.g. Bearne et al, 2003, Hardman et al, 2003; Pratt, 2006). This book is, however, primarily concerned with the principles and practice that apply across the curriculum and not to subject-specific teaching.

Interactive whole-class teaching is seen as an active teaching model promoting high quality dialogue and discussion between teachers and pupils. Different pupil contributions are incorporated, as they are encouraged to ask questions, suggest ideas and explain their thinking to the rest of the group or class and, where appropriate, demonstrate how an idea might work in practice.

There are numerous strategies used to engage pupils, such as bringing a pupil to the front of the class, using individual white boards and number fans, and computer-generated presentations. While applauding the principle of involvement, Merry and Moyles (2003) comment that *what still appears to be missing is any explicit discussion of the underlying rationale behind... interactive teaching* (p18). However, we can gain a fuller understanding of the concept by examining the two elements of the word interactive, namely 'inter' and 'active'. The 'inter' part represents the contact that takes place between two persons (child/pupil or adult/child); the 'active' part implies that the contact involves a dynamic relationship. In short, the concept of interaction is a 'blending' of the minds and personalities of participants to extend and enhance understanding.

Teachers have to become proficient in implementing a number of different interactive skills, such as demonstrating a range of techniques and practical procedures to pupils. *Showing and explaining* is a long-established means of introducing ideas, reinforcing learning and motivating pupils, especially if attractive visual aids are incorporated. Demonstrations can support learning when links are established with pupils' familiar experiences from everyday life rather than hypothetical ones. If a demonstration requires the use of specialist equipment or is potentially hazardous, teachers obviously have to be alert to possible health and safety considerations before and during the lesson.

Inexperienced teachers tend to avoid high levels of interaction with large groups of pupils because it can make class control more difficult to handle. Some pupils, in their eagerness to make a point or ask a question, become overexcited and exuberant. Others love to be in the limelight and, once they have gained their classmates' attention, start to show off or make deliberately 'risky' statements that draw gasps of admiration from their peers, sometimes accompanied by laughter or additional (unhelpful) comments. Teachers have to strike a balance between eliciting responses from pupils and ensuring that the situation does not become disorderly. Even if new teachers are keen to exploit the benefits that accrue from interactive whole-class or large-group teaching they normally find it advisable to begin by using a more didactic (direct teaching, adult-led) approach and only invite participation as and when they feel confident to do so.

Teaching approaches and teaching methods

Interactive teaching may usefully be described as an 'approach' (indicating flexibility), whereas other forms of teaching involving a unidirectional transmission of knowledge from adult to pupil are more accurately described as 'methods' (indicating a definable technique). Teaching approaches and methods can therefore be broadly distinguished as follows.

Teaching approaches (Q10, 25, 29, 31)

A teaching approach consists of the strategies that teachers employ to help pupils learn effectively, rooted in the belief that a teacher holds about the nature of learning. Thus one teacher may believe that pupils learn best when they are motivated by opportunities to explore ideas as a group, while another teacher may be convinced that they learn best when working alone with tasks that are closely targeted to their individual needs. Again, one teacher may employ a considerable amount of direct teaching, utilising question and answer supported by repetition of facts, while another teacher uses an investigative approach in which pupils are encouraged to raise their own questions and seek solutions or explanations. One teacher's style may be informal, using humour and repartee, while another teacher might adopt a more detached approach, and yet another encourages pupil participation under strictly controlled conditions. The particularity and innovativeness that characterises each teaching style classifies it as 'an approach'.

Teaching methods (Q10, 14, 25)

By contrast, a teaching method involves the use of a teaching technique that provides pupils with information, explains procedures, gives directions, organises work and uses question-and-answer technique as an assessment tool. However, teaching is conducted in such a way that the relationship between teacher and pupil is of relatively little importance. A visiting teacher could, in theory, enter the classroom and manage the learning process efficiently (rather like an invigilator during examinations) without forming a bond of understanding and empathy with the pupils. Such teaching tends to be strongly teacher-directed, with prede-termined and tightly defined learning outcomes. Although these definitions of teaching method and teaching approach are not watertight, they can be summarised as follows:

Teaching approaches tend to be:

* flexible;
* interactive;
* relational.

Teaching methods tend to be:

* prescribed;
* didactic;
* impersonal.

In practice, every teacher uses a combination of 'approach' and 'method'; the challenge for all practitioners is to know which one is appropriate and when it should be employed. Trainee teachers are more constrained in their teaching style for three reasons.

1. Pupils are used to the class teacher's and not the student's style.
2. Students need to explore different teaching styles as part of their training.
3. Students may not possess adequate class management skills to employ an innovative style.

As trainees often teach for only a proportion of the timetable, they may struggle initially to find a rhythm to their teaching because of the frequent 'inert' periods when they are only assisting. After a week or two has elapsed, trainees take greater responsibility for planning and teaching consecutive lessons, with the result that the situation settles and a regular pattern of teaching emerges.

Teaching skills and strategies (Q10, 15, 25)

The expressions 'teaching skills' and 'teaching strategies' are sometimes used in education literature as if they were independent processes. In fact, although they have distinctive features, they are largely interdependent. A helpful analogy is that of successful driving: the driver has to master the *skills* of handling the controls, steering correctly and so forth, but these skills are of little value without possessing the *strategies* to negotiate road conditions and cope with the vagaries of traffic with all its complexity and unpredictability. In the same way, teachers may have a grasp of the teaching skills needed to promote learning, but unless they also understand the strategies associated with implementation they will falter when faced with the realities of classroom life and pupils' reactions. Despite the synergy that exists between skills and strategies it is useful to consider briefly each one in turn.

A teaching *skill* is a specific ability ('able to do') that assists or enhances the quality of teaching. Some of the skills are passive, such as preparing worksheets for use in the lesson; the majority involve person-to-person interactions, such as discussions with teaching assistants and question-and-answer sessions with pupils. Classification of teaching skills can usefully be subdivided under three headings: (1) lesson organisation; (2) lesson management; (3) communication.

Lesson organisation (see Chapter 3) involves elements such as:

- deployment of apparatus and equipment;
- use of computer-assisted aids;
- allocation of work to a TA;
- preparing tasks and activities for pupils;
- grouping pupils for learning;
- establishing systems to process completed work.

Lesson management involves elements such as:

- clarifying the lesson/session purpose;
- engaging pupils in learning;
- monitoring pupil progress;
- maintaining discipline;
- summarising the lesson.

Communication (see Chapter 6) involves elements such as:

- quality of voice (tone, cadence, variety);
- articulation;
- eye contact;
- listening to pupils;
- systematic instruction;
- asking questions and handling responses;
- enthusing and praising.

The majority of teaching is concerned with verbally active rather than passive skills, but in practice the two cannot be fully separated; for instance, giving instructions may require use of previously prepared visual aids. Teaching skills require practice, thoughtful application, modification on the basis of experience and gradual refining over time.

A teaching *strategy* is a device for employing teaching skills effectively. For instance, to make better use of artefacts in teaching history a helpful strategy is to introduce the items one at a time, thereby inducing curiosity. Questioning can be energised if a teaching assistant is occasionally asked to select pupils to answer. Engaging pupils in learning can be enhanced by using examples from their own experience. An explanation of learning objectives is assisted by translating the formal language into child-friendly terms. Yet again, talking slowly and deliberately, including stressing consonants to improve articulation can enhance high-quality speech. Changing abruptly from narrowed eyes to wide eyes induces fascination in pupils. Moving physically closer to a restless pupil assists the maintenance of discipline, and so on. Teaching skill acquisition is never independent of the strategies chosen as the vehicle for their employment.

Some teaching strategies are harder to implement, for instance: knowing how long to persist with a particular teaching approach and when to desist; when to persevere with a verbal explanation and when to introduce concrete apparatus to illustrate the point; how much assistance to offer a pupil who is struggling; when to disregard pupils who are whispering when they should be listening; what response to make to a pupil who is cheerfully cheeky. Every teacher, whether vastly experienced or a complete beginner, is faced with constant choices about the best way to proceed in each of these and similar circumstances. Careful planning and thinking through the pattern of the lesson before the event helps to offset most problems, but sessions that glide along on well-oiled wheels without a trace of turbulence can sometimes lack creativity and vitality. As Jones and Wyse (2004) warn, *there is very little evidence to support the idea that the best teaching is always dominated by short-term lesson objectives* (p9). The ideal situation is to provide a lesson structure that offers adequate stability while leaving room for flexibility, thus allowing more innovative teaching and learning approaches to be safely explored.

PRACTICAL TASK PRACTICAL TASK PRACTICAL TASK PRACTICAL TASK PRACTICAL TASK

Selecting an approach

Given a free hand, what teaching approach would you ideally employ? How might the approach vary depending on the subject area? List the factors that influence your decisions.

Principles for lesson planning (Q14, 22)

In a previous publication (Hayes, 2003) I suggested that, as lessons are a means for helping pupils to organise their thinking, master skills and understand concepts better, lesson planning must take account of three factors:

1. what the pupils already know and understand;
2. what the pupils need to know and understand;
3. the best way to help them move from 1 to 2.

Lessons may incorporate a variety of different approaches. Thus a formal lesson might involve the teacher doing nearly all of the talking and the pupils doing most of the listening, followed by a silent phase in which the pupils work individually at tasks. On the other hand the lesson might be a 'large space' session on the school field, where health and safety and correct use of equipment are important factors. Regardless of the circumstances, however, there are some basic principles that apply to every lesson (see Figure 1.1).

- To use a systematic approach, assisted by a lesson outline.
- To concentrate on the things that the pupils need to learn or experience.
- To incorporate activities that will help to fulfil the lesson intentions.
- To specify the links with national strategy documents.
- To identify key vocabulary and questions.
- To specify the resources that will be needed.
- To write down the anticipated lesson process, step by step, including the introduction, the main body of the lesson and the conclusion.
- To ensure that plans take account of the learning needs of different pupils or groups, including the more able.
- To assess the pupils' attainment and progress.

Figure 1.1 Principles of lesson planning

Whereas a generation ago teachers were at liberty to teach in whatever way they chose, today's practitioner is constrained (or liberated, perhaps) by pressure to use approaches that yield the highest pupil test scores. However, skills and strategies to achieve lesson aims are only truly effective if they also promote social and moral learning, as there is little point in educating pupils to pass examinations if, at the same time, they become irresponsible and self-centred individuals!

Creativity and pupil learning (Q8)

In recent years there has been a growing acknowledgement that all learning is enhanced if adults and pupils in school are encouraged to think creatively and imaginatively. The government has contributed to the debate by the formation of creative partnerships, which offer a connection between schools and 'creative practitioners' (artists, authors, dancers, etc.) to provide pupils with opportunities to enrich their learning and to take part in cultural activities across the curriculum.

The sterile notion that 'all you have to do is to apply this or that teaching method and pupils will spontaneously learn' is being replaced by a view of learning that embraces and actively promotes initiative and lateral thinking. The thrust of the argument is that creativity is suited to the diverse needs of pupils because it fosters skills of adaptation, flexibility, initiative and the ability to use knowledge in a variety of situations. This thinking is based on the belief that human learning is highly complex and takes a variety of forms involving the intellect and the emotions, and sometimes both (Doll et al, 2004; Sternberg, 2003).

One current explanation about learning that receives some support from medical evidence is that the left part of the brain deals principally with language acquisition, sequences, analysis and number, and works to analyse information. The left part therefore responds best to structured and sequenced learning. By contrast, the right-hand part of the brain interprets images, looks for patterns, creates metaphors and strives to synthesise and consolidate information. Recent research findings suggest that interplay between the two parts of the brain is necessary for the development of deep understanding, creative expression and problem-solving (Sylwester, 2005). In short, creative learning necessitates a clearly formulated lesson structure within which opportunities for pupils to reflect, think and be innovative can mature and enlarge, supported by a language-rich environment.

Creativity is not a quality that a teacher or pupil either possesses or does not possess; like all attributes it has to be moulded and developed through perseverance, freedom to explore and thoughtful application. Chapter 7 focuses specifically on the development of creative and imaginative teaching.

The place of relationships (Q1, 2, 33)

There are countless texts about the effectiveness of particular structures, procedures and managerial systems in achieving desirable outcomes and meeting education targets. Fewer books place relationships at the heart of effectiveness in learning, though there are an increasing number of recent exceptions (e.g. Hook and Vass, 2000; Day, 2004; Matthews, 2005; Watkins, 2005).

It is true that pupils can learn regardless of their relationship with the teacher. For instance, it is perfectly possible for a child, with minimal adult contact, to be totally absorbed by a form of computer software and follow instructions in such a way that the experience aids understanding and extends his or her knowledge. The thrust of this book, however, is to emphasise that pupil motivation is enhanced if the adult–pupil relationship is secure. Pupils do not *have* to like their teachers; conversely, teachers do not have to like every pupil equally, but mutual adult–pupil respect and even a wholesome devotion is a powerful influence in promoting an eagerness to learn. As pupils who retain a sense of curiosity and are at ease about their lives in school are likely to be strongly motivated, teachers have a significant responsibility to create a learning environment in which children enjoy the work and prosper accordingly.

Young pupils benefit greatly from having immediate access to adults who are responsive to what they say and sensitive to their current level of language development. Pupils in nursery and preschool need positive and nurturing relationships with teachers who can model behaviours, engage in responsive conversations and foster enthusiasm to learn. In particular, new school entrants benefit from one-to-one interactions with caring adults who encourage and support their oral (spoken word) development. All pupils flourish in a classroom environment where there is an emphasis on language enrichment, promoted by opportunities to explore talk. All pupils need adults whom they admire and with whom they can share the joy of learning.

RESEARCH SUMMARY RESEARCH SUMMARY **RESEARCH SUMMARY** RESEARCH SUMMARY

The social role of the teacher

Vitto (2003) comments:

One might argue that building relationships and resilience is not the role of teachers. They might argue that it is the role of the parents to develop these skills or that there is no time to teach these skills in addition to an overloaded curriculum. However, as families experience increasing amounts of turmoil and stress, schools take on additional responsibility for the well-being of children. Learning, socialisation, and emotions are not mutually exclusive but are interrelated and inseparable. To be an efficient and effective learner, certain social-emotional skills must be present. If [pupils] do not have positive peer relationships, feel supported and cared for and possess problem-solving skills, beliefs that they can accomplish tasks and self control, they are not ready to be effective learners. (p9)

REFLECTIVE TASK
REFLECTIVE TASK

Enhancing the working relationship

Consider the following questions:

- What sort of adult–pupil relationship best motivates pupils and assists their learning?
- How might the relationship be spoiled?
- In what ways can adults convey to children that they are valued?
- What do pupils expect and want from teachers?

CASE STUDY

Rachel was a PGCE student teacher on placement in a Year 4 class. The following entry in her diary for the day exudes optimism. The high level of adult–pupil interactions and enthusiasm for learning is noteworthy.

Today was another good day. Tests are almost at an end. The pupils are still very keen about the Great Fire of London topic. I just can't get over how enthusiastic they have been. They say to me: 'Is it about the Fire of London today? Are we doing about the Great Fire of London?' One pupil turned around to me today and said: 'I like working with you; you make the lessons fun,' which I found very satisfying. So I'm feeling pleased and on top of things.

The art that I did with them today went really well. We've been working with images of the Great Fire of London. They've drawn them using a street theme or an image of the fire, which we then transferred onto polystyrene tile to do ink rollers and then print it on to black paper. It was just the pupils' expressions, very similar to when they had seen the egg the day before and said: 'Wow! Look at the white of the egg! It's gone huge!' And today it was the same when I peeled the paper off the inked polystyrene tiles and they shouted: 'Wow, look at that!' They just love it. They really enjoy doing all the artwork. They're just so thrilled about the Great Fire of London. Even one of the pupils that's got speech and language difficulties and has additional adult help because he finds it very difficult to concentrate came in, looked at one of the pictures and said: 'Look, that's Samuel Pepys, that is!' He hadn't seen that particular picture before but he'd seen the video with Samuel Pepys on it and we'd spoken about the diaries and he just walked in and identified him. That's what the job is all about for me. I'm just getting so much out of the pupils. It's just unbelievable, really great!

MOVING *ON* > > > > > > MOVING *ON* > > > > > > MOVING *ON*

As a new teacher in an unfamiliar situation, you have the challenge of quickly establishing and maintaining good relationships with children and adults. You will increase your chances of doing so by being organised, well-prepared and knowledgeable, in addition to being open, hard-working and personable. Both sets of attributes – practical and behavioural – have to be established quickly and explains why the first week with a new class is so exhausting. While you will want to 'get stuck in' and show that you mean business, it is easy to get over-tired. Pacing yourself and being self-disciplined (e.g. going to bed early) will help you to negotiate this important 'rite of passage' period.

REFERENCES REFERENCES **REFERENCES** REFERENCES **REFERENCES** REFERENCES

Bearne, E., Dombey, H. and Grainger, T. (2003) *Classroom Interactions in Literacy*. Maidenhead: Open University Press/McGraw-Hill.

Burns, C. and Myhill, D. (2004) Interactive or inactive? A consideration of interaction in whole class teaching. *Cambridge Journal of Education*, 34(1), 35–49.

Campbell, R. (2005) Primary education or primary schooling? *Education 3–13*, 33(1), 3–6.

Dadds, M. (1999) Teacher professional development and the sound of a hand clap. *Education 3–13*, 27(3), 38–44.

Day, C. (2004) *A Passion for Teaching*. Abingdon: Routledge.

Department for Education and Skills (2003) *Excellence and Enjoyment: A Strategy for Primary Schools*. London: Crown Copyright.

Department for Education and Skills (2005) *Every Child Matters: Change for Pupils.* Annesley: DfES Publications.

Doll, B., Zucker, S. and Brehm, K. (2004) *Resilient Classrooms: Creating Healthy Environments for Learning*. New York: Guilford Press.

Fisher, K. (2003) Demystifying critical reflection: defining criteria for assessment. *Higher Education Research and Development*, 22(3), 313–25.

Gage, J. (2005) *How to Use an Interactive Whiteboard Really Effectively in Your Primary Classroom*. London: David Fulton.

Hardman, F., Smith, F. and Wall, K. (2003) Interactive whole class teaching in the National Literacy Strategy. *Cambridge Journal of Education*, 33(2), 197–215.

Hayes, D. (2003) *A Student Teacher's Guide to Primary School Placement*. Abingdon: Routledge.

Hook, P. and Vass, A. (2000) *Creating Winning Classrooms*. London: David Fulton.

Jones, R. and Wyse, D. (2004) *Creativity in the Primary Curriculum*. London: David Fulton.

MacGilchrist, B. (2003) Primary learners of the future. *Education 3–13*, 31(1), 58–65.

Matthews, B. (2005) *Engaging Education*. Maidenhead: Open University Press/McGraw-Hill.

Merry, R. and Moyles, J. (2003) Scuppering discussion? Interaction in theory and practice. In: J. Moyles, L. Hargreaves, R. Merry, F. Paterson and V. Esarte-Sarries (2003) *Interactive Teaching in the Primary School*. Maidenhead: Open University Press/McGraw-Hill.

Pratt, N. (2006) *Interactive Mathematics in the Primary School.* London: Sage.

Squires, G. (2004) A framework for teaching. *British Journal of Educational Studies*, 52(4), 342–58.

Sternberg, R. J. (2003) *Wisdom, Intelligence and Creativity Synthesized.* Cambridge: Cambridge University Press.

Sylwester, R. (2005) *How to Explain a Brain*. London: Paul Chapman Publishing.

TDA (Training & Development Agency) (2007) *Professional Standards for Teachers: Qualified Teacher Status*. London: TDA.

Vitto, J. M. (2003) *Relationship-Driven Classroom Management*. Thousand Oaks, CA: Corwin Press.

Watkins, C. (2005) *Classrooms as Learning Communities.* Abingdon: Routledge.

White, J. (2002) Education, the market and the nature of personal wellbeing. *British Journal of Educational Studies*, 50(4), 442–56.

FURTHER READING FURTHER READING **FURTHER READING** FURTHER READING

Best, B. and Thomas, W. (2007) *Everything you need to know about teaching but are too busy to ask.* London: Continuum.

Brehm, K. (2004) *Resilient Classrooms: Creating Healthy Environments for Learning*. New York: Guilford Press.

Holmes, E. (2004) *Teacher Well-Being.* Abingdon: Routledge.

Hyland, R. and Jacques, K. (2003) The complete teacher. In: K. Jacques and R. Hyland (eds), *Professional Studies: Primary Phase*. Exeter: Learning Matters.

Medwell, J. (2008) *Sucessful Teaching Placement*. Exeter: Learning Matters.

Sedgwick, F. (2008) *1000 Good Ideas for Developing Thinking in the Primary School*. London: Continuum.

2
Characteristics of effective teachers

Learning outcomes

To understand:

- **what is meant by an effective teacher;**
- **how pupils characterise a good teacher;**
- **the importance of passion in teaching;**
- **ways teachers inspire pupils;**
- **effective pedagogy.**

Introduction

There is a difference between being an efficient teacher and a good or effective one. While an efficient teacher is diligent, well organised and able to teach in such a way that learning targets are met and pupils achieve what can be reasonably expected of them, an effective teacher possesses all of these qualities *plus* an ability to inspire and inculcate in pupils a love of learning.

Effective teachers try hard to make learning fun and effective; they take into account different pupil needs, yet maintain discipline and help pupils to achieve high standards of work. Their enthusiasm is reflected in a lively tone of voice, shining eyes, pleasant demeanour and active handling of the lesson content. Good teachers strive to ensure that every pupil feels confident to approach adults without hesitation to ask questions, clarify work routines and seek advice about problems with which they are grappling. Consequently, effective teachers teach in a way that makes the pupils feel relaxed and comfortable, yet alert and responsive to what is being said and done. Such teachers maintain a natural voice and never patronise pupils by 'talking down' to them.

An effective teacher observes and listens carefully to each pupil, assesses the learning and emotional needs of individuals, and tries hard to provide appropriate tasks and activities. Good teachers encourage pupils to become independent thinkers and self-motivated learners. They produce and make available a variety of resources, both to support their own direct teaching and to assist pupils' learning. Being an effective teacher means developing an ability to transfer information in such a way that the pupils will not only remember facts but absorb and process information so that they can apply the learning (referred to as 'deep learning'). A mark of pupils who have been influenced by a good teacher is their ability to transfer learning into new situations and their confidence to tackle unfamiliar challenges.

Born, bred or both (Q4, 7a, 9)

Today's training providers (such as university faculties of education and schools that are hosts for employment-based routes into teaching) are required to be rigorous in selecting candidates who possess the necessary academic and personal attributes to train to be teachers. The candidates' academic qualifications are revealed through examination results and grades, though the various access points and complexity of the certification process has complicated the situation in recent years. By contrast, candidates' personal qualities are much more difficult to assess and interviewers have to ask themselves questions such as:

- Will this person relate well to pupils and young people?
- Is this person amenable to receiving advice and guidance?
- Does this person have the potential to work as a member of a team?

When candidates come for interview to be accepted on a course of teacher training and are asked what comments other people have made about their intention to teach, their answers are often similar: *They say that I must be mad* (or words to that effect) invariably followed by: *But they think I will make a great teacher*. It is also significant that the people who write references for candidates tend to extol their personal suitability for teaching as much as their academic prowess. Consequently, they highlight characteristics such as being good with children, effective communication skills, willingness to learn, a pleasant manner and so forth. Perhaps the referees are detecting something important about the qualities needed by effective teachers that bureaucrats overlook, namely that effectiveness as a teacher resides as much in the heart as in the head.

PRACTICAL TASK PRACTICAL TASK PRACTICAL TASK PRACTICAL TASK PRACTICAL TASK

Teacher as example

To what extent do you agree with the following quotation from John Ruskin, the founder of Ruskin College, Oxford?

Teaching is painful, continual and difficult work; to be done by kindness, by watching, by warning, by precept and by praise, but above all by example.

Write down five specific ways in which you can 'lead by example'.

The belief that it is possible to 'spot' a good teacher is deeply engrained in the profession. Experienced practitioners are sometimes heard to say something to the effect: *I would employ this student tomorrow given half a chance!* On the other hand, if the placement is not going smoothly: *I had my doubts about this one from the start*. And there is plenty of anecdotal evidence that head teachers, induction tutors and governors quickly conclude that such-and-such a new teacher is going to do well or will struggle in the job.

An effective teacher is not faultless! There are always occasions when the session is mediocre, the pupils are restless and attempts to motivate the class are like water being emptied into a bottomless bucket. Periods of ill-health, times of self-doubt and emotional traumas can leave even the finest and most committed teachers gasping for air. It is fair to state that teaching mostly consists of happy days, but also a few disappointing ones. Teaching is such a personal endeavour that it is easy for teachers to blame themselves for everything that goes wrong, with a concomitant loss of confidence in their ability to cope. Even the most admired and respected teacher will admit, if asked, to moments of despair. The best way in which teachers can counteract negative thoughts about their teaching skills or personhood is by re-evaluating and affirming educational principles, examining classroom practice to see where adjustments need to be made and pressing on without recourse to morbid preoccupation with the job.

As teachers strive to make a difference to the lives of pupils and colleagues, it is vitally important for them to protect their own welfare, too. Pressures both from work and events outside school can easily wear down even the most committed person, resulting in mental anguish and physical strain. There are a number of strategies that help to relieve the stresses and strain and ensure optimum efficiency in the job and sound health (see Figure 2.1).

- Take regular exercise and practise steady deep breathing.
- Leave the school premises for a few minutes each day.
- Establish links with sympathetic friends and family members.
- Discuss specific discipline problems with a senior colleague.
- Eat healthily (e.g. fresh fruit) and regularly.
- Hesitate before agreeing to a request to do extra work.
- Concentrate on one task at a time.
- Do the least appealing tasks first.
- Do the difficult tasks when feeling fresh.
- Seek help from more experienced staff.
- Count your blessings!

Figure 2.1 Strategies to relieve tension

Pupil perspectives (Q1, 18, 25c, 25d, 27)

Educational research into the classroom environment is normally viewed through adult eyes, focusing on pupils' observable behaviour (e.g. the time they spend on task) rather than on the relevance of the pupils' perceptions and motivation. There is increasing recognition, however, of the value of listening to young people's views about education in relation to the school and classroom environment. Pupils of different ages can be perceptive, forthright and constructive in describing the sort of school they want.

The significance of context in affecting pupil learning and attitude towards school has long been recognised. A stuffy classroom generally drab in appearance is unlikely to inspire and motivate either adults or pupils. Again, an overbearing teacher who insists on rigid obedience and long periods of silence can hardly be surprised if pupils become unresponsive and show little initiative. On the other hand, very liberal teachers find that coping with disorder dominates proceedings at the expense of teaching and learning. There is a well established body of research on physical aspects of schools, classrooms and other learning environments, commonly focusing on the impact on pupil motivation of factors such as noise levels, seating arrangements and the organisation of resources (e.g. Jones, 1995).

RESEARCH SUMMARY RESEARCH SUMMARY **RESEARCH SUMMARY** RESEARCH SUMMARY

Supporting children's needs

Kershner and Ponton (2000) worked with 70 Year 5–6 (9–11 years) pupils from three schools and their three class teachers, in an inner-city environment with a diverse pupil population, including a high proportion of pupils with special educational needs. They were interested in finding out more about the way that classrooms are organised to support pupils' learning, bearing in mind the demands of the curriculum and the needs of the pupils involved. In particular, the authors wanted to probe the pupils' views of the classroom environment and contrast teacher and pupil perceptions. From the pupils' point of view the physical and social aspects of classroom life are demanding and they are obliged to develop a range of active coping strategies from the time they start school. An understanding of pupils' perceptions of the classroom environment assist in seeing how they view their task as pupils: for example, in social terms (e.g. getting on with each other), emotional terms (e.g. being secure and confident), as work-related (e.g. needing to concentrate) or learning-related (e.g. remembering, understanding and developing ideas). From the teachers' perspective, active engagement in such matters better helps them to grasp and take charge of the issues arising.

In surveys of pupils' opinions about what constitutes a 'good' teacher, the same points are mentioned on every occasion. Pupils like teachers who make it clear that they like *them*! They do not like teachers who treat them harshly and have little sense of humour. Pupils are attracted to teachers who have open faces, a pleasant manner and a helpful attitude. They are wary of teachers who tell them off rather than listening to their explanations. Good teachers make pupils feel secure because they are in control of the situation and sound confident. Following a class discussion about the attributes of a good teacher, a group of eight and nine year olds composed the descriptive poem illustrated in Figure 2.2 (below).

A good teacher

Smiles
Is generous
Listens to you
Has faith in you
Encourages you
Keeps things positive
Likes teaching children
Takes time to explain things
Enjoys teaching different subjects
Helps you when you are stuck
Tells you how you are doing
Does not give up on you
Lets you have your say
Cares for your opinion
Makes you feel clever
Treats people fairly
Makes allowances
Stands up for you
Tells the truth
Forgives you
Laughs

Figure 2.2 A good teacher

Pupils value teachers who provide well-prepared lessons such that they know they are learning something useful and can see that their teachers have made an effort to make the content interesting. They soon detect when sessions have been 'thrown together' or the teacher is substituting artificial enthusiasm for genuine preparation. They like lessons that have a clear focus and, particularly, where they see its relevance for their everyday experience. All pupils seem to enjoy lessons that have variety of pace and activities, including opportunities for practical work and collaboration with other pupils. The lesson needs to contain passages of intense focus balanced by clearly signalled moments of respite. Pupils appreciate teachers who can explain work well, give constructive feedback on their learning, assist them to resolve difficulties and maintain good discipline while avoiding coercion.

Personality, or however else we might define the deep-seated and persistent characteristics that are identified with people's behaviour, is a significant factor in teaching. It would be difficult to deny that teaching comes more readily and intuitively to some people than to others, but the overwhelming evidence is that inspiring teachers do not conform to a particular 'type'. There is, therefore, no single effective teacher personality, as successful teachers can have very different attributes and styles of working with their pupils. What *is* important is that the pupils recognise instinctively that the teacher or assistant is 'for' them.

RESEARCH SUMMARY RESEARCH SUMMARY **RESEARCH SUMMARY** RESEARCH SUMMARY

Teaching, learning and loving

Liston and Garrison (2004) claim that love, in all its forms and facets, is integral to teaching. Thus:

> *When we teach, we teach with ideas and feelings. When we interact with our [pupils], we react and they respond with thoughts and emotions. When we inquire into our natural and social worlds, we do so with desire and yearning. Teaching is an activity that brings one's emotions and mind to bear on subject matter and on connecting [pupils] with the subject matter.* (p5)

To what extent do you agree with Liston and Garrison that we are losing sight of the importance of emotion in teaching and have replaced it by an *instrumental, patriarchal logic of a bureaucratic, linear, means–ends rationality, one that demands teachers unquestioningly accept pre-assigned ends . . . and the means for obtaining them* (p2)?

Although pupils enjoy being with adults who are likeable and personable, it is a fallacy to imagine that pupils do not like teachers who insist that they work to a high standard. On the contrary, they respect and admire teachers who 'push' them firmly, providing that expectations are realistic and the tasks are sufficiently relevant to reassure the pupils that they are doing something worthwhile. Pupils enjoy the thrill that comes from tackling and overcoming work challenges that stretch their abilities but also allow them to complete the task and gain fulfilment in doing so. Classroom situations in which adult and pupils cooperate to achieve quality learning outcomes are invariably the happiest and most productive. There are various ways to enhance the adult–child relationship (see Figure 2.3).

---

1. Give pupils strategies to succeed.
2. Encourage them to think for themselves.
3. Help them to strive for self-sufficiency.
4. Show an interest in their life outside school.
5. React calmly when they get things wrong.

Figure 2.3 Enhancing the adult–child relationship

Brown and McIntyre (1993) summarised their research on pupil perspectives by suggesting that the best teachers:

- create a relaxed and enjoyable atmosphere;
- retain control;
- present work in a way that interests and motivates pupils;
- provide conditions so pupils understand the work;
- make clear what pupils are to do and achieve;
- judge what can be expected of a pupil;
- help pupils with difficulties;
- encourage pupils to raise their expectations of themselves;
- develop personal, mature relationships with pupils;
- utilise personal talents in teaching.

New teacher perspectives (Q2, 9, 10, 29)

Trainee and newly qualified teachers provide interesting perspectives on the ways that they view the concept of 'being good' as a teacher. The following examples are extracts from their written comments. Thus Amy uses a gardening metaphor:

Good teachers listen and learn and use what they hear in a constructive way. They need to be approachable, sensitive to individuals' needs, reflective and enthusiastic in teaching all subjects. A good teacher is like a skilled gardener, who plants seeds and nurtures the young plants until they stand tall and reach up to the sky and blossom. Good teachers are firm but fair, have a well-organised atmosphere in the classroom and allow the pupils to see those qualities in them.

Layla and Marlene emphasise communication and motivation:

When narrowing it down to one definition, a good teacher is one that is able to communicate with pupils effectively. By this they should be able to convey ideas to pupils in a way that they can grasp them and in the long term, master them. The teacher should use techniques that make pupils want to learn and, as well as using sufficient discipline, also have a caring personality.

A good teacher is a person who is able to communicate thoughts and concepts to pupils with a good degree of enthusiasm and knowledge. Good teachers are able to present lessons in a way that the pupils will enjoy and find interesting and stimulating. Ultimately, the teacher should be able to make the pupils think and, hence, learn.

Tony refers to independence in learning:

A good teacher is someone who enjoys the company of pupils and has patience to help and encourage them in their learning. The teacher needs to know a lot of knowledge in all subjects and do the best they can to make the lessons fun and exciting. Good teachers allow the pupils to take control of their own learning so that they become more independent in their academic endeavour.

Poppy points out the importance of enthusiasm:

A good teacher needs to have many qualities, but above all she should have the ability to see the potential in each child. Learning should be fun; I know from my own experience that I always learnt the most from teachers who were enthusiastic and passionate about their subject. I hope I will be able to generate the same kind of interest, not only in my specialist subject but also in all aspects of teaching.

Nasser and Fleur highlight the importance of enjoyment and respect:

A good teacher is one who can find the balance between constructing the lesson so that the pupils learn but also making it enjoyable. A good teacher should not have to shout or bully pupils to gain respect and must be able to adapt the lesson to the situation.

A good teacher is a person who will work hard to build and maintain a good relationship with all pupils. Good teachers can adapt their teaching methods to suit and satisfy pupils' abilities, as well as making learning fun.

Jack summarises the ideal situation as follows:

A good teacher should have open and accessible paths of communication to colleagues, parents and pupils alike. I hope I am able to make each child feel valued, happy and confident; to recognise potential and address any problematic areas. I want my classroom to be a relaxed, yet productive one, where I will be firm but fair in order to facilitate learning, while keeping it pleasurable.

Figure 2.4 summarises some of the personal characteristics you may have noticed in fellow teachers.

Outstanding teachers are ...
- Pupil-centred: devoted to the care and education of pupils.
- Passionate: work is a joy not a chore.
- Optimistic: problems are viewed as opportunities.
- Proactive: initiating rather than remaining passive.
- Curious: finding out about how systems work and why decisions are made.
- Persistent: never saying never.
- Knowledge-hungry: constantly striving to learn.
- Energetic: maintaining an enthusiastic approach.
- Flexible: responsive to changing circumstances.
- Self-responsible: refusing to blame others.
- Frugal: squeezing the most out of every situation.
- Meticulous: paying close attention to detail.
- Visionary: taking a long-term view.
- Collaborative: promoting team effort.
- Time-sensitive: putting most effort into priorities.
- Dream-makers: going for gold and enthusing others to do the same.

Figure 2.4 Personal characteristics of outstanding teachers

REFLECTIVE TASK

Becoming a memorable teacher

An anonymous student once commented:

We think of the effective teachers we have had over the years with a sense of recognition, but those who have touched our humanity we remember with a deep sense of gratitude.

Many teachers are memorable, but not all of them are memorable for positive reasons! What steps can we take to ensure that we do not only receive recognition from the pupils we teach but a deep sense of gratitude?

Passion in teaching (Q4, 8, 25b, 31)

Day (2004) argues that passion in teaching is not a luxury or frill, but is essential to all good practice, despite the fact that *bringing a passionate self to teaching every day of the week...is a daunting prospect* (p14). He insists that the most inspiring teachers are not content with teaching the curriculum to pupils in an effort to achieve government targets. Teaching can never be reduced to mastery of a technique, for the simple reason that *Good teaching is a complex job that makes exacting demands upon the heart and soul as well as the mind, which few other jobs can claim to do* (p59). An essential element of a teacher's job is to take some responsibility for pupils' moral development as well as their academic progress; consequently, professional accountability resides in helping pupils to cultivate ways of thinking, feeling and behaving. Thus:

> *For passionate teachers, professional accountability is about far more than satisfying externally imposed bureaucratic demands or annually agreed targets for action linked to government and school improvement agendas.* (Day, 2004, p25)

Passion in teaching is not about feebleness or weakness but about making learning a worthwhile experience all of the time, pleasant for much of the time and exciting for some of the time. It is adults conveying to pupils that everything possible will be done to make life in school happy and fulfilling. Every teacher has to expend a lot of emotional energy to establish and maintain a close relationship with pupils and with their colleagues; passion is a prerequisite if teachers are to inspire, motivate and engage with their pupils. Passionate teachers see pupils as curious and creative individuals who, with the help of sensitive adults, can be encouraged to explore new areas of learning.

Passionate teachers openly display a thirst for knowledge and revel in the opportunity to be with, and to teach, pupils. Passion can be seen in body language, the eyes and physical gestures, the vocabulary used and voice inflection. However, teachers need to dispense with unhelpful mannerisms during active teaching before they become too well established, for example flapping hands, tightly crossed arms, high-pitched responses, repetition of a pet word or phrase, and so forth.

Passion of itself does not guarantee an appropriate and suitable education or pupil learning. However, characteristics associated with a passionate approach, such as empathy, compassion, commitment, patience and sympathetic responses to pupils' concerns provide the best conditions for progress in learning in an atmosphere of trust and sincere respect between the teacher and the taught.

RESEARCH SUMMARY RESEARCH SUMMARY **RESEARCH SUMMARY** RESEARCH SUMMARY

Passionate teaching

The vastly experienced primary head teacher, David Winkley, argues that passion requires a long-term commitment and an intensity of interest by teachers in the pupils and in the subjects they are teaching. It *acts as an inner fire, burning away* (Winkley, 2002, p23). Winkley makes a number of other valuable points, as the following set of quotations make clear (all taken from p23).

- A passionate teacher may be quiet and fastidious, just as she may be tough and vigorous; but the pupils know about teachers who are committed to them and forgive them a lot.

- Such caring is signalled in a large number of small matters. It matters how you speak to me, how you mark my work, how you look at me.

- Caring motivates. It not only makes you feel better; it makes you work better. It oils the relationships in the classroom. It enhances the way you value yourself.

- Passion in teaching is not about showing pity or allowing children to please themselves. It is saying to children through word, action and gesture that because you care, you are going to do everything in your power to motivate and encourage them. Part of the unwritten agreement between you and the children is, however, that they have to respond reasonably and do their best. What more can you ask as a teacher?

Joys and sorrows (Q7)

Teaching is a skilled, complex and demanding job. When it works well it is a joy to be both a teacher and a learner. When a positive learning culture is established, competence is metamorphosed into something exceptional and teachers become creative artists, saturated with exultant moments. It even begins to looks easy! Trainee teachers, however, sometimes find that the pressure of training demands, adjusting to working in another person's classroom and aligning their approach and practice to that of the class teacher serves to detract from the pleasure of teaching. The wearisome job of completing college documentation and compulsory tasks, and providing evidence to demonstrate their compliance with the Standards, necessitates a lot of hard work. Being a teacher demands a deep emotional commitment and is bound up with self-identity, so fatigue, disappointment and anxiety inevitably have a detrimental impact. Conversely, successful classroom practice energises and promotes confidence, which in turn leads to greater achievement (Hayes, 2003). It is essential that teachers in training are aware of these powerful influences on morale and motivation, so that they do not confuse the temporary negative effects that a demanding school placement experience might have on their enthusiasm for teaching, with loss of vocation.

Surveys suggest that the majority of teachers have no regrets about entering the profession and are convinced that teaching is their true calling. In particular, they cherish the promise of a rewarding and varied job and the chance to work with pupils. There are a number of strategies that teachers at every stage of their career can use to 'keep the flame alight' and not allow the frustrating elements of the role to crush their passion for teaching (see Figure 2.5).

- Print a large sign in a prominent place saying 'Being a teacher makes my life count for something'.
- Smile at pupils often.
- Find things to laugh about each day.
- Tell pupils that they are wonderful and treat them as if you mean it.
- Don't make a drama out of a minor event.
- Persevere with time management to make the best use of every minute.
- Recognise the occasions when you are over-tired and force yourself to rest.
- Be open and accessible to colleagues.

Figure 2.5 Keeping the flame alight

When seeking to appoint a new member of staff, head teachers and school governors look for someone whose heart is open and receptive to new ideas and who believes beyond the shadow of a doubt that teaching is the greatest of all professions. Every head teacher wants to employ people who are keen to enrich pupils' lives through education and who cheerfully and enthusiastically demonstrate their commitment to the cause.

Teacher attitudes to learning (Q1, 8, 10, 28, 29)

The teacher has rightly been identified as a key factor in pupils' success in school. However, a minority of teachers unintentionally limit pupils' learning by their negative attitude, actions and comments. I shall refer to them as 'constrictors' because, rather like the snake of the same name, they squeeze the life and joy out of learning. Such teachers are often characterised by a belief that innate intelligence is the best predictor of pupil learning and achievement in schools. They view ability as a single and fixed attribute, such that a few pupils will achieve at a high level, the majority will be average and some pupils must resign themselves to failure.

In their teaching, constrictive teachers approach lessons with the attitude that there are some things that certain pupils are incapable of learning, so they have low expectations of them. Their teaching style tends to be predictable and mundane, based on a belief that pupils will learn the same things in the same way and at the same rate. Constrictors explain poor performance in school as being due to low personal motivation; it has nothing to do with the quality of the teaching! As a result, such teachers make only a token allowance for less able pupils, both in formulating lessons and designing tasks. Constrictive teachers commonly employ closed questions in which there is one correct answer or a single acceptable way of finding out. Mistakes are tolerated grudgingly and assumed to be due in large measure to a pupil's weak application to the task or inattentiveness, rather than genuine misconception or poor quality explanation by the teacher.

Pupils who are capable of working independently are valued by constrictors because they make few demands of them. Pupils who struggle with the work receive little sympathy because they are seen to benefit from receiving a dose of the hard reality that awaits them in the outside world. Constrictors see their main task as conveying subject information to pupils for mastery; pupils' failure to do so is considered to be due to negligence or a simple absence of ability that cannot be remedied.

Contrast the perspective of constrictors with the attitude of the majority of teachers who believe that every child has potential and talent waiting to be nurtured and exploited. I refer to these teachers as 'liberators' because they do their best to empower pupils to learn, have high expectations of all pupils and a firm conviction that each child has the potential to succeed.

Liberators root their actions and expectations in a belief that hard work and effective teaching as much as innate ability are the main predictors of pupil achievement. Consequently, they argue that all pupils are capable of improving their attainment and rectifying their areas of weakness if they can be motivated and assisted to do so. They accept that success can be demonstrated in areas other than traditional academic subjects, so pupils are offered varied opportunities to show what they have learned through creative means such as painting, drawing, technology, dance and drama. Far from being seen as a hindrance, incorrect answers and mistakes provide opportunities to gain insight and understanding.

Liberators believe that it is how well pupils learn that is important rather than how quickly, though they accept that speed at completing problems and finding solutions can be improved with practice. In their desire to foster deeper forms of learning, pupils are encouraged to raise questions, to extend their thinking beyond the immediate challenge and to grapple with dilemmas. Independence in learning is fostered, but pupils are also taught to collaborate and build group identity. Liberators provide detailed verbal and (where appropriate) written feedback on work and never give up on pupils, even when they disappoint. Sarcasm, shame and humiliation are never employed to gain control, address failure or subdue high spirits. Every liberating teacher views success in learning and self-satisfaction as more powerful motivators than external rewards.

To develop a liberating approach to teaching requires that teachers first be convinced that pupils have an infinite capacity to learn, though not necessarily from the formal curriculum or in the way that might be anticipated. Children never cease to amaze adults by their ability to grasp complex points. For example, a pupil may be (apparently) hopeless at formal computation, yet keep sophisticated scores when playing darts. Another pupil may have little idea about the geographical location of ports in the British Isles but know the position of every town and city with a major football team.

To become a truly liberating teacher does not happen overnight. It necessitates a reconsideration of educational and personal priorities. It certainly requires dedication, study, perseverance and determination. However, the end result, both in terms of effective pupil learning and adult satisfaction level, amply justifies the effort. Liberating teachers tend to share similar attributes – see Figure 2.6 below.

Liberating teachers are characterised by reference to five areas of their work and conduct:
1. They are child-centred, so that they:

   - see pupils as pupils, not mini-adults;
   - value the uniqueness of each child;
   - commit to establishing a relationship with each learner;
   - understand and value a child's point of view.

2. They have a positive outlook, so that they:

- believe in the worth, ability and potential of every child;
- honour the dignity and integrity of each learner;
- hold positive expectations for pupil behaviour;
- approach situations with a 'can do' and 'will do' attitude.

3. They possess a lot of self-confidence, so that they:

- believe in their own worth, ability and potential;
- see themselves as essentially dependable and capable;
- accept their inadequacies but strive to improve them;
- hold positive expectations for their own actions.

4. They are authentic in their dealings with others, so that they:

- strive for openness, honesty and genuineness in teaching;
- act naturally in formal as well as informal settings;
- stress the importance of openness and self-disclosure;
- use their personalities to enliven the curriculum.

5. They are visionary, so that they:

- uphold a strong allegiance to equality and freedom;
- interrogate issues with a view to gaining understanding;
- cherish mental, physical and spiritual development;
- encourage a search for truth.

Figure 2.6 Liberating teacher attitudes

PRACTICAL TASK PRACTICAL TASK **PRACTICAL TASK** PRACTICAL TASK **PRACTICAL TASK**

Restricting and liberating teachers

Think of the best teacher you have ever worked with or under. What aspects of the teacher's attitude would classify her/him as a liberator? Are there any aspects of your *own* work as a teacher that restrict rather than liberate? Make a list of these restricting elements and outline strategies for transforming them into liberating ones.

Effective pedagogy (Q22, 23, 25, 26a, 33)

In the earlier part of this chapter we explored the qualities that characterise good teachers and established the principles necessary for a vibrant learning environment. In this final section we turn to the challenge of pinpointing the way in which the attributes of good teachers might be reflected in their pedagogy.

The bedrock of academic success is found in creating an interactive learning climate in which pupils have self-confidence, feel relaxed in the company of other pupils in the class and enjoy an easy relationship with the teacher. It is now popular to refer to this kind of environment as a 'learning community' (e.g. Watkins, 2005). In practice this means that pupils do not hesitate to approach an adult about their concerns, ask questions to clarify areas of uncertainty and seek advice about the best strategy to employ in finding solutions. Adults do not see a need to be overbearing; pupils have no desire to upset the harmonious atmosphere.

In a vibrant learning community, pupils not only need relevant work but also a productive engagement with thinking and problem-solving that will equip them with skills of self-reliance when adult support is unavailable and they have to rely more on their initiative. Teachers can facilitate this environment by promoting an achievement-orientated attitude within which success is measured in terms of willingness to try hard as much as it is in discovering correct solutions. While it is true that good teachers vary in their teaching style, the following ten characteristics are commonly present.

1. **Good teachers plan their sessions/lessons thoroughly**, not only with regard to curriculum requirements, but also taking account of health and safety factors, stimulating a positive learning climate and giving pupils opportunity to expand and deepen their knowledge and understanding by grappling with relevant issues, asking questions and reinforcing knowledge. (Q22)

TEACHING HINT

Before you begin, mentally rehearse the session. Listen inside your head to the way that you will introduce the subject. Imagine pupils' responses. Give careful thought to lesson transitions. Think through the location and accessibility of resources. Anticipate hazards, possible interruptions and how you will respond to queries. A 'dry run' of the lesson can enhance the quality of your teaching in unexpected ways.

---

2. **Good teachers build on and work with the knowledge that a pupil already possesses** and do not make poorly informed assumptions about pupils' existing understanding. While it is not possible to know everything that a child has absorbed in fine detail, a firm grasp of it helps teachers to plan, organise and manage a lesson with greater efficiency. A lesson in which teachers spend time in reviewing previous learning or revising earlier knowledge will be different in character from one in which previous learning is secure and can therefore be safely built on without revision. (Q19, 25b)

TEACHING HINT

A characteristic of inexperienced teachers is a tendency to rush ahead with the immediate work without checking pupils' grasp of previous learning. Don't fall into this trap in your desire to inject 'pace' into the lesson. Take time to consider the minimum that pupils need to know and understand before they can grasp the new knowledge that you are about to introduce. Think in terms of four factors:

Content knowledge
For example, if pupils cannot add in multiples of two there is little point in attempting division by two. If content relies on pupils memorising previous work, some revision of earlier learning is necessary through question and answer, a simple game or teacher summary.

Vocabulary
Although pupils need to become familiar with a range of terms associated with a specific area of work (e.g. radius, circumference, diameter) they will not understand the meaning of the words unless you take the time to explain and explore them thoroughly.

Concepts

For example, you cannot assume that pupils will understand what is meant by 'air pressure' or 'orientation' or 'multiples'. Children become confused if you use the word 'subtract' when they are only familiar with 'take away' or 'minus'.

Tasks and activities

Most curriculum programmes and schemes of work are based on the assumption that it is possible to assess pupils' learning precisely and 'target' the task such that it 'matches' each pupil's need. Although the broad principle is commendable, it is unwise to overstate the precision with which the matching can be made. Every pupil needs opportunities to explore and investigate concepts, as well as completing the set work.

3. **Good teachers develop the ability to teach a class or group in a relaxed way but without losing authority and respect**. Being friendly is not confused with timidity or 'being one of the pupils'. The teacher's behaviour, conversation, responses and tone do not invite pupil ridicule or tempt them to take advantage of a situation. Friendly teachers lay down the rules unequivocally from the start and insist on compliance. This firm approach should not be confused with unreasonableness or harshness. (Q30, 31)

TEACHING HINT

Emphasise what you expect from pupils as much as, if not more than, what you do *not* expect. If possible, offer a balanced comment. For example: *Ben, please stop talking to Alan and finish the last problem by half past eleven. I will come and see how you are getting along in a minute*. Authority as a teacher resides in your ability to gain pupils' respect by being reasonable, calm, interested in what is said and fair in your dealings. If you want to emulate the quiet authority possessed by the best teachers and assistants, you must learn to evaluate situations quickly and discover what lies behind the behaviour as well as noting its outward manifestation.

4. **Good teachers are approachable when a pupil needs academic or personal help**, as well as accessible to parents and staff members. Every study of pupil attitudes towards teachers shows that pupils like teachers who are willing to clarify questions, explain carefully and show patience where there is genuine uncertainty. (Parents deserve to receive similar courtesies.) It is viewed as counter-productive to grumble or chastise unduly, even if a pupil is distracted and should have paid closer attention when the initial explanation or instruction was given. (Q2, 4, 5, 21b)

TEACHING HINT

Use pupils' names as much in situations of *approval* as you do in situations of rebuke. It is easy to say the name of a mischievous pupil a dozen times in a negative context during a session. Imagine that you are a pupil who struggles to behave, always in and out of trouble and hearing your name barked at you throughout the day. It merely contributes to low self-worth and may help to promote anti-authority attitudes. By contrast, if pupils associate their names with positive and affirming comments, they grow in stature and confidence. The world looks a better place!

5. **Good teachers use Standard English consistently**. This practice is important because young pupils, slow learners and pupils for whom English is an additional language particularly benefit from carefully articulated speech. Speaking carefully does not mean being artificial or elaborate or unnatural, just easy on the ear and clear. (Q19)

TEACHING HINT

When saying something important to pupils, slow the rate of speech and slightly exaggerate the words. Place an emphasis on consonants, especially at the ends of words. Don't be afraid to repeat key phrases or ask the pupils to repeat them in unison. Remember that even pupils for whom English is a first language do not always absorb what is said first time, so reinforcement is necessary for even the brightest ones.

---

6. **Good teachers talk to pupils in a way that they can understand**, using language which is appropriate to their age and experience. They are sensitive to the danger that their enthusiasm for the subject can result in them getting carried away with the sound of their own voices and failing to notice that their eloquent phrases and sophisticated vocabulary are making little impression on an increasingly bewildered group of pupils. (Q25c)

TEACHING HINT

Learn to hear the sound of your own voice and imagine that you are a pupil having to listen to it. Look for ways in which complex phrases and expressions can be simplified. In all forms of teaching you can gauge the impact of your words by observing pupils' faces: passivity often indicates confusion (though it may also indicate thoughtfulness); smiles and nods usually indicate a grasp of what is being said to them. You can ask the pupils to indicate their understanding non-verbally, for example 'nod twice if you understand'.

---

7. **Good teachers have belief in their teaching abilities and in the pupils as learners**. All successful teachers sound confident, even if they do not feel that way, and reassure pupils by giving every impression of being in charge of the situation. Confidence should not be confused with arrogance or a supercilious attitude that merely irritates both pupils and adults. It is especially important for novice teachers to be open to new ideas and willing to learn from colleagues, but this should be seen as a means of building on strengths rather than a form of professional remedial work. The greatest boost to confidence comes, of course, when teachers experience success in their teaching. (Q9, 29)

TEACHING HINT

Persevere with establishing and maintaining eye contact with pupils. When you speak, communicate the things you say in such a way that each pupil feels that you are speaking to him or her individually. It takes practice and experience to develop the habit of catching the eye of all the pupils and smiling reassuringly, but is a skill that merits perseverance.

---

8. **Good teachers take careful account of the needs of individuals**: academically, emotionally and physically. Every child is asking in her or his mind: 'Does this adult

care about *me*?' Primary aged pupils are often desperate to enjoy a good relationship with adults, though there are a few sad exceptions. Even in situations dominated by academic priorities, cheerfulness and an optimistic approach can transform a pupil's attitude and give much-needed hope. (Q21b, 25d)

TEACHING HINT

Watch a skilled teaching assistant at work. Notice how she listens carefully to each pupil and makes him or her feel special. Watch the TA's positive body language. Hear how her responses make it seem as if she is fascinated by what the pupil says. The truth is that she really *is* fascinated! Learn to treat everything a pupil says as if it were the first time that you had heard it. Demonstrate your delight by opening your eyes wide, smiling and declaring your amazement. If time permits and it seems appropriate, ask a follow-up question. For instance, a child tells you that she has two dogs at home and you respond by asking whether one of them is greedier than the other. Watch how the child explodes into life.

---

9. **A good teacher is able to work as a team member**, both contributing and receiving from others, because no teacher, however skilled and talented, can succeed by operating in isolation. Decisions that draw on collaborative action have a better chance of being correct ones. Trainee teachers are often judged by the extent to which they are willing to play their part in staff discussions, so if a teacher offers advice, they should be grateful and respond eagerly! Occasionally, trainees decide that the advice is inappropriate, in which case it is essential for them to discuss the matter further with the teacher, otherwise it may appear to the host that the trainee is being arrogant. (Q6, 7a, 20, 32, 33)

TEACHING HINT

During your teaching refer occasionally to conversations you have had with other members of staff; this strategy will reinforce in the pupils' minds the fact that adults talk to each other and that you are part of the network. Throughout the lesson, involve the teaching assistant or helper by asking for her thoughts, confirmation or reinforcement of the ideas being explored. This strategy greatly enhances your standing among the pupils *and* the adults.

---

10. **Good teachers use a great deal of encouragement and small amounts of praise**. It can be tempting to flood pupils with congratulatory comments when their effort, work, behaviour, answers to questions, and so forth do not justify such accolades. If adults are too liberal with their approval, pupils become blasé about striving for excellence, knowing that they will receive approval for modest effort. By contrast, regular encouragement promotes a climate of determination and perseverance to achieve the best outcome, which leads to praise and adult approval. (Q4, 27, 30)

TEACHING HINT

Develop the habit of occasionally asking pupils for their opinion of what they are doing. Initially, many will reply with a superficial comment, such as 'I think it is good' or 'rubbish' but, with careful prompting you can gradually elicit a more constructive response. For

---

example, you might ask for comment on a pupil's still-life drawing. In the discussion you might employ some of the following questions: *Are you happy with the proportions?* or *How pleased are you that you have shown all the details of the face?* When referring to a piece of descriptive writing you might prompt a more thoughtful response by asking: *How difficult was it to avoid making your writing into a list?* or *How satisfied are you that the reader will recognise your description?* It is generally better to ask more open-ended questions than questions that invite a single-word answer. It is also wise to avoid giving the impression that your questions are, in reality, a way of criticising or assessing the work quality – though, of course, it is part of your job to monitor progress and offer guidance about improvement.

RESEARCH SUMMARY RESEARCH SUMMARY **RESEARCH SUMMARY** RESEARCH SUMMARY

Impressions

Chaplain (2003) writes: *During the initial interactions with pupils or whole classes you will automatically make rapid assessments of them. If you couldn't make assessments of your pupils, you wouldn't be doing your job.* He then warns: *What you attend to will be influenced by a whole range of factors, including individual features of the pupils (for example, physical attractiveness, sex, volume of speech, dress) and cultural factors (ethnicity, social class) as well as the situation and your own characteristics.* (p41)

- What factors tend to influence your initial view of pupils, the way that you behave towards them and what you expect from them?
- What initial impressions do pupils receive of you?

PRACTICAL TASK PRACTICAL TASK PRACTICAL TASK PRACTICAL TASK PRACTICAL TASK

What sort of teacher do you want to be?

To what extent do you agree with the following quotation, attributed to philosopher Ralph Waldo Emerson?

> *To laugh often and love much; to win the respect of intelligent persons and the affection of children; to earn the approval of honest citizens . . . to appreciate beauty; to find the best in others; to give of one's self; to leave the world a bit better, whether by a healthy child, a garden patch or a redeemed social condition; to have played and laughed with enthusiasm and sung with exultation; to know even one life has breathed easier because you have lived . . . this is to have succeeded.*

Now write your own description of the sort of teacher you want to be.

CASE STUDY

We all have memories of teachers, some of which are inspiring and others, depressing. Here is one of the inspiring ones, written by a teacher:

> *I was nine years of age and it was the start of the new school year. I always felt nervous at the end of the summer holidays and used to wonder if I would cope with getting back into the routine. At the same time I was keen to see all my friends and meet the new teacher. His name was Mr Clerk and although he had been in to meet the class at the end of the previous term, I had been ill and therefore missed seeing him. I was filled with an irrational dread at the prospect of having him as my teacher. After all, the other teachers in the school were really nice, except for Mrs*

Gobby, as we used to rudely call her, who was irritable and loud. In fact my teacher in Year 4 had been a lovely lady called Miss Hooper, who was invariably helpful and relaxed. Would Mr Clerk be more like Mrs Gobby or Miss Hooper? My friends told me that he was friendly and liked football, but that did not quell my anxiety because I was a child that hated sport (though I pretended to like it in case my friends thought I was soft). On the first morning I was literally trembling with anticipation. I was a shy girl and had never had a male teacher before, so I did not really know what to expect. My mum sensed that I was unsettled but assumed that it was just 'new term nerves'. I said nothing to her.

I walked into the classroom as quietly as possible. Mr Clerk was chatting to a few pupils in the corridor and I slipped past like a ghost, hoping that he wouldn't see me. After we had all settled he strolled around the room and tried to remember everyone's name. When it came to my turn he pulled a funny face and said something about how he had a terrible memory. I went red and cupped my face in my hands to try and hide my hot cheeks. When the first lesson began I felt quite relieved. This was my chance to get my head down and keep out of sight. The day passed uneventfully (as far as I can remember) until it was time to go home. I suppose that I was in a hurry to escape from the classroom, but in doing so I managed to catch the handle of my bag on the teacher's desk and send papers, pencils and books crashing to the floor. To say that I was mortified was an understatement! Yet as I froze, awaiting Mr Clerk's furious reaction, I heard him laugh and say 'Oh, dear! That's the sort of thing that happens to me!' Whereupon he bent down and, with the assistance of some other pupils, picked up the scattered items and gave me a big smile. 'See you tomorrow, Laura,' he called out cheerily as I made my exit with a mumbled apology.

How wrong I was about Mr Clerk! After the trauma of that first encounter I can honestly say that I have never been happier at school. He read us delightful stories and amusing poems; he played games with us, sang to us, took us on walks and taught us how to make things. We did lots of science and 'finding out' and always seemed to be showing off our talents in assembly. The classroom was resplendent with artefacts, pictures, models and displays. There was something about the person of Mr Clerk that made me want to please him and do well. This feeling was shared by almost everyone (except Chris Green who seemed to hate all teachers). It's difficult to pinpoint just what qualities Mr Clerk possessed that made him special. He could be a bit gruff at times and occasionally lost his temper. Looking back I can also see that there were occasions when he had obviously not prepared the session very well and 'flew solo'. There was even the dreadful day that he made us sit in silence for a whole morning because he was so fed up with our behaviour!

But inwardly we knew that Mr Clerk was for us. He listened to our childish prattling about events in our lives as if they were the most interesting things that had ever happened. He spoke to us in a reassuring way and invariably encouraged us. His favourite expression was, 'Oh well, you can only do your best', and he didn't seem to mind if we made mistakes, as long as we had tried hard. On one notable occasion, after I had asked him for help for the third time with a maths problem, he looked at me and said in mock despair: 'Laura, I have a feeling that you and fractions are never going to get married! Don't worry, we'll have a go another time' and gave me something easier to do instead, which I completed with relish. When I had finished I recall rushing up to him to show what I had done. He greeted me with unrestrained joy and praised me by doing a silly jig that made everyone laugh. It was crazy but perhaps explained why all the kids in my class thought he was the best and most memorable teacher in the world.

Perhaps, above all, it was Mr Clerk's earnestness that touched our young hearts. He wanted us to do well and did not spare himself in offering advice, explaining things carefully and celebrating openly when we succeeded. I can still hear his chirpy voice, see his gleaming eyes and sense the warmth of his caring manner. It is no surprise that Mr Clerk's class was 'the place to be' and parents clamoured to get their children into it.

As well as having an enormous amount of fun that year it appears that the academic results were exceptional, too (or so my mum tells me). When, some fifteen years later or so I heard the sad news that Mr Clerk had died prematurely after a sudden illness, it took me days to recover from the shock. Although I had only seen him once or twice in the intervening time, it felt as if I had not only lost a wonderful teacher, but also a dear friend. I suppose that in many ways I had.

REFLECTIVE TASK

Discuss the following questions with a friend:

- What are the phrases used in this account that offer a clue about Mr Clerk's attitude towards the job of a teacher?
- What hidden fears and questions may lurk in some pupils' minds about teachers?
- What qualities made Mr Clerk special?
- Why did the academic results rise that year?

MOVING *ON* > > > > > > MOVING *ON* > > > > > > MOVING *ON*

The teachers you admire were not always so successful! Although some people seem to have more natural gifts than others, everyone has to strive and persevere to remedy weaker areas and reinforce stronger ones. You will be no exception. Don't allow temporary setbacks to undermine your confidence. Continue to demonstrate the sorts of personal qualities that endear you to colleagues, parents and pupils. Learn as much as you can from whomever you can. Be as patient with your own shortcomings as you are with children who struggle to succeed. Don't be so fixed on the end point of the journey that you fail to enjoy the scenery on the way.

REFERENCES REFERENCES **REFERENCES** REFERENCES **REFERENCES** REFERENCES

Brown, S. and McIntyre, D. (1993) *Making Sense of Teaching*. Buckingham: Open University Press.

Chaplain, R. (2003) *Teaching without Disruption in the Primary School*. Abingdon: Routledge.

Day, C. (2004) *A Passion for Teaching*. Abingdon: Routledge.

Hayes, D. (2003) Emotional preparation for teaching: a case study about trainee teachers in England. *Teacher Development*, 7(2), 153–71.

Jones, R. A. (1995) *The Child–School Interface: Environment and Behaviour*. London: Cassell.

Kershner, R. and Ponton, P. (2000) Children's views of the primary classroom as an environment for working and learning. *Research in Education*, 64, 64–77.

Liston, D. and Garrison, J. (eds) (2004) *Teaching, Learning and Loving*. Abingdon: Routledge.

Watkins, C. (2005) *Classrooms as Learning Communities.* Abingdon: Routledge.

Winkley, D. (2002) *Handsworth Revolution: The Odyssey of a School*. London: Giles de la Mare Publishers.

FURTHER READING FURTHER READING **FURTHER READING** FURTHER READING

Arthur, J., Davison, J. and Lewis, M. (2005) *Professional Values and Practice*. Abingdon: Routledge.

Cole, M. (2007) *Professional Attributes and Practice*. London: David Fulton.

Glasgow, N. A. and Hicks, C. (2003) *What Successful Teachers Do*. London: Sage.

Hayes, D. (2006) Effective teaching: an elusive concept. *Teacher Development*, 10(1), 43–54.

Lawrence, D. (2006) *Enhancing Self-Esteem in the Classroom*. London: Paul Chapman Publishing.

Panju, M. (2008) *7 Successful Strategies to Promote Emotional Intelligence in the Classroom*. London: Continuum.

3
Planning, organising and managing

Learning outcomes

To understand:

- **the links between planning and organising learning;**
- **what facilitates efficient lesson organisation;**
- **the factors that dictate teaching style;**
- **how learning can be managed effectively;**
- **factors to improve pupil attainment.**

Introduction

In Chapter 2 we explored the claim that pupils appreciate adults who are fair, interested in them as individuals, transparent in their dealings, clear about their intentions, helpful in their explanations, non-judgemental in their attitude, yet unflinching in confronting unsatisfactory situations. Pupils benefit from teachers who are prepared to listen carefully to what is said to them, leading to improvements in self-esteem, enthusiasm for learning and academic success. In this chapter we address issues relating to planning, teaching styles, organising the class and managing learning, all of which must be subject to the basic tenet established in earlier chapters: that is, to have a concern for individual well-being, motivation and corporate endeavour and to promote a positive working environment. In other words, planning, teaching, organising and managing must take close account of the educational and human beliefs that govern every area of school life and not be viewed as the 'real work', separate from emotions and relationships. The assertion made by those who espouse a narrowly objectives-driven curriculum that education is *solely* for the purpose of passing public examinations fails to take account of the many other dimensions of learning necessary for a civilised and morally responsible society.

As the most creative and imaginative teachers are those who possess a strong sense of what they want pupils to achieve and how it can be accomplished, preparation for teaching and active implementation during lessons needs to be of the highest quality if learning is to be purposeful and worthwhile. No one would set out on a car journey without knowing which way to go, the approximate time it will take and the resources required to get there. By planning thoroughly the driver can change route to avoid traffic, take rest breaks when needed, yet still arrive on time having enjoyed the journey. In the same way, a carefully planned lesson supported by adequate resources and a clear sense of purpose allows both teachers and pupils to make informed decisions, show initiative, be innovative and learn from the shared experience.

Planning and organising for learning
(Q14, 19, 22, 24, 26a)

A plan is merely a piece of paper outlining the lesson framework and providing reminders about things for teachers to say and do; as such it is inert and can only be brought to life when its content is put into practice. However, the process of *planning* to create the plan requires an understanding of subject matter, appropriate teaching strategies and how pupils learn. Some trainee teachers become so obsessed with completing the lesson pro forma that although they are clear about what has to be achieved they fail to give sufficient attention to how it will be accomplished. In practice, trainees who have attended to the planning process do not need to refer to the plan very often (if at all) during the lesson. Thorough preparation provides teachers with the confidence and flexibility to be spontaneous, though with due attention to time factors. Thus a lesson that follows an assembly may be shorter than anticipated due to the assembly overrunning; similarly, a lesson followed by a lunch break or the end of the school day creates additional time pressures that have to be accommodated.

The simplest but least satisfactory way to plan a lesson is by extracting one directly from a book or downloading it electronically. When trainee teachers first enter the new placement and have little knowledge of pupils' abilities or achievements, it is common practice for them to use the teacher's existing plans to ensure continuity in learning. However, as the trainee orientates to the situation, she or he assumes increasing responsibility for detailed lesson planning and relies less on the teacher for support. The transition time between relying completely on the host teacher and being independent is one that requires hard work and perseverance.

Inexperienced trainees who have spent very little time in school normally commence by having oversight for a group, as directed by the teacher; gradually, the trainee actively plans for a group and, perhaps, introduces a lesson to the whole class or reads a story or shares some information. Eventually, the trainee plans and teaches a complete lesson and then a series of lessons. The pace at which this process from group supervision to planning a series of sessions for the whole class occurs depends on four main factors:

- the trainee's confidence in his or her ability to teach and manage larger numbers of pupils;
- the speed with which the trainee orientates to the classroom routines and procedures;
- the teacher's confidence in the trainee and willingness to relinquish control;
- how quickly the trainee forms a bond of understanding with pupils.

Planning lessons does not take place in a vacuum. The more a new teacher can discern about the knowledge, understanding, skill level, perseverance, character and attitude of individual pupils, the easier it becomes to plan appropriately and respond to individual needs.

All teachers have to be acutely aware that the primary purpose of planning is to assist pupil learning, for it is a complex process and involves meaning-making, making sense of experiences, understanding and mastering emotions and the influence of context. Learners become increasingly aware of the thinking and learning processes that shape their understanding and, with encouragement, can gradually assume control over them. Learning is also enhanced through the development of social skills and qualities, such as perseverance and being aware of the needs and feelings of others. Pupils therefore require opportunity to discuss work with classmates and understand its implications for them and for others. As teachers spend time explaining the significance of the lesson content, they can show where it fits within the broader knowledge picture and clarify links with previous learning; they can encourage pupils to express freely what they understand, the things that puzzle them and ideas that emerge from careful thinking about issues. Such an approach must not only be underpinned by a positive attitude towards learning but also an acceptance that searching for creative solutions may result in temporary setbacks. Effective teachers make a determined effort to ask pupils what pleases them about their work and provide them with opportunities to share their enthusiasm with their peers.

Group planning and management (Q22, 25d, 31)

Planning for a single group is different from planning for the whole class and raises different issues as it is more intensive and nearly always involves engaging with a task or activity intended to reinforce knowledge or extend work from an earlier session. In addition, the intimacy of working with a single group often creates more noise than its size warrants because pupils frequently work collaboratively, with interchanges of ideas and discussion about key decisions. Concentration levels are also affected by the fact that every pupil is able to see what every other pupil does, thereby heightening the possibility of distraction. Whereas minor instances of unacceptable behaviour from individuals during whole-class sessions can be controlled through (say) a hard look from a distance or a disapproving shake of the head, such strategies are more difficult to employ in the close encounter of group work.

Supervision of a group takes a variety of forms. Most commonly the adult acts in a *monitoring* capacity in overseeing the task that pupils are carrying out. Sometimes the role is a combination of *describing and demonstrating* what has to be done followed by monitoring the task. The supervision may consist of an active *teaching* role using question-and-answer or story/poem, followed by monitoring of the task. Depending on the nature of the role (monitoring/describing/teaching) it is not always essential for the group to sit together around a nest of tables. It is sometimes preferable for supervision purposes to separate out the tables and place pupils in pairs, set apart physically from the other pairs. If, however, it is more appropriate to sit together 'face to face' for the purpose of sharing equipment or collaborative problem-solving, group harmony can be enhanced by means of the following strategies.

- Ensure that all the pupils are clear about the task.
- Specify whether the work has to be carried out singly or collaboratively, silently or through discussion.
- Check that there are sufficient basic resources (such as dictionaries) to avoid pupils squabbling over the availability of items.
- Insist on basic rules, such as taking turns, not calling out and paying attention when someone speaks.
- Avoid seating easily distracted pupils opposite one another.
- Set time limits for completion of the task.

Whole-class planning and management
(Q22, 25d, 31)

Planning for several groups or the whole class is more complex than planning for a single group as it has to take account of greater diversity in ability (even if the pupils are 'set' for the subject), access to more resources and, perhaps, the need to allocate tasks of varying degrees of challenge to different groups ('differentiation'). In very small primary schools children from several year groups may be present in the same class, which complicates matters further, as some younger pupils may be more academically capable than older ones, but also less mature. In multiple year classes there is often more emphasis on individualised work owing to the diverse nature of learning needs and maturity.

Trainee teachers often find that transfer from single-group to whole-class responsibility requires the application of new or enhanced skills.

- The trainee is in charge of all classroom operations from start to finish, including settling pupils and dismissing them at the end, monitoring work and ensuring the room is tidy.
- The introduction (see below) has to be planned in such a way that every pupil is involved, therefore requiring careful use of vocabulary and questions.
- Instructions for the tasks and activities that follow have to be given clearly at the end of the introduction to facilitate a smooth transition to the task phase.
- Teaching assistants have to be briefed beforehand so that they are familiar with the lesson content, the learning it fosters and the standards of work anticipated.
- Resources for the different activities have to be available and accessible, thereby minimising the potential for confusion and conflict.
- The trainee may be closely supervising ('guiding') a particular group but must also monitor the rest of the class.
- Time warnings have to be issued about work completion and reminders about procedures and standards of achievement.
- Completed and incomplete work has to be stored or, perhaps, brought to the final lesson phase (variously referred to as the review/plenary/summary; see later in this chapter).
- The final lesson phase has to be managed carefully to celebrate, evaluate and clarify learning.
- The room must be kept orderly and left tidy.
- At the end of the lesson, pupils have to be moved on to the next session, sent outside to the playground in an orderly fashion or, in the case of younger children, provided with milk and fruit.

If the lesson is located within a series (e.g. exploring a maths concept in depth) decisions have to be made about the time spent reviewing and revising existing knowledge. If the lesson is a 'one-off' or the first in a series, more time needs to be allocated to introducing the topic, explaining its relevance and indicating links with other areas of learning. The position of a particular lesson in the overall sequence is even more significant for trainees, who may not have taught (or even seen) the previous lesson, so at the start of the session it is essential to elicit from pupils what they remember and stir their recollections of its content.

Lesson introduction

The opening (introductory) lesson phase sets the tone for the remainder of the session and is normally dominated by five elements.

1. Explaining the purpose of the lesson in 'child-friendly' terms (Q25c)

Children are not interested in hearing the formal 'grown up' version of the learning objectives but are very interested in knowing what they are doing and its significance. The familiar procedure of writing lesson objectives on the board may impress a visiting inspector or tutor but serves little purpose unless they are explained to the pupils.

2. Reminding pupils of what they know (but may have forgotten) and encouraging them to share it (Q26b, 28)

The maxim that 'we do not know what we know until we hear ourselves say it' is relevant for pupils' learning. For young children the previous week can seem a lifetime ago and even older primary pupils do not tend to retain a lot of their earlier learning in an 'accessible' form (i.e. at the forefront of their thinking). Teachers have an important role to play in reminding them of key points and issues, and/or inviting pupils to probe their memories and retrieve key information. The process is greatly assisted by the teacher's use of pertinent questions.

3. Engaging pupils in the present lesson (Q25c, 28)

Engaging pupils' interest is a skill that takes considerable mastery and is a challenge for even the most experienced and enthusiastic teacher. The task of gaining pupils' attention is made easier if they are sitting still, attentive and curious. Some teachers use their voices 'musically' or mysteriously; others employ attractive visual aids; yet others root the learning in a story or familiar occurrence so that pupils find a point of common interest. A combination of voice, visual effect and story can be combined beneficially, though excessive use generates too much excitement and distracts from the main lesson purpose. Trainee teachers in particular must be alert when pupils employ maths paddles and wipeable boards, especially for instances of copying, unintentional number reversal (e.g. writing 12 instead of 21) and letter rotation (e.g. writing b instead of d), or for pupils who wait until the correct answer is confirmed and then hurriedly amend what they had originally written or shown.

4. Providing fresh information and knowledge relevant to the lesson (Q14, 25b)

Every lesson has the potential to generate new learning but even the most enquiry-based investigative approach necessitates that pupils have a grasp of certain knowledge, skills and understanding. As well as reminding pupils about previous work, teachers need to provide new information, offer different insights and offer strategies for completing tasks (see 5 below).

5. Allocation of tasks and activities, with accompanying explanation about procedures and expectations (Q1, 25d)

After the introductory phase, it is commonly the case that inexperienced teachers hurry their explanation about pupil tasks and activities, for one of three reasons.

- Pupils have been in the adult–pupil interactive mode for too long and are becoming restless.
- Teaching assistants are under-occupied as they wait to supervise their groups.
- An extended introduction means reducing the time spent on the remainder of the lesson.

While it is necessary to take these factors into account in determining the length of the introduction, over-hasty transfer of pupils to their tasks results in an unsettled start as pupils attempt to clarify the requirements.

The emphasis that needs to be placed on each of the five points noted above varies with the situation. For instance, if the pupils are confused about previous learning and their knowledge is insecure, more time has to be spent on revision. Again, if pupils show great enthusiasm for the topic, ask questions and respond positively to the teacher's explanations, teachers can seize the moment and discuss matters in depth. A characteristic of effective teachers is their ability to evaluate the position and adjust their teaching accordingly.

Some groups of pupils are invariably attentive, bright-eyed and eager to learn; others are much harder to involve. Yet even the hardiest learners are capable of losing interest and becoming distracted. To ensure that every pupil is participating, the use of 'wake up' strategies is sometimes appropriate, including a short song or recitation, read my lips, Simon Says, etc. It has also been claimed that what has become popularly known as 'brain gym' (using specific physical movements to clear neural pathways and improve mental and physical coordination) is useful to stimulate pupils' minds. Such activities might include a series of stretching exercises, hand–eye coordination manoeuvres such as writing patterns in the air in response to instructions or quick response actions. Although there is some dispute about the scientific evidence for the benefits of brain gym, it has the potential to assist learning by offering a break from the intensity of work and a chance to refocus efforts.

Some teachers enhance the introduction by use of question and answer (see Chapter 4) or involve pupils by bringing them out to the front to write on the board and demonstrate their knowledge. This strategy can be successful in that pupils generally love to be selected and it heightens expectation; it also suffers from three potential problems. First, in a crowded situation where pupils are seated on the carpet there is a danger of damage to fingers and toes as the chosen pupil steps forward; second, the process tends to arrest the lesson's momentum; third, the pupil standing by the board can obscure the view of some classmates. Teachers also have to be firm with anyone who takes the opportunity to show off and make it clear that such behaviour will not be tolerated. Selection is a privilege and pupils taking advantage of being chosen must be left in no doubt that they will have to prove their trustworthiness.

PRACTICAL TASK PRACTICAL TASK PRACTICAL TASK PRACTICAL TASK PRACTICAL TASK

Defining real work

Do not give the impression by your tone of voice that the fun has ended at the end of the introductory phase and the 'proper work' now begins! So avoid making comments such as, *Well we haven't any more time for asking questions so we had better get on with some work!* What impact might such a statement have on pupils' motivation for learning?

Monitor the way that you introduce the task phase over a period of (say) one week to help make the 'introduction to task transition' as smooth as possible.

Task phase (Q1, 12, 22, 23, 25d)

During the task phase of the lesson, teachers have to decide whether pupils work alone, in pairs or collaboratively, and the skills and resources they need to complete the activity. If the task involves writing, then practical considerations such as access to spellings, use of dictionaries and availability of written sources are all relevant. Before starting a written task, teachers have to clarify which aspects of the work are most important, for example neatness and conciseness, whether pupils should do a draft version first, how findings should be presented, and so forth. If the activity involves creating a visual image or structure (drawings, paintings, clay work, collage, etc.) then procedural considerations become a priority, such as suitable space for working, availability of the correct tools for the job, health and safety factors, and clearing up and storage of the finished or unfinished products.

Resources are particularly important during an enquiry-based session in which pupils have to investigate problems and discover solutions. The more open-ended and innovative the practical task the greater the need for a range of resources, for the simple reason that pupils may have ideas that can only be sparked into life if suitable aids and equipment are available. If the task is prescribed, the appropriate resources can, of course, be collected in advance of the lesson and allocated at the appropriate time.

If the task involves use of a worksheet (see Figure 3.1), its content must be carefully considered so that pupils do not become overwhelmed by the level of detail or confused by its complexity. It is useful to show pupils an enlarged version of the worksheet during the lesson introduction, demonstrating how the pupils should go about completing the task or simply familiarising them with its contents. This process should not be protracted; the intention is to ensure that the pupils can turn their attention to the work with minimal delay once they have been sent to their work areas.

- Title indicating the area of study *and* the purpose, for example: 'Recording temperature changes (area) to assess different insulators (purpose)'.
- Space for pupils to write their name and date.
- Sparing use of words, especially for younger pupils.
- Clear instructions about whether pupils have to write **on** the worksheet or use the information from it and record elsewhere (such as exercise books).
- Uncluttered layout with plenty of 'white space'.
- Straightforward element suitable for all pupils to tackle.
- Higher demand element to stretch more capable pupils.
- Open-ended element at the end to extend faster workers.
- A simple pattern or line drawing to enliven the sheet.

Figure 3.1 Layout of worksheets

Depending on the composition of the group or class, teachers have to make allowance for a variety of pupil types when they plan tasks: capable and less capable; faster workers and slower workers; conscientious and casual; self-sufficient and adult-dependent; innovative and conforming; settled and agitated; gregarious and isolated. Capable pupils require a more demanding level of work than less capable pupils, though teachers sometimes give all pupils the same work and adjust their *expectations* of work quality and progress on the basis of pupil competence. Faster workers should be commended for their endeavour but reminded that the completion of tasks is not competitive and that speed is never to be at the expense of accuracy. Conscientious workers may require reassurance that 'good enough' is acceptable, whereas slovenly workers have to be given highly specific direction about what constitutes an acceptable standard of work. Self-confident pupils can usually be given freedom of expression within the limitations of time and work completion but may need reminding to stay on task; by contrast, adult-reliant pupils need regular reassurance and encouragement to use peer support and to 'have a try'. A small percentage of pupils want to do things their own way and teachers have to decide the extent to which they are willing to permit such deviation from the norm. Conformist pupils normally concentrate for longer periods of time on a single task than restless ones, who need to be given a larger number of small-step targets for completion one at a time.

Uncooperative pupils are often labelled as 'troublesome', not least when they resist working in a pair or group or insist on working with particular individuals. However, it is often the case that such pupils feel vulnerable and under-confident, requiring close adult support and encouragement as they either struggle along independently or rely heavily on another pupil.

Whatever the subject area, all teachers have to be aware of how best to monitor pupils' understanding and progress. This process necessitates being clear about what constitutes an acceptable standard of work and how improvements can be suggested immediately (through verbal feedback) and in the longer term (by pinpointing areas for development and identifying targets for achievement). The vast majority of pupils make an effort to complete work satisfactorily; teachers and assistants have to do their best to ensure that they provide the best environment in which pupils can learn effectively.

REFLECTIVE TASK

Motivating less academic pupils

Less capable pupils and slow workers should not be deprived of involvement in open-ended and investigative work simply because they struggle to complete basic tasks. It is sometimes the case that slow workers never complete the basic tasks, thereby missing out on the more exciting activities. Take such factors into account when you plan lessons.

Lesson conclusion (Q25c, 26a, 27, 28)

The introduction of the literacy and numeracy strategies as a regular feature of primary schooling resulted in the word 'plenary' becoming a familiar term among teachers, denoting the end phase of the lesson (Watt and Burrell, 2006). The concept of bringing the whole class together for the final few minutes is not a new idea, but the highly prescribed and structured lesson format for teaching English and mathematics has highlighted the potential value of summarising the lesson, celebrating success and clarifying any misunderstandings about the work. A number of points are worth noting.

- The plenary phase was specifically designed for the 'literacy hour' and does not have to be used formulaically at the end of every lesson.
- A lengthy plenary can be at the expense of valuable task time.
- The plenary is not a magic formula to ensure a satisfactory end to the lesson.
- If several sequential lessons are closely related, it may be better to leave the extended plenary until the end of the last lesson in the series when there is something of substance to celebrate and discuss.

A failure to give pupils sufficient time to complete the allocated tasks owing to the pressing need for a plenary can be detrimental to learning as pupils hurry to finish, with an inevitable fall in work quality. Other pupils become frustrated because they are enjoying the work and want to feel the sense of fulfilment that accompanies completion. Over a period of weeks, insufficient time to end tasks can result in a series of half-finished products and little work of substance; it also provides no opportunity for pupils to concentrate for longer amounts of time on a sustained piece of work.

In addition to celebrating present achievement, effective plenary sessions are characterised by some or all of the following:

- they reinforce and extend learning;
- they alert pupils to alternative approaches;
- they rectify misconceptions and misunderstandings;
- they point to new areas of learning.

Some trainee teachers use the plenary to celebrate achievement but neglect other opportunities to explore not only what has been accomplished but *how* it has been done and the implications for future learning.

Bringing pupils together at the end of the session has many advantages but also some potential difficulties. Wise teachers give a few minutes' warning about the close of the task phase and allow the congregating to happen in a fairly unhurried and relaxed way. They avoid calling out across the room, quietly encourage pupils to hurry up and accept that it is not always possible for a pupil to end a written task abruptly. Settling pupils on the carpet can be quite challenging for inexperienced teachers, as children sometimes become excited as they gather with their classmates in a confined space. Some teachers of younger pupils allocate each one to a specific area of the carpet as a means of avoiding unnecessary disputes about where to sit. Every teacher has to develop strategies to ensure orderly behaviour (see Figure 3.2).

1.   Making the carpet zone a 'slow movement' area.
2.   Insisting that pupils sit upright, away from furniture.
3.   Inculcating habits such as folded arms, feet tucked in tightly and lips together.
4.   Using a small bell as a 'freeze' signal.
5.   Including a mildly competitive element to see who is ready first.
6.   Approving sensible behaviour and commending cooperative pupils.

Figure 3.2 Strategies to ensure orderly behaviour

Although most teachers gather the pupils on the carpet to conduct the plenary, this procedure is not always necessary. There are advantages in leaving pupils at their tables so that they can stand next to their chairs or remain seated when they are invited to participate. There is little point in pupils coming together on the carpet merely to receive a general commendation.

The length of time spent on the plenary will vary according to its purpose and content. Some plenaries have to be brief because of the lesson end; nevertheless, the following approximate periods of time are usually applicable:

- general congratulations to the class: 1 minute;
- general congratulations to each group in turn: 3 minutes;

- reinforcing key aspects of learning with the whole class: 5 minutes;
- clarifying a widely held misconception: 5 minutes;
- individually selected pupils to read aloud/report back: 5 minutes.

If several of the above are incorporated, the *total* time should not normally exceed 10 or 12 minutes.

RESEARCH SUMMARY RESEARCH SUMMARY **RESEARCH SUMMARY** RESEARCH SUMMARY

Task setting

Ainley et al (2006) conclude from the results of their research in mathematics that if teachers plan from pre-established learning objectives, the tasks they set may be unrewarding for the pupils and impoverish learning. Yet even if the teacher establishes an activity (based, say, on play or an investigation) and allows pupils to explore and develop their own thinking, it still does not guarantee that the pupils will engage with the task and master the concepts. Teachers need to resolve the tension between, on the one hand, classroom learning that seems to have little practical usefulness and, on the other hand, what the authors refer to as 'street mathematics' with direct relevance to everyday life. Tasks that have the potential to link purpose with utility need to have three dimensions:

- an explicit end product that pupils care about;
- making something for another audience (such as younger children) to use;
- being well-focused but containing opportunities for pupils to make meaningful decisions.

Involving the teaching assistant (Q32, 33)

In recent years there has been a considerable growth in the number of teaching assistants in UK schools and in the diversity and range of their roles and responsibilities. An increasing number of TAs work alongside teachers to support pupils' learning (Blatchford, 2004; Campbell and Fairbairn, 2005) and a high proportion of them are appointed to support pupils with special educational needs (SEN), including those with social, emotional and behavioural difficulties (SEBD). Other TAs draw on their knowledge of different languages in providing support for bilingual pupils' development and facilitating interaction between home, school and local communities. Relatively few TAs are employed principally to work with *more* able pupils. There are an increasing number of specialist teachers in larger primary schools who contribute in subject areas such as PE and art-based learning. Trainee teachers need to become familiar with the different specialist roles undertaken by assistants in school.

The TA can be involved at many levels of planning and organisation of learning, but is particularly valuable in the active teaching situation, even if it is only through the use of comments such as: *We think that's a great idea, don't we, Mrs Wright?* or *I know Miss Keen had a suggestion about how we might begin*. This inclusive approach is not to patronise the TA but to demonstrate publicly for the pupils' benefit that all the adults are working together. It is sometimes appropriate at the end of a lesson for the TA to speak on behalf of the group that s/he has been managing or support them as pupils do so.

Teaching assistants should be treated with great courtesy. Trainees have much to learn from them and should not feel discouraged if TAs seem to know as much about pupils' learning as the teacher does; sometimes they know more!

Higher level teaching assistants (Q3b, 5, 20)

The national agreement on raising standards and tackling workload recognised that school support staff already make a vital contribution to pupils' learning and achievement and higher level teaching assistant (HLTA) status is a formal recognition for the skills, knowledge and experience that TAs have gained. As part of the remodelling of the workforce strategy, many schools deploy HLTA staff to carry out an enhanced role in supporting qualified teachers as a means of improving pupil achievement and the work/life balance for staff. The professional standards they have to meet are formulated with reference to three areas:

- professional values and practice;
- knowledge and understanding;
- teaching and learning activities.

The HLTA role is more demanding than that of other classroom support staff. HLTAs are expected to participate in the full range of teaching and learning activities, such as contributing to the planning and preparation of lessons, monitoring pupils' participation and progress, providing feedback to teachers, and giving constructive support to pupils as they learn. They have opportunity to work with individuals, small groups and whole classes where the assigned teacher is not present. Taking responsibility for a whole class marks a significant change from the system as it previously pertained in as much as the HLTA is, in such circumstances, assuming the role of temporary teacher. The extension of the HLTA role also means that the relationship with teachers is closer to one of 'fellow professional' rather than subordinate. Teachers have to collaborate closely with the HLTA to ensure continuity of learning for pupils. Some HLTAs become highly skilled in subject areas such as technology, craft and reading recovery, and are able to assist in mentoring TAs.

RESEARCH SUMMARY RESEARCH SUMMARY **RESEARCH SUMMARY** RESEARCH SUMMARY

Teaching assistants

Watkinson (2003) refers to the necessity of establishing and maintaining good relationships (p24, extracts). She writes:

> Basically it boils down to treating others as you would like to be treated, putting yourself metaphorically in the others' shoes. A mutual trust has to be built up. Effective communication is essential in good relationships. This not only means listening, but also giving clear, appropriate and if possible unambiguous instructions or messages. Be explicit (politely) about needs and misunderstandings; implicit messages can be misunderstood, causing hurt or delay. Write things down for yourself and others where you can, being as concise as possible. Maintaining positive attitudes such as trying to see the good in people or pupils, trying to understand, smiling where you can, all help relationships to work.

Watkinson's wise advice for teaching assistants applies equally to trainee teachers!

Teaching modes (Q25, 31)

Teachers can employ a variety of teaching modes in classroom teaching, of which three are most commonly used:

- direct transmission teaching;
- interactive transmission teaching;
- participative teaching.

Direct transmission teaching, as the name suggests, involves imparting knowledge and understanding to pupils unidirectionally (adult speaking, disclosing and demonstrating; pupils listening and receiving). The success by which this form of transmission is achieved depends upon teachers presenting the information in a structured way, using appropriate vocabulary, engaging the pupils by speaking enthusiastically, varying the speed of delivery and making the content relevant. The process can be enlivened by utilising visual aids, as younger pupils especially find it difficult to pay attention for lengthy periods of time.

Interactive transmission teaching is similar to the direct transmission model but includes interludes for teacher questions and pupil answers. Interactive teaching requires more skill than direct transmission because the teacher has to alternate between imparting information and managing pupils' responses to questions.

Participative teaching takes place when teachers encourage active pupil involvement, not only by answering questions but also in offering suggestions, providing insights and supplying examples. Participative teaching requires considerable teaching acumen because, although it is often creates the most invigorating sessions, it also provides opportunities for disorder among pupils who do not possess the self-discipline to wait for their turn, listen to the ideas of classmates or attend to noise levels. Teachers who employ participative teaching have to work hard to clarify the rules about when and how pupils can make contributions and how they should respond to the views of others. It is not advisable for inexperienced teachers to use this third mode with the whole class before they are competent with the other two modes. Figure 3.3 shows a summary of the characteristics of the three modes.

Direct transmission teaching
- adult initiates, pupils attend;
- acts as a vehicle for the rapid transfer of knowledge;
- relies on close pupil concentration;
- relatively easy to manage over a short time frame.

Interactive transmission teaching
- adult initiates, pupils respond;
- knowledge is interrogated through question and answer;
- relies on pupil responsiveness;
- successful management depends on establishing clear rules.

Participative teaching
- adult introduces, adult and pupils both contribute;
- knowledge is extended through discourse;
- relies heavily on pupil initiative;
- adult acts as mediator and arbiter.

Figure 3.3 Teaching modes

Increasing the level of pupil involvement
(Q1, 4, 10, 28)

Some teachers find that over a series of sessions, they develop their teaching approach from one that relies primarily on adult initiative to gradually increase the contribution made by pupils. In the first few encounters with the group/class it is advisable for a new teacher to maintain a firm grip on proceedings, whereby pupils 'speak when they are spoken to', answer questions when selected and respond to invitations for a simple acknowledgement from them (hands up, nods, yes and no). As new teachers learn more about the pupils' knowledge, capability and personalities, they can invite a limited amount of pupil participation. The level of participation is a matter for the individual teacher to determine, but it is probably wiser to begin by using specific invitations, such as:

- pupils put a hand up if they agree/disagree with the idea/statement;
- they use a thumbs-up/thumbs-down/thumbs-central to indicate whether they are clear about what has been said;
- they nod their head if they prefer A to B;
- they raise both hands if they wish to make a different suggestion.

Other, more imaginative, pupil responses to specific invitations can be employed when the teacher is certain that the situation can be redeemed if the pupils become over-exuberant. Alternative strategies to hand raising and offering public comment, while still retaining pupil interest, include the following.

- whisper in the ear of the person next to you what you think;
- shake the hand of the person next to you if you are pleased;
- pat yourself on the back if you were going to say the same (as the person who answered correctly);
- blow out a candle flame to a count of three if you don't agree (gentle blowing);
- breathe fire if you agree (a 'breathy' ha-aa sound).

These response procedures not only inject fun into the proceedings, they also allow for a modest degree of pupil involvement while allowing the teacher to retain tight control over the interaction. It is still necessary, of course, to monitor behaviour and explain what is and is not permissible. Over time it is possible to extend the range of pupil contributions until a harmony has been achieved between adult and pupil contributions. Some teachers feel uneasy about this more collegial environment and worry that they might lose control or that the pupil contributions will deviate from the principal learning objectives. However, high pupil initiative in a whole-class/large-group teaching situation should not be confused with pupil dominance. The teacher acts in the role of mediator, ensuring that the comments, questions and suggestions are appropriate and relevant.

Additionally, there is only one teacher in the room (plus a teaching assistant, perhaps) and 30 pupils, so it is unrealistic to imagine that events can be left to run along unsupervised, the only exception being when a designated pupil is given responsibility for directing affairs within a group. There are also occasions when a chosen pupil 'in the hot seat' answers questions from the other pupils about an interest, hobby or experience. In such cases, the chosen pupil selects another on the basis of hands up. Another variation is for the pupil to choose a classmate to ask a question; once the answer is given, the pupil who asked the question selects another to ask a further question, and so on around the class until questions are exhausted (see Figure 3.4).

1. Pupil is chosen by teacher for role as respondent.
2. Pupil respondent selects a classmate (X) to ask a question.
3. Classmate X asks a question.
4. Pupil respondent answers the question.
5. Classmate X selects another pupil (Y) to ask a question.
6. Classmate Y asks a question.
7. Pupil respondent answers the question.
8. Classmate Y selects another pupil (Z) to ask a question, and so on.

Figure 3.4 Pupil involvement in asking questions

A high level of pupil involvement makes heavy demands on a teacher but can be extremely rewarding, both in terms of the learning that occurs and the social benefits, as pupils develop patience to take turns, listen to other points of view, evaluate comments, ask questions and enthuse about ideas. These skills do not come naturally to most pupils, so it is important for teachers to spend time beforehand and during the interaction in spelling out the procedures and then enforcing them. Over time, pupils will self-regulate, but there is often a transition time when individual transgressions are met with petulant ripostes from the rest of the group that require calm but firm adult intervention. Teachers have to decide how much they are willing to persevere through this transition phase to tap deeply into the benefits of having a highly motivated group that is actively contributing to the discussion without fear of derision. Inexperienced teachers who yearn for a more egalitarian learning climate sometimes find the practical challenge of exercising control over lively and eager youngsters too much to cope with and hastily revert to a more teacher-directed approach.

REFLECTIVE TASK

Practising and rehearsing teaching

It pays to practise the interactive phase beforehand in the empty classroom or at home, thinking about the very first statement that you will make, which is likely to be a request that the pupils pay attention to what you say. Imagine yourself giving information, asking questions and receiving answers. Anticipate the sorts of responses you might receive from the pupils and how you will handle them. What strategies will you use to:

- Gain pupils' attention and settle the class?
- Select pupils to answer questions or be asked questions by classmates?
- Evaluate the quality of responses?

Interaction continuum (Q17, 25a, 28, 30, 31)

Pollard (2005) suggests that the characteristics and qualities of interaction between teachers and learners can be represented in terms of a continuum of high to low adult involvement, and low to high pupil initiative.

1. *High adult involvement, low pupil initiative*. This form of interaction is 'teacher-driven'. The adult directly manages pupil learning.
2. *High adult involvement, high pupil initiative*. This form of interaction is 'learning-driven'. The pupils as well as the adult make active contributions.
3. *Low adult involvement, low pupil initiative*. This form of interaction is 'resource-driven'. The effective use of resources underpins learning.
4. *Low adult involvement, high pupil initiative*. This form of interaction is 'pupil-driven'. Pupils accept a high degree of responsibility for their learning.

Pollard's reference to the character and qualities of interactive teaching suggests that situation 1 is likely to involve a considerable amount of didactic teaching, where teachers provide information, ask questions and present issues. Pupils are expected to respond to the adult initiative rather than to be initiators. In this context it is interesting to note that in their research about effective classroom talk, Myhill, Jones and Hopper (2006) explain that talk may facilitate learning but is not necessarily interactive or participatory in the way that the teacher intends or imagines because teachers tend to dominate the spoken agenda. Pupils merely respond to teacher-initiated talk and have little opportunity to introduce their own ideas or ask questions. Situation 1 is tightly structured and involves frequent reinforcement of key points through repetition and rehearsal of arguments. Teachers insist on conformity to the rules; pupils do as they are told; learning is prescribed; activities are non-negotiable; pupils are expected to absorb knowledge passed to them by adults. By contrast, situation 2 allows pupils to contribute to decisions about learning, such that they are viewed as active participants; teachers tend to facilitate learning rather than drive it; learning outcomes are predetermined by the teacher but there is flexibility to accommodate unanticipated learning; activities provide opportunities for dialogue; pupils often work collaboratively rather than individually. Situation 3 relies on the availability of resources as the vehicle to promote learning. A lot of adult effort is channelled into setting up equipment and learning aids so that pupils can be self-sufficient and do not need to call on adult help too often. Programmes are self-explanatory and rely on pupils following instructions. Situation 4 is characterised by adults deliberately retreating to the margins while pupils actively seek answers through experimenting, enquiring and problem-solving. Pupils tend to work in pairs or groups; discussion and decision-making is strongly encouraged. In contrast to situation 3, situation 4 offers the likelihood of different finishing points and learning outcomes. Situation 4 differs from 2 in that adult intervention is more subtle and less assertive.

Teachers have to decide which of the four approaches is best suited to their lesson aims. If a lot of information has to be transmitted in a short time, situation 1 is likely to dominate. If the class is highly motivated and already possesses a lot of knowledge and insight about the topic, situation 2 may pertain. If learning is (say) technology-based or involves working through 'practice papers' in advance of tests, situation 3 might be appropriate. If the teacher wants pupils to gain independence in learning and explore ideas for themselves, then approach 4 is used. This summary is tabulated in Figure 3.5.

Most teachers tend to start with 1 to introduce the lesson, continue with 2 by means of question-and-answer or by inviting pupils to submit their ideas and, in the task/activity phase, to employ 3 or 4 depending on whether the tasks require the use of a worksheet or computer program, in which case 3 is relevant, or from an enquiry-based activity, in which case 4 is relevant. Assessment of pupil progress and understanding also affects the selection of 3 or 4. If all pupils are given the same or similar task so that the teacher can objectively compare and contrast attainment, then 3 is more appropriate because of its tight

Characteristics of interaction	Lesson intentions
High adult involvement, low pupil initiative	Transmission of knowledge with predetermined outcomes
High adult involvement, high pupil initiative	Gaining understanding through the interrogation of concepts and ideas
Low adult involvement, low pupil initiative	Systematic procedural learning using available resources
Low adult involvement, high pupil initiative	Enquiry-based learning with varied outcomes

Figure 3.5 Links between levels of interaction and lesson aim (after Pollard, 2005)

structure, allowing an *outcomes-based* assessment. If the assessment focuses on *process* then 4 is better suited because learning is more collaborative and relies on social interaction as well as intellectual engagement with the activity.

RESEARCH SUMMARY RESEARCH SUMMARY **RESEARCH SUMMARY** RESEARCH SUMMARY

Teacher types

Galton et al (1998) found that teachers dominate talk in the classroom and most of the things they say are associated with organising and managing lessons or issuing instructions. Although teachers asked numerous questions, the amount of time they spent engaging pupils in challenging discussions was comparatively short. What would the Galton team discover in your classroom?

As new and inexperienced teachers become more confident in teaching and get to know the pupils better they adapt their approach to suit the prevailing conditions, taking account of pupil understanding, experience and enthusiasm, resource availability, additional adult help and time factors.

● If pupils have forgotten key facts or have incomplete understanding or are unclear about skills for completing the task, teachers have to spend more time reinforcing knowledge.
● Resource availability will affect the number of pupils able to work on (say) skill acquisition. It sometimes becomes obvious that apparatus or equipment that appeared to be adequate for a given number of pupils (e.g. the number of glue sticks) is, in fact, inadequate. Some teachers divide the class in such a way that groups of pupils take it in turns to access resources, sometimes supervised by a TA, while the remainder of the class gets on with a different task that does not require the resources.
● The availability of adult support is not judged simply on having an extra 'body' in the room; the adult's knowledge and experience has to be taken into account in planning the lesson. Thus, while having a TA is usually an asset, her or his level of expertise has also to be considered and exploited.
● Time factors relate not only to the length of the session; the time required to introduce the lesson and organise the pupils also has to be taken into account. It soon becomes obvious whether the tasks and activities can be completed in the available time or whether more time is needed. Teachers have to be precise in explaining the standard of work that they are willing to accept but also to recognise that some pupils, equally capable of achieving the desired standard, are slower and more meticulous workers.

Physical factors (Q21a, 25d, 30)

Despite the teaching approach employed, attention to basic points, such as ensuring that pupils are physically comfortable and visual aids are accessible, pays rich dividends. When interacting with pupils, teachers need to consider their physical location and as far as possible ensure that every face is looking directly at them. Most interactive sessions with younger pupils take place 'on the carpet', with the teacher seated and the pupils clustered around her or his feet. The teacher has close physical proximity to the pupils, so that eye contact is easy and few problems exist in hearing what is said. However, there is a temptation for restless pupils to move position, touch other pupils or make whispered comments, all of which must be dealt with firmly by making explicit what is allowed and enforcing rules consistently.

To prevent pupils becoming uncomfortable after being seated on a hard floor for too long, some teachers develop a regular system for stretching based on (say) an action song, rhyme or chant. A controlled procedure is preferable to merely telling the pupils to 'have a stretch', which invites silly behaviour. For health and safety reasons pupils should never be allowed to flop down on the floor, especially in a restricted space where clumsy actions can result in damage to toes and fingers.

When given a choice, it is nearly always the case that a few pupils will regularly choose to sit as far away from the teacher as they can manage; others will sit to one side, out of regular eye line. In tracing an invisible triangle, with the adult at the apex and the furthest pupil at the other two corners, the pupils sitting inside the triangle are in the adult's immediate vision, while those outside the triangle are not instantly visible – see Figure 3.6, based on Pye (1989). In practice, this usually means that pupils sitting near to the front but immediately to each side of the adult are 'less visible' than the other pupils. The implications for the quality of the interactive phase is that (a) the teacher is less likely to have direct eye contact with the pupils outside the triangle; (b) the teacher is less likely to choose these pupils to answer questions or offer a comment, thereby reducing their immediate involvement. Inclusion of every child can be improved by using a technique of accepting answers only from 'children on the left' and 'children on the right' or 'children directly in front of me'.

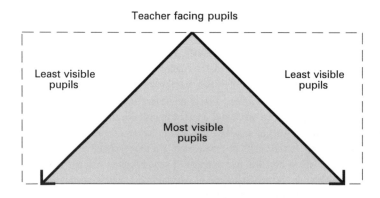

Figure 3.6 Pupil visibility

Different physical arrangements have implications for the way in which the interaction between adult and pupils is conducted. In the situation where pupils are sitting at tables and the teacher is mobile it is less easy for the teacher to gain direct eye contact simultaneously with most of the group or class; in addition, the physical distance across the room means that the person speaking needs to use a stronger voice in order to be heard. However, the adult standing and pupils seated is advantageous in that each pupil can see the teacher and vice versa.

Whatever the physical organisation, access to visual aids and a computer keyboard is a key consideration. If the teacher is seated, resources must be within arm's reach. If the teacher is standing, it is tempting for novice teachers to stay rooted to the spot. On the other hand, by moving around the room it is possible for teachers to find themselves in the wrong location when they need immediate access to a particular resource. These apparently minor points can distract from smooth lesson management and lead to unhelpful interruptions.

PRACTICAL TASK PRACTICAL TASK PRACTICAL TASK PRACTICAL TASK PRACTICAL TASK

Communicating through eye contact

If you are communicating directly with pupils it is important that you can see the eyes of every pupil with ease and every pupil can see you comfortably. Use the technique of saying to children, 'Please look into my eyes' as a means of gaining attention and sealing your relationship with them. Monitor the impact of this strategy over a period of several days.

When a teacher is teaching a class or large group using an interactive transmission approach incorporating questions-and-answers (see earlier) it is common for the level of pupils' concentration to rise because there is less opportunity for social contact (chit-chat) and the teacher is demanding full attention. A whole-class teaching situation in which pupils are seated around nests of tables can be awkward because the proportion of them with their backs to the teacher have either to swivel on their chairs to see what is happening or turn the chair to face the front. The conventional practice of seating pupils in groups around tables to undertake individual tasks, while enhancing opportunities for collaboration, also increases the likelihood of off-task talk. When individual tasks occupy a significant proportion of classroom time, the practice of seating pupils in groups may therefore work against effective learning.

Instead of nests of tables, alternative seating arrangements, such as parallel rows, can help to improve pupils' concentration levels and behaviour. Some teachers employ a U-shaped (horseshoe) seating plan to bring about physical separation but retain the possibility of open interaction. The horseshoe arrangement is ideal for a formal interactive session such as the question and answer phase in a numeracy lesson but is not always suitable for other forms of learning (e.g. collaborative problem-solving) and certain curriculum areas that require access to a large area (e.g. map work). It is not always straightforward to change furniture arrangements for different activities without creating some disruption and noise, but it is essential to use a seating arrangement that is appropriate for the style of teaching and learning being undertaken. Teachers new to a classroom benefit from spending a few minutes becoming familiar with the room by using a simple mapping technique (see Figure 3.7).

- Draw a simple plan view of the room with key features.
- Shade in *zones of activity*, such as carpet area, sink area, book area, and *pathways* (major 'routes').
- Mark access/exit points.
- Superimpose different table arrangements and pupil positions.
- Consider the impact of the design on teaching and learning.

Figure 3.7 Studying the room layout

Managing and evaluating learning
(Q19, 22, 25d, 26, 28, 29)

Planning and most organising take place before a teaching session begins; managing and evaluating learning occupy the major proportion of lesson time, though some adjustments to plans and organisation may be necessary as the lesson unfolds. The successful managing of learning is based on three principles.

- Teachers have a right to teach.
- Pupils have a right to learn.
- Teachers cannot coerce pupils into learning but must employ strategies to make learning seem worthwhile (Hook and Vass, 2002).

Teachers can promote pupil enthusiasm by ensuring that lessons are relevant, accessible, engaging and interesting, and organising the classroom such that pupils are so engrossed in the tasks that they have little or no desire to be mischievous. When managing the learning, teachers must find ways to stay calm and relaxed, without appearing passive or feeble.

Examining the link between what teachers do in classrooms and the learning outcomes for pupils has received a lot of attention since the 1970s. This link has been described in terms of the relationship between 'product variables' and 'process variables'. *Product* variables are significant educational outcomes that increase and strengthen pupils' knowledge and skills, interest in the subject or topic, motivation to learn, academic self-confidence, creativity and social development (e.g. team work). *Process* variables refer to those things that teachers do to help achieve the product outcomes, such as:

- careful organisation of resources;
- enthusiasm for the subject area;
- showing relevance of subject area;
- well established routines;
- use of different teaching approaches;
- using a variety of question types (see Chapter 4);
- use of encouragement and praise;
- encouraging pupils to think deeply;
- promoting independence in learning;
- providing pupils with constructive feedback.

Part of the curriculum agenda is driven by the fact that it is easier to test *academic* or 'cognitive' variables than it is to test *affective* or 'non-cognitive' variables. In recent years, what pupils learn has tended to be defined in terms of cognitive performance, through official tests and examinations. There is considerable debate about whether the recent focus on such testing has been too narrow, but the benefit of concentrating on measurable academic performance has allowed pupil progress to be compared within and across schools. As a result, external judgements (chiefly through inspections) about whether teachers in school are working effectively and the setting of targets for improvement have been made simpler. However, less easily measured product variables, such as the ability to investigate problems and find solutions or demonstrate empathy, figure very weakly in assessments of teacher competence, and critics complain that important social, moral and spiritual learning outcomes are being neglected.

The principle of 'personalised learning' is to tailor education (curriculum content, teaching approach, learning opportunities) so that every pupil reaches his or her full potential. Personalised learning should not be confused with pupils working alone or pupils being left to their own devices without adult support. It is not the same, therefore, as *individualised learning*, in which a pupil works autonomously.

Good classroom management helps to make personal teaching possible, not only because it keeps pupils on task but also because it frees the teacher to provide the individual help that a pupil needs. Effective management allows a teacher to spend time with a particular group while others work independently. Clear routines and careful organisation give teachers the flexibility to respond to the spontaneous and unpredictable events that arise in the class-room, which in turn facilitates creative thinking and action. If expectations are made explicit it gives pupils confidence to take risks as a means of enhancing learning. If expectations are weakly explained by the teacher, pupils spend too much of their energy trying to interpret the instructions. In practice, teachers need to spend much more time explaining what pupils need to do than they may realise is necessary. There is, however, a tension between spending additional time ensuring that pupils understand what is required of them and allowing them to engage with their tasks before they become restless. This balance is not easily struck, but on the whole it is better to err on the side of giving a fuller and more complete explanation.

PRACTICAL TASK PRACTICAL TASK PRACTICAL TASK PRACTICAL TASK PRACTICAL TASK

Clarity of your explanations

To check that the pupils understand what is required of them, use one or other of the following strategies:

- ask them to tell a friend what they think they have to do;
- choose some capable pupils to 'play teacher' and tell the rest of the group what is required.

Think of variations on these themes.

Despite careful organisation and explanation of the task, teachers who become too wrapped up with a single group of pupils are not available to provide support elsewhere in the room. The situation where pupils are left to their own devices in the hope that they can self-direct their learning is only possible under the following circumstances:

- when the task involves the use of a tightly structured worksheet rehearsing familiar knowledge;
- when pupils are provided with resources and jointly asked to investigate a problem in accordance with a predetermined format;

- where older pupils are used to working with the same partner and have become highly self-sufficient;
- where young pupils are involved in self-directed play.

Effective class management is not only a mechanism to facilitate the smooth running of a lesson; it also provides the structure within which to nurture the warm relationships teachers require if they are to offer pupils targeted support. Once classroom procedures and expectations are established, teachers are able to spend their time in promoting pupils' learning rather than worrying about procedural issues and behaviour. A settled environment increases the likelihood that pupils will receive more of the individual help they need to gain success; equally, teachers tend to enjoy teaching much more than when they are constantly distracted from their work by having to deal with trivial concerns.

A test of a well-organised classroom is to observe what happens when the teacher leaves the class unattended. How do your pupils react when you are otherwise engaged?

RESEARCH SUMMARY RESEARCH SUMMARY **RESEARCH SUMMARY** RESEARCH SUMMARY

Improving learning outcomes

Torrance and Pryor (2001) offer suggestions about improving classroom practice and focus on features of interactions, including:

- developing more open-ended forms of questioning;
- placing a greater emphasis on observation: identifying what activity to observe and why, as a foundation for effective feedback;
- clarifying criteria for both task and quality.

The authors found that *weak teaching* was characterised by the following teacher actions:

1. They frequently closed down opportunities for exploring pupils' understanding.
2. They did not make clear the purpose of classroom activities to pupils.
3. They gave little explanation of what represented quality in pupils' work as distinct from task completion.
4. Their communication with pupils tended to focus on behaviour and classroom management, rather than on the quality of learning.
5. Their feedback was often about presentation rather than content.

Reggio Emilia (Q5, 30, 31, 32)

A philosophy of teaching and learning in which the curriculum is originated by the child and framed by the teacher is frequently associated with the Reggio Emilia approach. Reggio Emilia is a small town in the north of Italy where, for the past generation, educators, parents and other interested members of the community have developed an innovative public system of child care and education. Children from all socio-economic and educational backgrounds have access to the programmes, with priority given to children with disabilities.

The expression 'negotiated curriculum' is preferred to explain the approach to learning, as opposed to (say) emergent or child-centred, as it better captures the constructive, ongoing and reciprocal relationship between teachers, pupils and parents. The teacher's role is principally to explore the learning experience with the pupils by provoking thinking, shaping problems for resolution and resolving points of conflict. To do so, they start with pupils' ideas and interests, shape them verbally and further explore them with the pupils. At the same time, adults ensure that the classroom is arranged to be aesthetically pleasing and child-friendly with accessible resources, assisting and encouraging pupils to make considered decisions about their usage.

Teaching and learning is rooted in an exploration of materials and objects to discern their substance, function and potential. It is seen as beneficial for learning if there is variation in the colour, texture and pattern of items, with a view to helping pupils to become sensitive to the differing tones and hues. For example, an important dimension of tactile learning is when children are able to distinguish between materials by feeling and comparing their textures. To encourage children to be attracted by and handle items, displays are presented artistically, so that children are excited and inspired by what they see. The approach emphasises the importance of revisiting ideas and situations, based on the concept of a 'spiral' curriculum.

An important facet of the Reggio Emilia approach is for adults to help children see the interconnectedness of their learning experiences and express it through a variety of representations (art, construction, music, writing and so forth). Parents are involved as closely as possible in the educative process so that they are aware of the sorts of projects being undertaken by pupils in school. Assessment of pupil progress relies on a variety of documentation, including close observation, taping, video and maintaining individual portfolios.

As well as the familiar interests of children, such as sport, parties, pets and the like, topics for study are drawn from children's conversations and from community and family events. The topic selected can also be provoked by teachers by reference to themes that they know are likely to be familiar to pupils drawn from the natural world, the local environment, games and the like. The topic must be of sufficient substance to develop it, introduce new ideas, discuss, raise issues and ascertain progress. The best topics are based on real experiences that have significance to pupils yet are sufficiently expansive to explore a range of ideas and have potential for creative expression through play, construction, art and drama.

CASE STUDY

Latisha was mid-way through her one-year PGCE training and placed with a 28-pupil combined Year 3/4 class in a medium-sized primary school. The main task was to construct mathematical three-dimensional shapes from sheets of templates that were ready on tables. Latisha did not have a TA to assist. The pupils gathered on the carpet for the introduction and Latisha reminded them about previous work and asked them a number of questions to clarify understanding. She had put a variety of solid 3D shapes in a bag and asked individuals to come forward and feel in the bag to see if they could identify the shape they were touching. After giving several pupils the opportunity to feel the shapes and describe them for others to guess their names, and providing a brief revision of terminology, Latisha sent the pupils to their tables, where they were soon busy in cutting, folding and gluing the 3D templates. Most pupils were enthusiastic to complete the task but some found that the dexterity required to finish the shapes was beyond their capability. Glue sticks had to be shared between three or four pupils, and scissors between pairs. The atmosphere was purposeful and Latisha moved around the room offering practical help where needed. The task demands were such that time slipped past quickly. The lesson summary was cursory, followed by frantic clearing up prior to assembly.

Positive features of the lesson included a thoroughly prepared lesson plan, specified assessment criteria to evaluate progress, careful use of terminology in the introduction, close monitoring during the task phase and perseverance to complete the session in a strictly limited time frame. However, the session would have benefited from the following:

- thinking more carefully about the demands on the teacher of such an intensive, practical lesson;
- talking to pupils more about the properties of 3D shapes during monitoring of the task;
- paying much closer attention to clearing up and orderliness.

The end product would also have been improved if pupils had received more precise guidance about task procedures, for instance:

- cutting out the shape along the lines with care;
- scoring the creases before folding them into position;
- ensuring that each glued seam was dry before proceeding to the next step.

Other small but important details had also been overlooked:

- some pupils finished more quickly than others and did not have an extension activity to occupy them;
- pupils were not told to put their names or an identifying mark on the shape template, which caused confusion about ownership once the shapes were built;
- storage of completed work had not been considered, with the result that some of the shapes were crumpled as they were casually thrown in a pile;
- the pupils had to walk across the room to the same place to deposit litter in the single available rubbish bin. The availability of several smaller bins or sacks would have simplified the procedure.

The lesson was far from disastrous but due to Latisha's inexperience in handling such an involved practical session, the amount of mathematical learning was limited. By contrast, Latisha learnt a lot about the need for detailed classroom organisation and management!

MOVING *ON* > > > > > > MOVING *ON* > > > > > > MOVING *ON*

In recent years there has been a lot of emphasis on 'learning outcomes' and the importance of the teacher in ensuring that these aims are fulfilled lesson by lesson. The reality is that you have to strike a balance between organising teaching and learning to achieve these stated goals and organising lessons to allow for unexpected outcomes and spontaneous ('serendipitous') learning. The link between teaching and learning is far less precise than official documentation claims, so relax, enjoy the experience of working with children and allow learning to grow naturally rather than trying to 'force-feed' it.

REFERENCES REFERENCES **REFERENCES** REFERENCES **REFERENCES** REFERENCES

Ainley, J., Pratt, D. and Hansen, A. (2006) Connecting engagement and focus in pedagogic task design. *British Educational Research Journal*, 32(1), 23–38.

Blatchford, P. (2004) *The Role and Effects of Teaching Assistants in English Primary Schools*, Research Report RR605. Nottingham: Department for Education & Skills.

Campbell, A. and Fairbairn, G. (eds) (2005) *Working with Support in the Classroom*. London: Paul Chapman Publishing.

Galton, M., Hargreaves, L., Comber, C. and Wall, D. (1998) *Inside the Primary Classroom: Twenty Years On.* Abingdon: Routledge.

Hook, P. and Vass, A. (2002) *Teaching with Influence*. London: David Fulton.

Myhill, D., Jones, S. and Hopper, R. (2006) *Talking, Listening, Learning: Effective Talk in the Primary Classroom*. Maidenhead: Open University Press/McGraw-Hill.

Pollard, A. (2005) *Reflective Teaching*. London: Continuum.

Pye, J. (1989) *Invisible Children*. Oxford: Oxford University Press.

Torrance, H. and Pryor, J. (2001) Developing formative assessment in the classroom: using action research to explore and modify theory. *British Educational Research Journal*, 27(5), 615–31.

Watkinson, A. (2003) *The Essential Guide for Competent Teaching Assistants*. London: David Fulton.

Watt, H. and Burrell, A. (2006) Making the plenary session count. *Education 3–13*, 34(1), 11–18.

Further reading

Baines, E., Blatchford, P. and Kutnick, P. (2008) *Promoting Effective Group Work in the Classroom*. Abingdon: Routledge.

Barnes, R. H. (2006) *The Practical Guide to Primary Classroom Management*. London: Sage. See Chapters 1 and 2.

Edwards, C., Gandini, L. and Forman, G. (eds) (1998) *The Hundred Languages of Children: the Reggio Emilia approach*. Westport, CT: Greenwood.

Hughes, P. (2008) *7 Principles of Primary Education*. London: David Fulton.

Kendall-Seatter, S. (2005) *Primary Professional Studies: Reflective Reader*. Exeter: Learning Matters. See chapters 5 and 6.

White, H. (2006) *Every Day a Good Day: Establishing Routines in Your Early Years Setting*. London: Sage.

4
Effective questioning

Learning outcomes

To understand:

- **the purpose for asking questions;**
- **question types;**
- **what pupils learn from being questioned;**
- **when questioning is most effective.**

Introduction

It is no exaggeration to say that if teachers are unable to use question and answer effectively in their teaching they are unlikely to succeed at the job. Teachers ask many questions throughout the day, most of them concerned with eliciting responses from pupils, reminding them of key facts and issues, or simply acting as a spur to participation. Informal questions are commonly used as teachers enquire about events in pupils' lives or seek to resolve their concerns. When a question is asked it is reasonable to assume that an answer is sought, but adults in school occasionally ask questions that take the form of barely concealed cautions or rebukes.

Although the importance of questioning as a teaching technique has been promoted as an essential part of every teacher's armoury, its utilisation does not guarantee learning. Questions can be 'great deceivers' because by using them in front of a captive audience they make teachers feel that they are doing something that has educational benefit. In fact, questions may or may not be a useful teaching tool, as this chapter reveals.

Purposes of questions (Q12, 14, 25c, 30, 31)

The key purpose for asking questions is to promote learning, either through introducing new concepts and skills or, more commonly, revising old ones. When teachers employ a question-and-answer strategy it tends to be used for one or more of five purposes:

- to involve pupils in the lesson;
- to discover whether pupils possess specified forms of knowledge;
- to encourage pupils to think deeply about an issue;
- to open up fresh areas of a theme or topic for discovery;
- to inspire creativity and imagination.

The type of question will vary according to which of the five purposes are most significant. Thus questions that are principally to *involve pupils* in the lesson are likely to be straightforward ones that every pupil can answer. Questions to discover *whether pupils possess knowledge* are best carried out through formal written means (a 'test') or, with younger pupils, asking them on an individual basis. Questions that *encourage pupils to think deeply* will be open-ended, allowing for a variety of responses. Supplementary questions are often needed to prompt a fuller range of answers from the pupils. Questions to *open up fresh areas* tend to be of the 'suppose that' types. The use of allegory, stories and real events can be valuable vehicles for stimulating the 'gasp factor' (a sense of awe and wonder). Questions to *inspire creativity* are likely to be of the 'can you find ways to' type. These questions are commonly used in connection with designing, constructing and investigating activities, especially in science and design and technology (D&T).

Questioning technique is therefore valuable at many levels and contexts; however, it can also suffer from shortcomings, of which the following are a selection:

- asking too many superficial questions;
- asking too few questions that make pupils think hard;
- asking rhetorical questions in the presence of very young pupils;
- use of inappropriate vocabulary;
- questions that are poorly expressed;
- framing or delivering questions in a way that alarms pupils because they fear that wrong answers might cause them to be scolded;
- several questions contained within a single statement;
- answers that can only be answered by clever and confident pupils;
- 'read my mind' questions that move from pupil to pupil in an effort to find someone who knows!;
- questions that begin hard and get harder;
- questions that are too simple and are therefore perceived as babyish;
- endless lists of unrelated questions that lead nowhere and end abruptly.

Questioning is widely used by teachers in whole-class and large-group situations and under-pins much of the interactive teaching process as a means of enhancing pupils' learning. Thus teachers ask a question, select a respondent, affirm or refute the response, comment further on the points or issues that have been raised or alert the pupils to the errors in their reasoning. The need to teach within a given time frame means that there is a limited amount of time available for pupil-initiated points. In practice this constraint means that adults begin nearly all the verbal exchanges and pupils' opportunities to respond are governed solely by the teacher's question rather than questions that might arise in their own minds. Ideally, the effective use of questions should encourage pupils to ponder and reflect on issues and problems as a means of aiding their conceptual development, opening up fresh areas of the topic for consideration and thereby stimulating pupil initiative, creativity and innovation.

Teachers have to consider carefully whether it is better to *tell and explain* something directly to the pupils or to employ question and answer techniques. Inexperienced teachers some-times use questions as a substitute for direct teaching, so it is essential for them to consider whether there is more to be gained by transmission teaching than in assailing pupils with a plethora of questions to 'drag out' the correct or appropriate response. Giving information to pupils as a substitute for questioning does not have to be dreary and tedious; even in a formal session a teacher can make a few questions thought-provoking, for instance in a maths lesson asking, 'What would happen if everyone woke up tomorrow morning one metre taller than they are today?' In determining the balance between 'tell them' and 'ask them', the following are relevant:

- questions are an important teaching tool but should be treated more like grains of pepper to add 'bite' to a meal than lashings of gravy to saturate it!;
- a balance of question types (closed, open, speculative – see later in this chapter) is most powerful;

- telling pupils facts can be activated by the use of pictures, short poems, snatches of songs, spontaneous role-play and so forth;
- pupils love to have details pointed out to them, to be enthralled by fascinating questions and to see the excitement on a teacher's face;
- even during the telling phase, an occasional question can be inserted to involve all the pupils;
- the whole group/class can be involved by using phrases such as:
  - put your hand up if you think this/if you think that (offering a choice);
  - hands up how many of you were going to say the same thing (as the pupil who answered correctly)?

A piece of information can be energised if it is followed by a question; for instance, explaining the importance of hygiene in cooking might involve giving information about ways in which germs can be harmful, followed by a question: *What would be the effect if someone with a nasty cold sneezed into the air?* Similarly, a pupil might provide a piece of knowledge that forms the basis of a question. For example, a pupil explains how maps help travellers to find their way; the teacher acknowledges the pupil's statement, adding: *What signs could you use to find your way to safety if you were in the middle of a strange country without a map?* If pupils are seated in groups, questions for discussion can be placed in envelopes for them to open at a given signal. The question in the envelope can be the same for everyone or a series of different ones. After a given time, a pupil from each group can be selected to report back to the class.

It is also essential that employing questions to help enforce discipline does not undermine their status. For instance, a question such as, *Shall we all line up quietly by the door?* is, in truth, a command to do so. The attempt to cloak an authority statement in the guise of egalitarianism is contrary to the transparent, interactive environment in which learning prospers.

REFLECTIVE TASK

Selecting a pupil to answer

When you ask a question, consider whether it is better to (a) put a pupil's name at the start, such as *Chelsea, can you think of any other reason for . . .* or (b) asking the question then selecting someone to answer. The first approach is orderly but may disengage the other pupils; the second approach keeps the class on its toes but is more challenging to manage. What factors influence your choice of method?

Basic question types (Q25c, 26)

When dealing with a wide ability range of pupils, teachers find that it is preferable to start with more straightforward questions to involve all the pupils, rather than beginning with conceptually challenging ones that limits the number of pupils who can participate. In a 15 or 20 minute session it is not unknown for 50 or more questions to be posed by a teacher. The impact on less astute pupils can only be imagined! Even where fewer questions are asked it is unusual for pupils to be given more than a few seconds of thinking time to cogitate or raise questions of their own.

The principal reason for this intense teaching approach is the tendency for teachers to use 'closed' or 'single answer' questions, where each question has a specific answer, so that a pupil's response will be judged either correct or incorrect. For instance, multiplication tables and spellings are in this category. The overall question rate is inflated if teachers ask the same question of numerous pupils before receiving the correct answer. In such circumstances the large total number of questions may, in practice, consist of (say) only 20 questions, oft repeated.

Questions that are not 'closed' are referred to as 'open' or 'multi-answer', some of which are 'speculative'. For instance, an open question might invite pupils to provide a range of alternative words or ideas about the best way to undertake an activity. Speculative questions encourage pupils to make informed guesses and employ their imaginations. Thus the teacher might encourage pupils to anticipate what life will be like one hundred years from now if the earth's climate warms, or to predict which bridge design will be strongest. While all open questions allow for longer turns, speculative questions in particular offer the chance to construct a lengthier reply, as pupils explore and justify their ideas. Teachers need to be aware, however, that the larger the number of open questions, the fewer can be asked in a given time period, which may limit curriculum coverage. Figure 4.1 summarises basic question types.

Question type	Involvement	Typical length of response	Next step	Reason for asking the question
CLOSED	One pupil at a time to find correct answer	Single word or short phrase	Teacher asks another question	To find out what pupils know and do not know
OPEN (general)	Pupils offer answers in turn	Depends on the extent of pupil's understanding	Teacher invites further responses to the same question	To find out the variety of responses within the group
OPEN (speculative)	Selected pupils explain their ideas in depth	Expansive	Teacher invites other pupils to comment	To find out what pupils believe and envisage

Figure 4.1 Summary of basic question types

Figure 4.1 is a useful means of describing open and closed questions but a closer scrutiny of question types shows that there are many other variations available for teachers to employ. Thus, in their exceptional book about asking better questions, Morgan and Saxton (1994) not only emphasise the difference between open and closed questions, and between higher-order and lower-order questions, but also list a glossary of terms describing a wide range of types.

The authors emphasise that producing a typology of questions is intended to stimulate teachers to consider how they are using the technique of questioning. In the following section some names and descriptors in the list have been changed from the original; most of the examples given with each entry are not taken from the original typology.

Question typology (Q19, 25b, 25c, 31)

The typology that follows includes a large number of question forms that serve, to a greater or lesser extent, as a means of extending thinking and promoting learning.

- *Overt* – direct questions that demand a single answer, for example: 'Which tower is taller?'
- *Recall* – questions that require pupils to draw from their existing knowledge and experience, for example: 'Can anyone remember the different methods we used to work out this subtraction?'
- *Inciting* – a question that invites elaboration, for example: 'Can you explain why you believe that?'
- *Polar* – questions that require yes or no, true or false, for example: 'Do you want to choose this one?'
- *Branching* – questions that offer alternatives, so that pupils have to make choices, for example: 'Shall we use this shape or that shape first?'
- *Confrontation* – questions that challenge the validity of a statement, for example: 'Is it really true that taller people are always stronger than shorter people?'
- *Critical* – questions that open up issues, sometimes by being provocative, for example: 'Would it be better if girls and boys had separate playgrounds?'
- *Deductive* – questions in which the pupil answering has to provide evidence to support a statement, for example: 'What makes you say that motor bikes are dangerous?'
- *Inductive* – questions in which the pupil has to summarise a series of related and accepted facts and widen the scope of enquiry, for example: 'What makes a story or a person into a legend?' (The teacher is trying to show how legends are different from, say, myths and fairy tales.)
- *Heuristic* – questions that guide pupils to discover answers for themselves, for example: 'What will happen if we fill these bottles with water or sand before rolling them down the slope?'
- *Productive* – questions that lead pupils into new areas of enquiry, for example: 'Can you think of a way to paint the picture without using brushes?'
- *Liberating* – questions in which the adult makes it clear that there is no single correct answer, for example: 'How many different ways can we think of to organise the books?'
- *Hypothetical* – questions that encourage imaginative replies, for example: 'What sort of questions would visitors from Mars want to ask about life in school?'
- *Divergent* – questions that invite a range of concrete and abstract answers, for example: 'What would happen if all the teachers got bad throats and could not talk for a week?'
- *Research* – questions that invite pupils to look for solutions, for example: 'How can we reduce the amount of litter in the playground?'
- *Enactive* – questions that drive the pupils into further thought, for example: 'If we continue to damage the equipment, what will be the result?'
- *Social* – A question that reminds pupils of their responsibilities towards one another, for example: 'How can we show someone that we want to be his or her friend?'
- *Rhetorical* – questions designed to affect the emotions but not necessarily to provide answers, for example: 'I wonder what would happen if we all behaved as selfishly as the man in the story?'
- *Reflective* – questions that necessitate periods of time for deliberation before answering, for example: 'How did it feel on your first day in school?'
- *Illuminating* – questions that clarify a pupil's previous answer, for example: 'Are you saying that every triangle has three sides?'
- *Synopsis* – questions that assist pupils in crystallising their thinking, for example: 'So if we want to run faster, what skills must we develop?'
- *Elaborating* – questions that encourage a pupil to embellish a bald statement, for example the pupil says: 'The note gets higher and then lower'; the teacher asks: 'Are you saying that as we tighten the string, the pitch of the note is raised, and as we loosen the string the pitch falls?' Note that this type of question involves a subtle form of direct teaching.

- *Reviewing* – questions that invite pupils to retrace their steps in learning, for example; 'What did you have to find out before you could complete the chart?'
- *Evaluating* – questions that invite pupils to examine their work critically, for example: 'Can you think of other adverbs that you might have used to make the description more graphic?'
- *Leading* – questions that prompt the desired answer, for example, to work out the answer to 10 add 12, a teacher might say, 'So if 10 add 10 is 20, then 10 add 10 add 2 equals what?'

Some question types are often less helpful in promoting learning.

- *Serialised* – questions fired off rapidly that require immediate answers and allow no thinking time (though this form of questioning can be considerable fun for pupils if the learning climate is relaxed).
- *Marathon* – long and involved questions.
- *Ambiguous* – questions that lead to uncertainty in the pupils' minds.
- *Restrictive* – questions in which unhelpful alternatives are offered.
- *Prompting* – questions accompanied by heavy clues about questioner expectations.
- *Contrapuntal* – questions that are confused by unnecessary additional comment.
- *Legitimising* – questions that require respondents to justify their position.
- *Profound* – deep-seated theological questions.
- *Judgemental* – questions asked by an adult as someone with authority, in which the pupil response is spontaneously evaluated.

A scan of the amended Morgan and Saxton typology (above) emphasises the key point that questions can serve a variety of purposes, so their framing and relevance to the area of learning is of the utmost importance. For example, a teacher may wish to discover what pupils know, or to rehearse previous learning, or to reinforce ideas, or to probe an issue, or even to rouse a sleepy bunch of pupils! All too often, an inexperienced teacher is instructed by a tutor that it is essential to ask questions but then gives little thought to the purpose for doing so. This unthinking approach tends to have four consequences:

- a surfeit of superficial questions that do not enhance pupils' understanding;
- a lack of continuity and progression in the questioning;
- vague or unhelpfully complex questions;
- question fatigue.

If a teacher wants to *discover what pupils know* it can be helpful to use a 'whisper what you think to your neighbour' approach and then request hands up, or use an either/or, asking pupils to opt for one or the other, rather than a 'hands up who knows'. This method involves all the pupils rather than a selected few.

If a teacher wants to *rehearse previous knowledge* it is useful for teachers to employ a 'tell them a little, ask pupils for more' approach, thereby providing sufficient information to remind pupils of basic facts, but also leaving opportunity for them to add to what has been said.

If a teacher wants to *reinforce ideas* the questions can invite the pupils to speculate and use their imaginations, for example asking them how they would direct someone from the school to the fire station if the High Street were closed.

If a teacher wants to *probe an issue* the questions must offer an alternative perspective so that pupils re-evaluate the accepted wisdom, for example whether it is necessarily true that grown-ups always know best.

Quick-fire questions are appropriate if a teacher wants to *make pupils more alert*, possibly incorporating a competitive element, especially for juniors. For example, each pupil receives five points if he or she *would* have given the correct answer, even if not chosen to provide it. At the end of the quick-fire time the teacher asks pupils to raise their hand if they accumulated more than 5 points, 10 points and so on. Inexperienced teachers should be aware that this approach invites a high level of eager participation, rivalry and celebration!

PRACTICAL TASK PRACTICAL TASK **PRACTICAL TASK** PRACTICAL TASK **PRACTICAL TASK**

Depth of questioning

Some teachers use questions to probe knowledge deeply, like a mineshaft driven down through tough rock to reach the richest coal seams. Other teachers use shallow questions, more akin to opencast mining in which a thin layer of poor quality coal is skimmed effortlessly from the surface. Ask a colleague to monitor the time you allocate to using 'mineshaft' and 'open mining' questioning styles. Evaluate whether you need to adjust the balance.

Questioning and higher-order thinking (Q25b, 28)

If pupils are to be encouraged to learn in creative and varied ways, they benefit from being asked a range of questions that extend their thinking. One way in which variety can be achieved is through the use of a 'taxonomy' of learning to promote what is referred to as higher-order thinking skills, the best known of which is attributed to Benjamin Bloom. In 1956, Bloom headed a group of educational psychologists who developed a classification of levels of intellectual behaviour that were considered significant in learning (Bloom, 1956). Bloom found that over 95 per cent of questions required learners to think only at the lowest cognitive level, namely the factual recall of information. He identified three domains (or categories) of intellectual behaviour, sometimes referred to as KSA (knowledge, skills, and attitude):

- cognitive domain: mental skills (*knowledge*);
- psychomotor domain: manual or physical skills (*skills*);
- affective domain: growth in feelings or emotional areas (*attitude*).

The model they produced does not consist of 'absolute' divisions and is open to interpretation. Nevertheless, Bloom's taxonomy is easy to comprehend and is probably the most widely applied one in regular use today. There are six major categories, beginning with those making the simplest intellectual demands and progressing to the most complex, on the assumption that the first one must be mastered before the next one can be addressed, though the reality is more complex.

1. Knowledge
2. Comprehension
3. Application
4. Analysis
5. Synthesis
6. Evaluation

Bloom's taxonomy of learning is a useful guide to enhancing the quality of questioning skills because it helps teachers to focus on the demands that a particular set of questions makes of pupils. The relationship between Bloom's categories and questioning is most clearly seen through the use of actual examples, as the following sections demonstrate.

Questions that test knowledge (Q26)

The majority of questions that test knowledge demand straightforward recall: the teacher asks a question that has a single correct answer or a very limited range of alternatives. Pupils sometimes answer knowledge questions simplistically, when a teacher is hoping for greater intellectual rigour; this situation particularly pertains in science. For instance, a teacher might ask why different weights drop at the same speed, only to be told by the pupils that it is because they hit the floor at the same time. The answer is correct but makes no reference to the force of gravity concept involved. Again, a question about why birds are able to fly might elicit a range of answers from 'fear of cats' to 'because it is quicker than walking', rather than a scientific explanation about bone and feather structure affecting the aerodynamics. Plain answers to complex questions may indicate that pupils have not grasped the basic concepts and that the teacher would have been better advised to 'explain and tell' rather than seek clarification through questioning. Knowledge questions can be broadly divided into four categories:

- *Where an answer is either true or not true*
  - What number do we get when we add 10 to the first number?
  - How do you spell a particular word?
  - When did the first man walk on the Moon?

- *Where there are several correct possible answers*
  - What are the names of three nineteenth-century prime ministers?
  - Which month has 30 days?
  - What is the best way to keep warm?

- *Where answers require fuller knowledge*
  - How are African and Indian elephants different?
  - Why do sunsets come in a variety of colours?
  - How do you use a map to find your way from point A to B?

- *Where answers require discernment*
  - How would you describe the sound made by a rattlesnake?
  - Who were the most important generals in the Second World War?
  - Why do most people enjoy the sound of rainfall on a roof?

Questions that test comprehension (Q25c, 26)

A glance at the knowledge questions classified above, especially under the final category (answers that require discernment), shows that there is overlap of questions that test knowledge with questions that test comprehension because they both require a degree of understanding about external factors that impinge upon the solution. Comprehension questions as a group are difficult to classify but can be listed under *restricted comprehension questions* (RCQ) and *elaborated comprehension questions* (ECQ). Restricted comprehension questions only need to take account of the available knowledge and information, while elaborated comprehension questions require extended thinking and elucidation of the principle. The two types of questions are frequently used in conjunction.

RCQ: How would you classify the two-dimensional shapes on the chart?
ECQ: What does this tell us about how we use shape to classify objects?

RCQ: How would you summarise the class rules in your own words?
ECQ: How would you decide whether someone was keeping the rules satisfactorily?

RCQ: How might you rephrase the last two sentences in the paragraph?
ECQ: Is what the author claims in these sentences necessarily true?
If not, why not?

RCQ: What evidence is there that the character in the story is frightened?
ECQ: Nevertheless, who thinks the character behaved bravely, and why?

RCQ: How is the writer making use of adjectives in the story?
ECQ: Are there other adjectives that she might have used?

RCQ: Which parts of the poem make us laugh?
ECQ: What techniques does the poet use to create the humour?

RCQ: What makes the picture scary?
ECQ: How has the artist applied different colours to 'paint the mood'?

Questions that test application (Q25b, 26)

Pupils tend to respond more enthusiastically to questions that have a purpose other than the teacher finding out what they know or remember. In particular, the use of questions linked to practical activities serves to focus attention, stimulate creativity and foster imagination.

- *To focus attention*
    - Which of these creatures have more than two pairs of legs?
    - How would you use the sound patterns to create background music for our assembly performance?
    - How would you arrange the cubes to make an interesting shape?

- *To stimulate creativity*
    - What can you do to work out the problem in a different way?
    - How would you draw a diagram to show the procedure?
    - Can you make use of the facts to set your friend a challenge?

- *To foster imagination*
    - What would happen if you performed this movement without first warming up?
    - What questions would you ask in an interview with your favourite pop star?
    - What design would you use to build a magic castle made of chocolate?

Application questions serve to shape pupils' thinking and make them engage deeply with the task. Just as some knowledge questions overlap with comprehension questions, it can be seen that some of the extended comprehension questions overlap with application questions. It is noteworthy that creative and imaginative forms of application questions are often used in association with exploratory forms of learning (finding out) as opposed to specified, objectives-orientated learning (being told how).

Questions that test analysis (Q23, 26)

'Analysis' is a term that has a variety of definitions, including:

- an investigation of the component parts of a whole and their relations;
- a form of literary criticism in which the structure of a piece of writing is scrutinised;
- the process of splitting up an action, an event or an idea to understand how it works.

Analysis relies heavily on pupils having good comprehension; however, once the meaning has been grasped, pupils need to separate out the component elements that constitute the knowledge. Analysing a situation, text, argument, procedure or performance is more demanding than mere comprehension because it necessitates organising and structuring ideas in such a way that they can be communicated so that others are able to understand, appreciate or make judgements. Examples of questions that invite analysis include the following.

- What were the key features of the play?
- What advantages and disadvantages accompany the different ways of working out the maths problem?
- What criteria would you use to classify the leaves we collected?
- How would you explain the factors that influence the relationship between elves and hobbits?
- What parts of speech are present in this passage?
- What are the different instruments used in the music?
- What evidence can you find that one type of paper absorbs water more quickly than another?
- What links can we establish between healthy eating and fitness?
- What are the points in favour of and against the suggestion?

Questions that test synthesis (Q25b, 26, 28)

Synthesis consists of combining separate elements, thoughts, ideas or information to form a coherent whole. Just as an analysis involves comprehending and separating out the components, so synthesis is the opposite process of drawing together separate points to create something new, either by using old ideas creatively or employing new ideas imaginatively. The most powerful synthesis has the capacity to inspire innovative and creative practice. Examples of questions that invite synthesis are as follows.

- Can you think of a different way to take the attendance register?
- How can we improve the safety of pupils crossing the road?
- How would you teach a bully to be kinder?
- Can you think of other ways to mix the colours to represent the sky?
- How can you use the string, paper and clips to make a simple flying machine?
- Can you suggest alternative methods to find the answer?
- How would you change the layout of the school garden so that people with poor sight could enjoy it?
- How can we make sure that no pupil is lonely in school?
- How would you go about designing a new school uniform?
- How would you estimate how far different toy cars will travel down different gradients?
- Can you draw a diagram to summarise all that you know about weather patterns?

By contrast with questions requiring analysis that tend to begin with the word 'what', synthesis frequently starts with 'how' to emphasise the problem-solving requirement. Whereas when pupils carry out an analysis it tends to produce similar outcomes, synthesis exposes a range of outcomes.

Questions that test evaluation (Q26, 28)

An evaluation involves making a decision or judgement about the significance, value or quality of something, based on a careful study of its features. A more formal evaluation can also be defined as the process of determining whether an item or activity meets predetermined criteria. The evaluation process may consist of reviewing the basic premise (was this the right thing to do?), efficiency (did we do it in the best possible way?) and effectiveness (did it achieve what we hoped for?) of an enterprise. Pupils need a lot of adult guidance in forming conclusions, as they often have neither the experience or wisdom or insight to reach a well-reasoned decision. As evaluations of situations and decisions sometimes involve a moral judgement, teachers have to be willing to combat pupil prejudice, misunderstandings and immaturity. In doing so, teachers may need to confront their *own* uncertainties and be open with pupils about the dilemmas that are attached to many decisions. Examples of evaluative questions are as follows.

- To what extent do you agree with the policy of making slow workers stay in at playtime and finish their work?
- How would you evaluate the success of a holiday?
- What is your opinion of school dinners without chips or French fries?
- What would you say to someone who claims that boys are greedy and girls are bossy?
- What would you say to someone who had recently moved into the area and was looking for a good school for their children?
- How can we decide who is the best teacher?
- What would you do about a starving person who stole food?
- What would guide your choice in selecting an animal as a pet?
- How would you choose the winner of a fancy dress competition?
- How well are you doing in maths this year? How do you know?
- If you were the head teacher, how would you decide what to say in assembly?

Utilising Bloom's taxonomy in teaching (Q25b, 25c, 26, 28, 29)

It is worth reiterating that Bloom's categories are not intended to be wholly distinctive; there are inevitably overlaps between them, as easily seen by examining the sample of questions noted above. Some teachers will work their way through the levels, making a string of questions increasingly demanding. For example, a series of questions based on regular addition in multiples of five might take the following form.

- *Knowledge:* What number do we get if we add 15 to 35?
- *Comprehension:* Explain how we reach that answer.
- *Application:* How much would it cost if we bought two items from a sweet shop, one costing 15 pence and the other costing 35 pence?
- *Analysis:* What combinations of coins can be used to make up the 50 pence?
- *Synthesis:* How many different methods can we use to work out the answers to these sums?

- *Evaluation:* Is one candy lollipop and one gobstopper worth paying 50 pence for? What else could you buy with the money that would be better value?

Some areas of work lend themselves more naturally to higher-order questioning, requiring pupils to speculate about outcomes and consequences. The key point is that teachers should give careful consideration to the types of questions that they want to employ and link them to different forms of learning.

Sequences of questions based on Bloom's taxonomy can be used for differentiation and diagnostically. With respect to *differentiation*, knowledge-based questions and comprehension questions (as opposed, say, to analytical questions) provide opportunities for less academic pupils to respond correctly and gain confidence from doing so; similarly, more intellectually challenging questions can form the basis of questions to stretch the more able. Used *diagnostically*, categories of questions that begin with knowledge-based types and work through levels of difficulty towards evaluative types have the potential to provide assessment information as pupils provide (or fail to provide) varying responses at each level of difficulty.

Using the taxonomy as the basis for differentiation *and* diagnosis is a formidable challenge for even the most experienced teacher. For novice teachers it is often beyond their capability, which explains why so many inexperienced teachers prefer to differentiate *written* tasks to take account of and assess pupil capability rather than use verbal questioning. A TA who would otherwise sit passively and observe the teacher–pupil interactions can make effective use of her time by making notes about the nature and quality of individual pupil responses while the teacher concentrates on asking the questions and fielding the answers. The notes can later be shared and recorded more formally to provide evidence of an individual pupil's understanding and grasp of content.

RESEARCH SUMMARY RESEARCH SUMMARY **RESEARCH SUMMARY** RESEARCH SUMMARY

Using questions

Wragg and Brown (2001) emphasise the importance of questioning technique:

Undirected questions often lead to chorus answers and lack of control. Hence the importance of directing questions, when this is appropriate, by name, gesture, head movement or facial expressions. Distributing questions around the group rather than concentrating on one or two willing respondents not only involves more pupils but also reduces the risk of losing attention and class control. Some teachers often subconsciously favour the approach of asking mainly knowledgeable pupils, if only because their answers come more quickly or seem more rewarding. (p31)

Adult responses to pupils' answers (Q2, 27, 30)

Pupils learn through question and answer but can also be disillusioned or dismayed if the session is too intensive, confusing or threatening. Phrasing a question in such a way that the pupils discern which answer is expected does not stretch their thinking but merely makes them 'mind-readers'. The best questioning enhances pupils' confidence, encourages them to think creatively and invites them to raise their own questions. There are two things for teachers to be aware of, and cautious about, when receiving replies. First, although most pupils are keen to answer questions, a sizeable minority are anxious that they will get something wrong and be ridiculed by their classmates. By involving them in a 'whole class' response, such pupils can get used to making a public response without being singled out. Second, although giving a correct answer is important in some instances, there are also many occasions when a question that invites opinion is more useful in promoting learning. However, timid pupils who venture an opinion may have to be protected from more asser-tive pupils who are all too ready to disagree or contradict! There are also more subtle ways in which teachers may inadvertently mishandle pupil responses. For example:

- negative body language: leading to pupil insecurity;
- ignoring the answer: resulting in bewilderment;
- use of faint praise: promoting uncertainty;
- use of 'yes but' responses: dampening enthusiasm;
- rejecting the reply out of hand: lowering self-esteem;
- overreacting to inappropriate answers: causing alarm;
- responding by asking a difficult question: fostering subordination;
- inviting whole-class responses in unison: inviting potential discipline problems;
- interjecting with a subsidiary question while the pupil is speaking: creating confusion;
- rejecting valid answers that are not the desired one: narrowing thought.

Of course the teacher's response also depends on the pupil and the nature of the adult–pupil relationship. Self-confident pupils are able to brush off setbacks and eagerly seek a further opportunity to answer a question whereas insecure pupils may be reluctant to risk further exposure. Sensitive teachers do not allow other pupils to contradict a pupil's answer 'in mid-flow' as this can be demoralising for the pupil concerned. Instead, they inculcate a 'wait until the person has finished speaking' policy.

Experienced teachers ensure that some questions are open-ended and provide for a variety of answers, each of which can be commended. However, even incorrect answers can serve a useful purpose as they reveal misconceptions and incomplete understanding. Teachers have to find a way to respond to an inaccurate response so that it clarifies the incorrectness or incompleteness of the answer while commending the pupil's willingness to contribute. Such balanced responses might include:

- *Thank you, Sarah; that is not the answer but I'm pleased you had a try.*
- *I don't agree with you, Alfie, but you have certainly given us something to think about.*
- *How interesting, Faisal; I wonder how you reached that conclusion.*
- *Oh, Imogen, you are so close!*
- *Ah, I see what you have done, Barry; it's an easy mistake to make.*

Teachers must ensure, of course, that any wrong thinking is ultimately corrected, but sensi-tivity in the way that it is done makes a considerable difference to the class ethos, morale and motivation.

Improving your questioning technique
(Q18, 25c, 29)

Ineffective questioning is normally due to poor technique, characterised by one or more of the following.

- *Asking superficial questions that make few demands upon pupils*, other than having to raise a hand and utter an answer. The only time to ask such questions is to elicit a full response early at the start of the session by encouraging less confident pupils to participate.

- *Asking too few questions that make pupils think hard.* While it is unreasonable to expect pupils to think deeply all the time, the lack of probing questions creates an atmosphere of low expectation.
- *Use of inappropriate vocabulary* (too advanced, too vague or too specialised). It is easy to forget that pupils do not possess the concepts to understand sophisticated language that is more suited to adult exchanges. While avoiding 'baby-talk', it is important to phrase the questions in such a way that pupils will grapple with how to give a suitable answer and not be expending brainpower trying to interpret the question!
- *Poorly expressed questions* (especially the use of 'double negatives' in the sentence). For instance, imagine the confusion that is caused by a question such as: *When is it unsuitable not to do what a grown-up has told you not to do?*
- *Framing or delivering questions in a way that alarms pupils* because they fear that wrong answers might cause them to be scolded. A bright tone of voice and open body language is essential to avoid the problem occurring.
- *Including more than one question within a single statement.* For example, the following question is, in reality, composed of three questions: 'What sort of creatures might live in the stream and how will they avoid being eaten, and do they all swim the same way?' It is essential to deal with one question at a time.
- *Answers are only sought from clever and confident pupils.* Some pupils like to be 'invisible' (see Chapter 3) and either sit out of immediate eye range or remain completely passive, never venturing an answer; however, such pupils are not necessarily incapable of doing so.
- *Mind-reading questions.* If it quickly becomes clear that the pupils do not know the answer, it is better to stop and tell them, but also to provide more information about the point to reinforce learning.
- *Asking endless lists of questions* that get nowhere, end abruptly and have no connection with the work that precedes or follows.

Regardless of the care with which teachers formulate questions and the enthusiasm that they pour into the interaction, pupils sometimes offer low-level or unexpected responses. There are a number of possible explanations for these superficial replies. First, pupils may simply need more time to think and discuss. A question may appear simple but have implications for pupils that would never occur to an adult. For instance, imagine asking a class of ten-year-olds how the Pilgrim Fathers might have felt when they landed in America. A teacher might hope for answers that referred to relief, celebration, happiness and apprehension. In their minds, however, pupils might associate America with adventure parks, hurricanes, Indians and cowboys, and answer accordingly. Questions that explore feelings and emotions, especially those that require empathy rather than personal disclosure, inevitably require more time and thoughtful consideration than questions that deal with facts or opinions.

Second, the pupils may need more information about the context. For instance, suppose that a teacher asks how many pupils can 'think of another word that we can use instead of *nice*'. At first there is little enthusiasm, so the teacher encourages the pupils to try. One shy girl suggests 'good' as an alternative; the teacher was hoping for a more profound example but decides to commend her answer and request further instances. Another pupil ventures 'very nice' and the teacher reminds him that it must be a single word. By now the class seems paralysed, so the teacher prompts them with 'delicious'. A few more weak examples are suggested by the pupils before the frustrated teacher reads out the list of appropriate adjectives that he had prepared earlier. The reason for the tentativeness was that the pupils needed to hear concrete examples of words used within the context of a sentence before submitting alternatives. For example, If the teacher had offered, 'the two pupils had a nice time playing in the nice park' as the example, the pupils would have had a template sentence structure as a guide for offering suggestions.

Sometimes a stimulating question can generate excitement that needs to be managed before the lesson can proceed. For instance, a question about the best way to get to a holiday destination conjures up for pupils memories of sandcastles, discos, fairgrounds and ice creams; the route to the holiday has relatively little significance for a pupil who is desperate to tell about when his brother was sick on the merry-go-round or when his little sister got lost. Every teacher has to decide whether to allow time for pupils to express their animated thoughts or to curtail them abruptly and insist that the primary question is answered.

A closed question can inadvertently invite a higher-level response. For instance, the teacher might show the class a picture of animals in a natural setting and point to a badger (say) and ask the pupils to put up their hands if they know what it is called. Most of the class respond correctly, but a pupil calls out that her dad told her that badgers are a pest because they spread disease and should be killed. The girl has inadvertently supplied the answer to the question but also introduced a new layer of learning (sometimes referred to as 'deep' learning – see, for example, Stoll, Fink and Earlthat, 2002) that is hard to ignore or dismiss. The teacher intended to identify a number of animals in turn but now the parameters of learning have been extended. Instead of a series of straightforward answers to the (apparently) closed questions, the teacher is faced with a dilemma about how to proceed. Several other pupils are already exchanging comments with the girl, who is busy defending herself and her father from their protestations.

The use of questions in classroom teaching is a powerful teaching tool that has the potential to unlock knowledge, motivate pupils and cement adult–pupil relationships. Used unwisely, however, it can be a frustrating constraint, fail to have the intended impact and even create discipline problems. However, it is no exaggeration to say that the quality of all interactive teaching depends in large measure on the standard of the questioning.

CASE STUDY

When Asha was placed with a bright Year 5 class she was delighted that it contained so many articulate and confident pupils, as she was keen on fostering dialogue and discussion as a means of exploring key issues. For the first few days Asha observed the class teacher working interactively with the whole class, offering insights, asking questions, fielding pupil comments and summarising their responses. It seemed to Asha that the teacher helped every pupil to be involved and the working atmosphere was relaxed and purposeful. In her previous school placement Asha had been commended for her work with a reception class, so she felt motivated and eager to show what she was capable of doing with the older pupils. Asha assembled the class on the carpet and explained that they were going to think about the issue of 'fairness' and 'equality' with special reference to the work they had been doing about pupil labour in the nineteenth century. Initially all went smoothly; the pupils listened intently as she reminded them of some things that they had learned. It was when she began to ask questions that class management issues surfaced. Asha thought that she would start with some apparently simple 'yes or no' questions and gradually increase the complexity so as to provide for a differentiated approach, allowing less able pupils to answer the straightforward questions and the more able to cope with the more probing ones. She soon became aware that the strategy was flawed. Asha first asked: *Were children in the mines happy or unhappy?* and pointed to Raj, who stared blankly for a moment then whispered doubtfully, *not happy*. Asha had no sooner begun to congratulate him for answering correctly when Devon called out that Raj was wrong. Asha was startled and asked what Devon meant. He replied with conviction that, *Some of the children were happy, Miss, because they could earn money for food*. Two or three other pupils protested that they disagreed with Devon, who became quite defensive and looked to friends for support. A few seconds of comment and counter-comment followed and Asha found herself shush-shushing them to restore order. It wasn't until the class teacher spoke sternly from the back of the room that they settled. Asha swallowed hard and tried again. *Now, put up your hands if you think you know the answer to this one: 'Why did Lord Shaftesbury get involved?'* Lots of arms shot into the air, together with an assortment of grunts to indicate a willingness to respond. Asha chose Paul, who replied that it was because Shaftesbury wanted to help the poor. A few pupils said that he was wrong and Asha then selected Brian, who offered that Shaftesbury helped pupils because he was sad that they were getting injured and killed in the factories and mines. A few of his friends giggled. *Okay, settle down*, Asha insisted, her confidence waning. *Let's see who can answer this hard question: 'Who was angry when children began to go to school instead of working in the factories and what did the parents think and what happened as a result?'* No sooner had pupils begun to call out random suggestions than the class teacher intervened. *I am sorry, but I think we need to stop answering questions and move on to the next part of the lesson*. Asha glanced up at the clock and was horrified to see that the introduction and handful of questions had occupied over ten minutes. As previously agreed, the class teacher took over at that point in organising the task phase. Asha felt deflated. In her lesson evaluation she later wrote the following.

- Using question and answer technique with a new class requires considerable skill and patience.
- I must clarify the rules before launching into the lesson.
- Simple questions sometimes turn out to be complicated ones.
- I selected too many boys to answer questions.
- My 'hard question' was ridiculous because it consisted of three parts!

After receiving advice from the class teacher and having several more attempts, Asha gradually became adept in questioning older pupils, especially after she imposed three rules.

- Pupils remain at their tables and do not come to the carpet.
- Pupils have to use a thumbs-up (sure of the answer) or thumbs-down (no idea) or make a circle with thumb and finger (unsure) before raising an arm.
- Disagreement with the previous speaker is indicated by raising both arms in the air and keeping them still.

MOVING *ON* > > > > > > MOVING *ON* > > > > > > MOVING *ON*

Try to emulate experienced teachers who weave questions into the lesson in such a way that the children don't feel threatened or intimidated and are willing to risk their answers being wrong. Such teachers use questioning as a natural part of teaching in the same way that a skilled chef prepares and mixes ingredients to produce a nourishing meal. A question is not an end in itself; rather, it flavours and enhances learning to feed eager minds; it stimulates thinking; and it provides information. Questions can also act as a 'spice' to enliven dull content and energise children's imaginations.

REFERENCES REFERENCES **REFERENCES** REFERENCES **REFERENCES** REFERENCES

Bloom, B. S. (ed.) (1956) *Taxonomy of Educational Objectives: Handbook I: The Cognitive Domain*. New York: David McKay. Note that Bloom et al were responsible for various other associated publications until 1964.

Morgan, N. and Saxton, J. (1994) *Asking Better Questions*. Markham, Ont: Pembroke Publishers.

Stoll, L., Fink, D. and Earlthat, K. (2002) *It's About Learning and It's About Time*. Abingdon: Routledge.

Wragg, E. C. and Brown, G. (2001) *Questioning in the Primary School*. Abingdon: Routledge.

FURTHER READING FURTHER READING **FURTHER READING** FURTHER READING

Baumfield, V. and Mroz, M. (2004) Investigating pupils' questions in the primary school. In: E. C. Wragg (ed.), *Teaching and Learning*. Abingdon: Routledge, 49–59.

Browne, N. and Keeley, S. M. (2006) *Asking the Right Questions: A Guide to Critical Thinking*. Englewood Cliffs, NJ: Prentice Hall.

Walsh, J. A. and Sattes, B. D. (2005) *Quality Questioning: Research-Based Practice to Engage Every Learner*. Charlestown, WV: Edvantia.

5
Control, behaviour and discipline

Learning outcomes

To understand:

- **the principles that underpin a purposeful learning environment;**
- **how a purposeful environment can be established and maintained;**
- **how pupils know what is expected of them;**
- **strategies teachers use to foster good behaviour;**
- **the place of rewards and sanctions.**

Introduction

The working environment in classrooms varies considerably from class to class, even within the same school. Occasionally a room resembles a dentist's waiting area; pupils are quietly occupied and orderly but the atmosphere is lifeless. In other situations a classroom is more like an open market; pupils work noisily and there is lively activity. Yet another classroom feels like a court in session; pupils and adults interact but there is an underlying tension and the teacher acts like the presiding judge. From time to time a classroom is akin to the manic atmosphere in the Stock Exchange; pupils compete with one another, argue about the rights and wrongs of a situation and seem unable or unwilling to cooperate; the teacher struggles to cope. Thankfully, the majority of classrooms are orderly but not unduly so; pupils are intent on doing the tasks well; adults and pupils work harmoniously; there is a sense of constrained urgency but no panic, strident voices or harsh comments. The teacher has instilled in the pupils a desire to think, gain knowledge, understand situations, explore uncertainty, exploit learning opportunities, take calculated risks and celebrate one another's successes. The factors that contribute towards the creation of such a learning environment form the substance of this chapter.

Terminology (Q31)

There is a strong tendency when discussing pupils' actions and attitudes to use the phrase 'behaviour management' rather than discipline. The word 'discipline' has negative connotations and is reminiscent of harsh treatment, authoritarianism and meek compliance on the part of pupils, a notion that is far removed from an emphasis on interpersonal relationships and mutual respect that permeates this book. Despite these connotations, effective discipline facilitates interaction and creativity rather than suppressing it, for the simple reason that without firm boundaries and structures the learning environment is unstable. Although a definition is only ever a loose guide to the meaning of terms, the following is generally agreed.

- *Behaviour* is what the child does.
- *Discipline* consists of the structures the adult imposes to assist the child's behaviour.
- *Control* is what the child learns to exercise to bring about satisfactory behaviour.

Principles (Q1, 2, 3)

Robertson (1996) claims that it is in such skills as organising, presenting, communicating and monitoring that teachers' true authority rests; without these qualities the interest and respect of their pupils will never be gained. Consequently, all teachers need to ask how much pupil misbehaviour is due to their own shortcomings or inexperience, how much is due to the pupils; and how much is due to the prevailing classroom and school systems. In doing so, however, it is important to remember the following.

- Children are just that, children!
- They possess limited and narrow perspectives on life.
- They tend to be spontaneous rather than cautious in their responses.
- They do not always see the implications of their actions.

Pupils sometimes get confused and in the excitement of the moment may behave as if they were at home rather than at school. In certain respects this confusion is a positive signal that the child views the classroom as a 'second home', though it has to be accepted that some children are deliberately awkward and a few are wilfully naughty. Nevertheless, it is undoubtedly the case that the vast majority of children want to be sensible and appreciate adults being persistently and consistently firm. Novice teachers should constantly remind themselves of this truth.

If children who are normally compliant behave inappropriately, it may be that they do not respect the adult concerned or do not fear the consequences of their mischievous behaviour, but it is more likely that they are confused about boundaries, unmotivated, bored or lacking confidence. Some children perceive themselves as failures and do not wish to reinforce negative experiences, so cloak their anxiety in frivolity and gain a bad image by being uncooperative or unhelpful when, all the time, it is a plea for help.

Trainee teachers have special challenges, for although they may begin to think, dress, walk and talk like a teacher, they still have to convince pupils that they are the 'real thing'. The time that it takes for acceptance will vary, depending on the age of the pupils (very young ones tend to accept any adult as a teacher; older ones are more canny) and the attitude of the trainee. A few pupils will never quite accept the newcomer and in extreme cases may resent what they see as the intrusion of an outsider upon their territory, despite the trainee's very best efforts to fit in.

A small percentage of older pupils view trainees as a source of entertainment and enjoy baiting them and testing the boundaries of behaviour. Trainees become discouraged when the mischievous pupil that causes them so much trouble is far more compliant and reasonable for the regular teacher. New teachers need to understand that gaining authority as a teacher takes time and perseverance. It is not a sign of imminent failure for novice teachers to encounter difficult teaching situations, though it is far from easy for them to stay upbeat and cheerful and refuse to become depressed by negative pupils' responses. However, every new teacher has to be willing to engage with individuals directly, make lessons interesting and win over reluctant learners.

Clarifying boundaries (Q30, 31, 33)

Contrary to how it might seem to an inexperienced teacher, pupils yearn for specific and clearly stated rules to govern their behaviour and work. Unless adults clarify expectations, younger pupils in particular become confused and older pupils can get resentful, especially if they are told off for doing something when they did not realise it was prohibited. This situation is different, of course, from wilful disobedience, and a small number of pupils are capable of pretending that they were confused about the regulations as a way to conceal poor work or naughtiness. It soon becomes obvious to any new teacher that unless pupils have a firm understanding of what is and is not permitted, supported by decisive action when there is an infraction of a rule, the situation deteriorates rapidly. By contrast, a well-structured day with established routines gives pupils a framework within which to explore and test the boundaries of acceptable behaviour without adversely affecting the learning climate.

Younger pupils do not always perceive a connection between their level of effort and academic and behavioural outcomes; they think that events are controlled by adults or subject to random circumstances and fail to grasp their responsibility in the matter. Other pupils do not have the maturity to recognise that their behaviour is unacceptable (perhaps reinforced by permissive attitudes at home) and are genuinely puzzled when adults become exasperated with them. It is commonly found, however, that the extent of the troublesome behaviour moderates in situations where teachers make an effort to provide pupils with strategies to alter their unacceptable ways. A discipline approach in which pupils are actively involved in planning and shaping their behaviour often has more long-term impact than the imposition of a punishment which, though settling the immediate problem, does little to address underlying issues. Through participation in the negotiation and drawing up of 'behaviour contracts' with their teachers and self-monitoring and evaluating their behaviour, pupils gradually understand that they must take responsibility for the way they act or accept the consequences. Very disturbed children, however, require specialist support through the agency of the school SENCO (special educational needs coordinator) or an outside agency such as the psychological service.

PRACTICAL TASK PRACTICAL TASK **PRACTICAL TASK** PRACTICAL TASK **PRACTICAL TASK**

Contracts not capitulation

Drawing up an individual behaviour 'contract' with a pupil should not be confused with capitulation. In the end all pupils must behave reasonably, and while teachers make allowance for their age, personality and disposition, no pupil can be allowed to harmfully dominate a situation.

- Identify a child who tries to dominate the classroom.
- Deprive the child of the oxygen of publicity by briskly dismissing his/her silly comments and moving on quickly.
- Enthuse openly about other children's sensible comments.
- Work closely with a colleague to evaluate the impact of the strategy.

Mischievous pupils (Q21b, 31)

Although few pupils are actively devious, inexperienced teachers in particular need to be aware of the strategies that a minority of mischievous pupils use to manipulate situations and, as a consequence, establish a degree of control over adults.

- *Pathetic voice to gain sympathy*. Pupils pretend to be submissive to gain sympathy but revert to their previous unsatisfactory behaviour once the crisis has passed.
- *Innocent question to sow seeds of doubt*. Pupils ask a question about procedures or the appropriateness of a decision so that trainee teachers in particular wonder if they have inadvertently broken an unspoken classroom rule.
- *Gormless response*. When asked a question, pupils adopt an attitude of feigned ignorance as a barrier to further questioning.
- *Blaming another child*. Pupils deflect attention from their own misdemeanours by accusing another child.
- *Referring to a parent*. Pupils imply that their parents have criticised the teacher's methods or decisions.
- *Sidestepping the issue*. Pupils begin to talk about a different topic, stare into space or simply wander off.
- *Introducing a teacher's pet subject*. Pupils suddenly raise the teacher's favourite subject in the hope that it makes the teacher more agreeable.
- *Asking a challenging question*. Pupils suddenly discover a fascination with work that they had previously ignored in the expectation that the teacher will be impressed by their change of heart and overlook the poor behaviour.

Inexperienced and trainee teachers are especially prone to the kinds of tactics outlined above. Pupils rarely try the same approach twice if teachers state unequivocally that they are unimpressed by the pupil's action and deal with the original transgression. If, however, actions *are* repeated, despite warnings and sanctions, trainees should not hesitate to seek advice from the host teachers.

Behaviour, teaching and managing
(Q1, 12, 25a, 31)

New teachers find that it is wise to teach in a more highly directed way initially, only allowing pupils to participate in decisions and exercise autonomy when the overall situation is under control. Once classroom management and organisational routines are secure, the teaching can become more adventurous because the adult–child relationship has been forged and pupils know what to do and what is expected of them. The teacher demonstrates that he or she is ready and willing to offer help, talk about learning, teach in an interesting way, give constructive feedback, set personalised goals and gradually set higher expectations. As the intellectual demands on the pupils grow, so they become increasingly aware of the need to think deeply and engage with the lesson content; children also come to appreciate how they can use adults as a source of knowledge, advice and encouragement. Good classroom management considerably assists the maintenance of discipline and inspiring teachers are characterised by specific attributes.

- They hold and communicate sensibly high expectations for pupil learning and behaviour. Through the personal warmth and encouragement they express to pupils and the classroom procedures they establish, effective teachers make sure that pupils know that they are expected to learn well and behave appropriately.
- They teach appropriate behaviour in much the same way as they teach any area of knowledge, including regular revision and review of progress. Although teachers often display classroom rules on the wall, experience shows that pupils take little account of them unless they are referred to frequently and used in a variety of contexts.
- They specify the consequences of pupil misbehaviour and explain the links between actions and sanctions (or rewards).

- They enforce classroom rules promptly, consistently and equitably, responding quickly to misbehaviour and imposing sanctions without angst.
- They inculcate in pupils a sense of belonging by referring to 'our' class and 'our' standards.
- They maintain a brisk but unhurried pace to engage pupil interest and make smooth transitions between activities to minimise the likelihood of unruly action.
- They monitor classroom activity, providing regular and specific feedback and encouragement, while ensuring that their comments are factual rather than accusatory.
- They observe and comment on pupil behaviour and reinforce appropriate action by the provision of verbal, symbolic (e.g. thumbs-up) and tangible rewards (e.g. stickers).

All teachers have to decide what *kind* of teacher they aspire to be (see below) but school policies and the pressure of work can operate against them achieving their goal. For instance, a teacher may want to increase the amount of collaborative investigation but feel driven to use more didactic methods (formal teaching, transmission of knowledge, objectives-based approach) as a means of ensuring that pupils gain high test marks. Trainees often have to put some of their ideals on hold to an extent until they are qualified and responsible for their own classes; even then, school policies and staff agreements influence practice. No teacher can be wholly autonomous.

PRACTICAL TASK PRACTICAL TASK **PRACTICAL TASK** PRACTICAL TASK **PRACTICAL TASK**

Giving specific commands

In the early stages of getting to know a class, instead of asking a question such as *Who is looking this way?* insist: *Look this way please.* Instead of saying *We are waiting for a few people to settle*, give an order: *Please sit still, Jack and Patricia.* Monitor yourself and see how often you fail to be specific when giving commands.

Teacher types (Q2, 3a, 7a)

There are three broad teacher types, each of which is characterised by certain traits, both in active teaching, relationship with pupils and behaviour management: (a) authoritarian; (b) compromiser; (c) classroom director. If teachers seek to be *authoritarian*, their teaching will be characterised by five features.

1. They see control over pupils as being an end in itself.
2. They are prepared to humble pupils to achieve their goals.
3. They view teaching as an 'us versus them' combat.
4. They believe that adults must gain the ascendancy at all costs.
5. They blame pupils when things go wrong.

If teachers aspire to be *compromisers*, their role can be characterised in four ways.

1. They strive to be popular with pupils.
2. They encourage pupils to participate in moulding the learning climate.
3. They take close account of pupils' opinions.
4. They negotiate situations and try to reach consensus.

Many teachers are uncomfortable with authoritarianism and reluctant to be seen as a compromiser. They prefer instead to be seen as the *classroom director*, in which case their role is characterised as follows.

1. They adopt a calm but decisive approach, even under provocation.
2. They negotiate with pupils but insist on being the final arbiter.
3. They address rule infractions directly, explaining their actions but not apologising for them.
4. They employ humour to defuse situations.
5. They ensure that the positive, purposeful learning atmosphere is affirmed regularly.

In reality, it is rare for any teacher to fit snugly into one of the above three categories, though one will invariably dominate. Some experienced teachers advise novices to begin at the authoritarian end of the spectrum and gradually work through the compromiser phase before becoming established as the classroom director. Some class teachers insist that, with respect to behaviour management, the trainee teachers replicate their own approaches as closely as possible. While it is true that novice teachers sometimes attempt to run before they can walk and promote an egalitarian climate before they have established themselves in the classroom, excessive authoritarianism leads to a tense learning climate. In particular, the use of ridicule and fierceness as a means of exercising control are contrary to the spirit of effective interaction; such strategies are invariably self-defeating.

Although a domineering teacher attitude damages the harmonious environment that teachers desire to establish, compromise and negotiation must not be confused with feebleness. A teacher's willingness to listen and, perhaps, take on board a point raised by a pupil when making a decision is not a sign of weakness but of strength. Some children are adept at manipulating adults, either by being uncooperative, pleading, complaining, contradicting or arguing. If teachers want to stay open-minded when discussing an issue with pupils, they have to make it clear that only sensible and polite contributions will be heeded. When a pupil begins to contravene the rules of engagement, use of the following comments (or similar) can be effective:

Please speak normally and do not shout at me.

I am only going to listen if you say things politely.

Or if several pupils are trying to make points at the same time:

My ears are burning, so everyone stop talking now, please.

I will only choose pupils with their hands up/arms folded/finger on lips.

Some pupils find it extremely difficult to contain their ideas or control their tongues. While it is commendable for pupils to demonstrate enthusiasm and a wish to contribute, a surfeit becomes irritating and spoils the working atmosphere.

Building a class culture (Q18, 21, 30, 31)

Building a culture depends on many factors, notably whether the teacher is experienced, new to the class or a trainee working alongside the resident teacher for a specified period of time. For the first few weeks with a new class, teachers have to focus on establishing procedures and reinforcing pupil expectations, which can be broadly divided into things they can do for themselves and things they can do for others (see Figure 5.1).

What pupils can do for themselves...
- Make sure the work is of the best possible standard.
- Improve the quality of work every day.
- Work steadily to complete work.
- Finish work properly rather than finishing first.
- Persevere and refuse to give up when the work is hard.
- Enjoy learning.

What pupils can do for others...
- Help them to enjoy learning.
- Encourage them to do well.
- Celebrate when they succeed.
- Listen carefully to their concerns.
- Be a true friend.

Figure 5.1 Key expectations of pupils

A list of good intentions will not, of itself, create a positive classroom environment, but it provides a basis for discussion with pupils and a reference point for reviewing progress. Some teachers have a list of desirable behaviours but rarely, if ever, refer to them or spend time exploring them with the pupils in terms of how the aspirations can be achieved.

As teachers attempt to create a positive ethos and maximise opportunities for effective learning, it is essential for them to take close account of pupil motivation. Without having a desire to succeed, every learning task becomes a chore and adults have to resort to coercion and lavish use of external rewards to maintain momentum. In addition to relevant work content, a variety of other factors contribute towards positive motivation, such as how adults look and sound, the full attention they offer pupils, their affirmative comments, endless encouragement and the way in which they celebrate success and publicly but genuinely communicate their pleasure to pupils who persevere with tasks and make an earnest attempt to understand the work. Misbehaviour most often occurs because pupils find being naughty more interesting than the lesson or more rewarding than another experience of failure. Pupils may also misbehave when they are not involved in the learning activity, do not understand the task or cannot obtain assistance when it is needed. See Figure 5.2 for a list of techniques to minimise disruption.

- Scan the class frequently to detect and deflect potential problems.
- Ensure that pupils are aware of the consequence for deliberate violations of the rules and procedures.
- Praise positive behaviour before criticising negative behaviour.
- React calmly and quickly to a pupil's inappropriate behaviour.
- Remind pupils of the classroom rule or procedure.
- Make the consequences of inappropriate behaviour plain.
- If a sanction is needed, apply it consistently.
- Offer pupils a chance to redeem themselves.

Figure 5.2 Techniques for minimising disruption

While they need to be vigilant in combating inappropriate behaviour, it is important that teachers do not adopt a defensive posture, anticipating trouble at every turn and thereby failing to applaud and reward responsible behaviour and positive attitudes. When asked what it is like to be in the class, every pupil should be able to answer with at least a modicum of approval!

Maintaining order requires that pupils are clear about what is expected of them and teachers are specific where detail is important (e.g. safety factors during gym) and flexible in situations where pupils are free to explore options (e.g. collaborative problem-solving). Good order demands a confident adult presence that is transmitted through speaking directly and forcefully in a measured but resolute tone.

Focusing on positive aspects of pupils' behaviour is far more satisfying for teachers than relying on threats and punishments, as engaging pupils in the process of learning while threatening to punish them if they step out of line sends contradictory messages. Pupils become confused in that they perceive that on the one hand the teacher wants to foster an interactive relationship based on mutual respect, positive values and negotiation, but on the other hand is all too ready to dispense punishments if displeased.

Practical points in maintaining order
(Q3b, 21b, 25d, 31)

Discipline is always easier for trainees after they have learned the pupils' names; otherwise, pupils can hide behind their anonymity and the newcomer is unable to respond quickly to a situation by naming the individual. Until new teachers get to know pupils better it is appropriate to have a short period of time in which selected pupils are only allowed to offer their ideas when they have first stated their names.

There are a number of points to consider in maintaining an orderly yet dynamic atmosphere during the many adult-initiated interactions that occur during every lesson. First, during 'carpet time' it is essential to watch for pupils who escape to the wings of the area to avoid being involved in the session, either because they are extremely shy and prefer anonymity or they want to avoid being asked questions and do not wish to participate during whole-class responses (see Chapter 3). A small number of pupils may want to be mischievous. Teachers have to learn to sweep their eyes across the whole group and not merely on the pupils sitting directly in front of them. Less responsive and restless pupils usually only require a steady look to settle them and, perhaps, a little affirmative nod of the head to acknowledge their compliance.

Teachers should avoid turning their backs on pupils or writing on the board with their bodies at an awkward angle, which often results in a slanting scrawl and can lead to muscle strain. Where possible, it is better to have words and phrases and simple facts written on cards or electronically registered in advance of the lesson. Equipment and resources should not be placed on the table in front of the pupils when they are meant to be concentrating on what the teacher is saying. It is far too tempting!

Lesson junctures must be monitored particularly closely, as the chances for disorder are increased when pupils are going to their tables, accessing their trays and selecting resources. Simple strategies help to make this process smoother, for example sending only a few pupils at a time from the carpet to tables following the lesson introduction.

Sensible organisation facilitates an orderly move from one lesson phase to the next, in particular having resources ready and in position and ensuring that the TA knows what is taking place and what is required of the pupils.

Successful teachers decide in advance that they are not going to allow calling out while they speak, bearing in mind that some pupils become so enthusiastic that they find it difficult to hold back. Inexperienced teachers soon learn that it does not pay to allow a few silly pupils to shout advice (helpful or otherwise). Even when sensible pupils offer a helpful comment it is important for trainees not only to thank them but also to remind them about the correct procedure. If a particular child is 'hooked' on calling out, novice teachers should not fall into an action–reaction mode; that is, the pupil calls out, the teacher tells the pupil not to do so; the pupil calls out, the teacher repeats that this is unacceptable, and so on. Instead, pupils should be given two warnings, after which they are informed that further transgressions will mean that their name will be written on the board. If they violate the agreement during (say) the next five minutes, a sanction is imposed. If the pupil exercises self-control, the name is removed without fuss.

Correction and rehearsal is a technique that can be used effectively with young pupils, by which appropriate behaviour is modelled by an adult for the child, who then copies it until mastery is gained. For example, if a pupil slams the classroom door, the adult shows how to shut it quietly and the pupil is then told to practise doing the same. If successful, he or she is commended; if not, the pupil is told to try again until an acceptable result is achieved and imprinted in the pupil's mind. This rehearsal technique is most effective if the instructions are transmitted in a pleasant, firm tone of voice, together with an explanation that the process is not a punishment but a chance to be successful.

In practice it is sometimes necessary for a teacher to employ punishments and warnings as well as praise and reward. To be effective, however, teachers need to be realistic in their expectations of the class and individuals, and place more emphasis on commendation than on blame. Teachers who maintain a light but eager touch and do not take themselves too seriously are better able to facilitate purposeful learning environments. They find the humour in situations and distinguish carefully between deliberate (wilful) behaviour and unintended acts (born of pupil inexperience). They use sanctions very sparingly (though unapologetically when it becomes unavoidable). At the same time they never try to ingratiate themselves with pupils, show favouritism or allow impertinence. Wise teachers understand that there is a difference between the desirable 'light touch discipline' that avoids humiliation but leaves the adult firmly in control of the situation, and the undesirable 'tentative discipline' that does not.

RESEARCH SUMMARY RESEARCH SUMMARY **RESEARCH SUMMARY** RESEARCH SUMMARY

Assertive discipline

Canter (1998, p44) refers to the application of assertive discipline in the classroom and stresses how teachers must effectively communicate the behaviour required of their pupils.

> This [assertive discipline] approach is based on the idea that pupils and teachers have rights as well as responsibilities. Pupils need and respond to limits set by teachers, and teachers therefore should ensure those limits are established…A positive classroom atmosphere is established through meeting pupils' needs, planning and implementing classroom rules, teaching pupils how to behave appropriately, providing

positive attention and engaging in productive dialogue with disruptive pupils. Teachers are described as assertive if they effectively communicate the behaviour required of their pupils and the actions by which they intend to achieve this behaviour. Appropriate actions must follow words; otherwise responses are non-assertive and therefore ineffective. Teachers must respond positively to pupils who display appropriate classroom behaviour, thus recognising their efforts to achieve the teachers' goals. It is important that teachers are sincere when recognising pupils' attempts to meet their expectations.

Rewards and sanctions (Q1, 3b, 5, 31)

Praise and reward systems have their origin in behavioural psychology and have spawned a variety of commercial packages on promoting effective discipline in school. Strategies are based on the principle that by setting out clear rules and specifying rewards and sanctions for breaking them, schools can make a positive difference to children's behaviour. Underpinning the praise and reward systems is a belief that pupils can choose how to behave and, therefore, must accept responsibility for their actions. Teachers spend time explaining to a pupil what is and is not acceptable behaviour and the consequences of making a bad choice. The emphasis is always upon calm explanation; angry threats are avoided. Pupils who make sensible choices are encouraged and occasionally rewarded.

A quiet firm word generally has a more positive impact than irritability and also maintains the teacher–pupil relationship; similarly, a smile, nod or a symbolic reward such as a sticker have their place in promoting a secure learning climate. The vast majority of pupils respond sensibly if they are spoken to courteously and, where appropriate, the significance of their present misbehaviour is explained to them.

A limitation of using a praise and reward approach is that it may not take sufficient account of the *context* in which the behaviour occurs. During times of great excitement, such as the build-up to an important festival or prior to a class assembly, unfitting behaviour invites greater tolerance than on most other occasions. Similarly, it may not be appropriate to give a pupil who had previously been rude to a teacher a reward, even though the pupil's work merited it.

Concerns have also been aired about the way in which rewards can make pupils rely on external motivation instead of completing work for the pleasure of doing so. Similarly, criticisms of set punishments can create a climate of undue caution or even fearfulness, thereby stifling spontaneity and pupils' natural eagerness to attempt something different. Regardless of these objections, praise and reward systems operate in many primary schools. Teachers and pupils find security in such a system if it is perceived as fair and used consistently, with beneficial effects on pupil behaviour.

Despite the success of praise and reward systems in altering external behaviour, no policy, school rule or package can, of itself, change deep-seated attitudes. It is the quality of the adult–pupil interactions in the use of rewards and other incentives that makes a lasting difference. Behaviour that interferes with another pupil's basic rights or contravenes a rule cannot, of course, be overlooked, but pupils who take ownership of their own behaviour learn self-control that will prove to be invaluable during their time in school and beyond it.

According to a study conducted by Harrop and Williams (1992) there is a disparity between pupils' and teachers' views about the most effective punishments and rewards. Their survey indicated that whereas teachers believe that the most influential punishments are telling a pupil off or informing the parent, pupils put telling the parent, being stopped from going on a school trip and being sent to see the head teacher as the top three. The variance between teacher and pupil perspectives with respect to rewards is even more striking. Teachers thought that praise in front of other pupils, merit/house points and a mention in assembly were the most influential rewards; pupils selected informing parents, good written comments and good marks. The use of merit and house points was well down the pupils' list. The emphasis that pupils placed on parental involvement is noteworthy.

The Harrop and Williams study was conducted before the imposition of national curriculum tests (popularly known as SATs), league tables and target setting in schools. A more recent study involving slightly older pupils (Shreeve, 2002) found that in schools where students are motivated by an intrinsic desire to learn and achieve, formal systems of rewards and penalties were usually not necessary. Good teachers were able to motivate pupils and manage their behaviour by using praise and offering helpful feedback. Behaviour management depended in the main on a positive relationship between the teacher and pupil, good lesson planning and interesting work. Formal sanctions were rarely used by teachers to signal disapproval.

The Shreeve study also indicated that boys and (especially) girls agreed that being kept in at break, a letter or phone call home and extra work were the most successfully used sanctions. Warnings and being moved temporarily to another class were rated as the least effective penalties, especially by girls, who were generally punished less than boys. The process of actively involving pupils in discussing which sanctions are most effective under which circumstances appears to improve behaviour and reduce the need for strong disciplinary measures.

PRACTICAL TASK PRACTICAL TASK PRACTICAL TASK PRACTICAL TASK PRACTICAL TASK

Pupils' views about sanctions

Find out the views of children about rewards and punishment based on the Harrop and Williams study, either through discussion or by using a questionnaire or using a questionnaire followed by discussion. The categories are:

REWARDS

1. Praise in front of other pupils.
2. Private praise.
3. Good marks.
4. Good written comments.
5. Mentioned in assembly.
6. Praised by other pupils.
7. Whole class praised.
8. Merit/house points given by the teacher.
9. Parents informed about good behaviour.
10. Having work on display.

PUNISHMENTS

1. Being told off in front of the class.

2. Being told off in private.

3. Being sent to see the head teacher.

4. Teacher explaining what is wrong with the behaviour in private.

5. Teacher explaining what is wrong with the behaviour in front of the class.

6. Kept in at playtime.

7. Being moved to another seat in the classroom.

8. Parent informed about naughty behaviour.

9. Taking unfinished work home.

10. Being stopped from going on a school trip.

Discuss the findings with a colleague and consider the implications for your practice.

Social and emotional aspects of learning
(Q3a, 18, 21a, 30)

Whatever the scheme or approach devised to address issues of pupils' social and emotional development, the best primary classrooms are those characterised by purposeful work that is enjoyable and motivating for pupils and allows them opportunities to interact with other pupils in group activities. The emotional attachment that exists between teacher and the pupils is a strong motivating factor and provides adults and pupils alike with a sense of fulfilment.

The government's Primary National Strategy Unit provides resources that help to promote the social and emotional aspects of learning (SEAL) as part of its national primary strategy (DfES, 2005). SEAL materials are used by schools where the social and emotional aspects of learning have been identified as a key focus for their work, addressing pupils' difficulties in understanding and managing their feelings, working as a team member and coping with disappointment. The resources focus on five social and emotional aspects of learning:

- self-awareness;
- managing feelings;
- motivation;
- empathy;
- social skills.

Pupils are helped to develop skills such as acknowledging other viewpoints, group cooperation, perseverance, conflict resolution and dealing with anxiety. SEAL builds on existing initiatives such as circle time or buddy schemes, the curriculum for personal, social and health education (PSHE) and citizenship. The SEAL materials are organised under seven themes:

- new beginnings;
- getting on and falling out;
- say no to bullying;
- going for goals!;
- good to be me;
- relationships;
- changes.

Each theme is designed for a whole-school approach and includes an assembly and suggested follow-up activities in each area of the curriculum. The colour-coded resources are organised at four levels: Early Years Foundation Stage; Years 1 and 2; Years 3 and 4; and Years 5 and 6.

RESEARCH SUMMARY RESEARCH SUMMARY **RESEARCH SUMMARY** RESEARCH SUMMARY

A settled working environment

Arthur et al (2005) report in detail on a lesson in which there was an almost total absence of any challenging behaviour by pupils. They go on to analyse the main reasons.

- The teacher's personal organisation and planning for the lesson was strong and transparent to pupils.

- The teacher was decisive in driving the lesson along with confidence and with sufficient changes of activity to sustain pupils' interest.

- The teacher had good command of verbal communication, mastery of material and an understanding of how pupils learned.

- There was a strong rapport between teacher and class, between whom there were high levels of mutual trust and respect.

- Pupils appreciated that the teacher was genuinely interested in them as individuals and enjoyed being with them.

- The teacher gave pupils controlled space and conditions in which to explore their role as learners.

CASE STUDY

Clare was on her final school placement and had been placed in a Year 4 class in a large primary school. The following account shows how difficult it can be to act fairly and decisively while maintaining a positive learning climate...

Nine-year-old Howard was supposed to be doing his writing but kept sniggering and making silly comments to his friend Toby, who was sitting opposite. They were in the 'independent' group, without immediate adult supervision, and were supposed to be selecting from a list of describing words and using each one in a short sentence. Clare was working with some pupils on a different table. She noticed the two boys being mischievous and decided that a simple reprimand would suffice. Clare walked over to them, leaned across the table towards the boys and said quietly, *Make sure that you have finished your work before assembly in 15 minutes. If you fail to finish to my satisfaction you will take your books with you and when the head asks what's going on, you can explain to her why the work hasn't been done.* The boys looked closely at the expression on her face to see if she was joking and realised that she meant business. They quickly settled to work.

A few minutes later Clare noticed that Gareth had put his head on the table and was making a grunting sound. Gareth was capable of being troublesome but recently he had been trying very hard to be cooperative. His mother had mentioned to Clare that Gareth's aunty had offered to take him to a theme park next month, but only on the condition that he had been a good boy at school. Clare moved across to Gareth and asked if he was alright. (She was well aware of his uncertain temperament but wanted to check that he wasn't ill.) Gareth muttered something from the tabletop that Clare had to ask him to repeat. He barked out the same incoherent phrase, but did so with vehemence. Clare hesitated. She did not want the other pupils to think that Gareth was getting away with it but knew that if left alone he would recover after a minute and continue with his work as if nothing had happened. Clare noticed that Howard and Toby were watching intently and remembered the severe warning that she had given to them about wasting time. Now they were waiting to see what action she would take with Gareth.

In that moment a number of thoughts flashed through Clare's mind: her own status as a teacher; the impression that she would make on the other pupils and on the TA; the need for fairness; avoiding a confrontation with Gareth. Time hung heavy for a few seconds. General advice that she had been given by tutors and class teachers seemed irrelevant for this particular situation. *Stay calm*, she said to herself *and try to resolve the situation rather than score points*. Clare made her decision. *Gareth, I cannot hear what you are saying and other pupils are waiting for me. When you are ready to start work again come over and ask me for my help.* She knew that the two other boys might perceive her actions as fainthearted, but that could not be avoided.

She went back to her group and picked up the thread of the work. Patty, a shy little girl, whispered to her, *Gareth is pulling a face at you, Miss!* Clare nodded to acknowledge the comment and continued with the session. In her mind she felt pleased about the way she had handled the situation. The class had settled to work and assembly was only five minutes away when Gareth suddenly stood up and announced, *I'm going to the toilet* (something for which permission had to be granted by an adult). Miss Kaur, the TA, asked if Clare wanted her to follow Gareth and bring him back. Clare hesitated. Now what? The main options seemed to be:

- Allow Gareth to go to the toilet, but ask Miss Kaur to make sure that he gets there and returns to the classroom afterwards.
- Stop him, insist that he sits down and make him ask permission properly before allowing him to go to the toilet.
- Stop him and insist that he remains in the classroom.

In an instant, Clare decided on the first strategy. Miss Kaur followed Gareth, who came back about two minutes later and slumped down at his desk. A number of the other pupils were amused by Gareth's behaviour. Clare decided that she had to speak to Gareth publicly or the rest of the class would think that he had escaped being disciplined. She told the class to clear up before assembly and, when the pupils were lining up, spoke forcefully but calmly to Gareth and told him that he was never to go to the toilet without permission again. He would now walk with her at the front of the line and sit by her feet during assembly. Clare added, for effect, *I do not know what your mother would say if she knew*, but felt guilty as she saw the look of horror on Gareth's face and heard his cringing apology.

Key issues:

- What factors might have triggered Gareth's behaviour?
- Should Clare have been firmer with him from the start?
- Was she right to let him walk off to the toilet?
- Should she mention his behaviour to Gareth's mother?
- What principles about effective behaviour management emerge from this incident?

MOVING *ON* > > > > > > MOVING *ON* > > > > > > MOVING *ON*

Fear of losing control is heightened if the class contains a number of boisterous pupils, who have a disproportionate impact on the learning environment. At some point in your career you are bound to encounter such circumstances and need to be aware of the possible impact on you and the rest of the children, and how to implement coping strategies, both practical and emotional. First, don't lose sight of your basic principles as a teacher in your eagerness to be 'tough'. Second, be highly insistent without becoming agitated. Third, offer incentives, not bribes. Fourth, don't allow the rest of the class to suffer negative repercussions as a result of your firm stance; get them on your side. Finally, use all the support and advice available . . . and stay cheerful.

REFERENCES REFERENCES **REFERENCES** REFERENCES **REFERENCES** REFERENCES

Arthur, J., Davison, J. and Lewis, M. (2005) *Professional Values and Practice*. Abingdon: Routledge.

Canter, L. (1998) The assertive discipline approach. In: H. Ayers and F. Gray (eds), *Classroom Management*. London: David Fulton.

Department for Education and Skills (2003) *Excellence and Enjoyment: A Strategy for Primary Schools*. London: DfES Publications.

Department for Education and Skills (2005) *Excellence and Enjoyment: Social and Emotional Aspects of Learning*. London: DfES Publications.

Harrop, A. and Williams, T. (1992) Rewards and punishments in the primary school: pupils' perceptions and teachers' usage. *Educational Psychology*, 7(4), 211–15.

Robertson, J. (1996) *Effective Classroom Control*. London: Hodder & Stoughton.

Shreeve, A. (2002) Student perceptions of rewards and sanctions. *Pedagogy, Culture and Society*, 10(2), 239–56.

FURTHER READING FURTHER READING **FURTHER READING** FURTHER READING

Adams, K. (2009) *Behaviour for Learning in the Primary School*. Exeter: Learning Matters.

Brownhill, S. (2007) *Taking the Stress out of Bad Behaviour*. London: Continuum.

Hart, S. and Kindle Hodson, V. (2004) *The Compassionate Classroom*. La Crescenta, CA: Center for Non-Violent Communication.

Kendall-Seatter, S. (2005) *Primary Professional Studies: Reflective Reader*. Exeter: Learning Matters. See Chapter 8.

Rogers, B. (2006) *Classroom Behaviour*. London: Paul Chapman Publishing.

6
Effective communication

Learning outcomes

To understand:

- **how speaking and listening contribute to learning;**
- **strategies to improve meaningful pupil dialogue;**
- **the essential communication skills for teachers and pupils;**
- **how listening can be improved;**
- **how to enhance the level of adult–child interaction.**

Introduction

In earlier chapters we noted how effective interaction is largely dependent on establishing and maintaining a verbally active teacher–pupil relationship in which there is ease of communication within agreed boundaries. Regardless of how carefully plans have been constructed, resources made available and activities organised, the effective teaching of primary-age children relies heavily on creating mutual bonds of trust and respect. Moreover, teachers and assistants need to develop insights into the things that children find significant and motivating if they wish to create communication networks that will promote learning. This chapter explores many of these key issues.

Quality of speech (Q25c)

It goes without saying that incoherent speech and muddled thinking affect the quality of communication and cause frustration among pupils, most of whom are genuinely interested in the things teachers are trying to tell them. Poor speech compounds problems for pupils who are already disaffected with learning or feel uninspired; it can lead to restlessness and misbehaviour.

Some teachers speak quickly but are so articulate that pupils are still able to follow what they say. However, it is important that adults speak at a reasonable pace, especially when talking to younger pupils. Equally important is to give pupils opportunity to absorb and mentally process what is said by use of occasional pauses to allow for scanning the group, making eye contact with as many pupils as possible and smiling. The pauses should last for only for a few seconds at the end of each block of speech or momentum is lost and the pupils' interest wanes. Teachers have to strike a careful balance between conveying the necessary information to the class and not overwhelming them. Inexperienced teachers are often so intent on transmitting facts that they forget to take account of the listeners' needs, but there are two simple strategies to engage pupils' interest. First, the speed of speech is varied to emphasise points, repeating key phrases as necessary and lowering the pitch slightly to stress important words. Second, without undue exaggeration, variety is injected into the voice tone through:

- inculcating a sense of mystery and suspense;
- slurring particular words gently;
- sounding a note of caution or uncertainty;
- whispering loudly;
- speaking briefly in a staccato manner.

Clarity of speech is achieved by avoiding slipshod language and taking particular care over the use of consonants. For instance, the loss of the letters 't' and 'd' from words leads to an incoherent form of speaking that makes it more difficult for pupils to grasp what is being said. As a result the pupils spend more effort attempting to follow the adult's words than in absorbing their meaning and implications. A teacher will sometimes rebuke a pupil who requests further explanation for not listening when, in truth, the pupil was not only confused by *what* was said but *the way* in which it was communicated. Children are also unimpressed by adults who try to emulate contemporary expressions as a means of ingratiating themselves. Playground talk between older pupils in particular will often incorporate the latest catch-phrase or slang expression; teachers are not expected to follow suit!

Listening to pupils (Q2, 4, 27)

There are many occasions when teachers have an opportunity to hear a pupil speak, including their formal responses to open-ended questions, class discussions and informal conversation (often outside regular lesson time). If teachers are convinced that pupils learn through the process of expressing their thoughts and benefit from being taken seriously by an adult, then time spent listening to them is justified. It almost goes without saying that no adult will want to tolerate unkind comments, tittle-tattle or negative talk from children, however eloquently expressed.

All adults need to persevere to become good listeners because it lies at the heart of effective communication and is an essential teaching skill for every teacher because:

- it is courteous to listen carefully;
- every pupil appreciates an attentive adult;
- pupils have important things to say;
- it helps to seal adult–pupil relationships;
- it models appropriate behaviour for pupils to emulate;
- it enables adults to learn more about what pupils know and understand;
- other pupils learn from what their peers say;
- pupils may need to convey their fears and concerns;
- the teacher or TA may be the only adults in a pupil's life prepared to show a keen interest.

Listening has to be learned and practised because most people prefer to talk rather than to hear what others have to say. Furthermore, adults can become so preoccupied by the *feelings* being aroused in them that they 'stop hearing'. Consequently, sympathetic listening is not sufficient; the brain also needs to be alert and fully engaged. However, as the human brain works about three to five times faster than the tongue, it is possible to be listening carefully, yet to find that the mind is wandering. Listening, then, relies both on self-discipline and being convinced that the speaker has something worth hearing.

If teachers want to improve their listening ability, they must make an effort to minimise distractions, which tend to come from three different sources: the environment, the listener's mind and the speaker. Environmental distractions include noise, passers-by and a stale atmosphere. Distractions from within the teacher's own mind are largely due to competing thoughts: wanting to listen to the pupil but preoccupied with other duties and priorities. The pupil can also be a source of distraction due to factors such as accent, mannerisms, clothing, cleanliness, language use and so forth. Because teachers are trained to take note of mistakes and errors, it is easy for them to be sidetracked by trivial factors, such as a pupil's appearance, to the detriment of concentrating on the message that a pupil is trying to convey.

Each of the three forms of distraction (environmental factors, listener's thoughts, speaker's traits) can be reduced or constrained by employing specific strategies to combat their intrusion and negative influence on the quality of listening. Environmental factors are often outside the immediate control of teachers but they can make a deliberate decision to 'shut out' extraneous noise and other distractions and to concentrate on the pupil's words. Controlling their own thoughts can be helped by closely following the pupil's speech and mentally summarising the key points. Focusing on the pupil's face can help to minimise distracting factors such as unkempt appearance or irritating mannerisms. Steps to improve listening are also listed in Figure 6.1.

---

1. Develop a genuine interest in the speaker and what is being said.
2. Concentrate on the words and ideas that are being expressed.
3. Resist the temptation to 'fill the unspoken words'.
4. Think about what the words mean to the speaker.
5. Grasp what meaning is being conveyed beyond the words.
6. Keep a mental record of key points.
7. Ask questions to clarify what has been said.

Figure 6.1 Seven steps to better listening

Teachers can help pupils to gain confidence in speaking and expressing their ideas openly and with confidence by employing the following strategies:

- listening with an open mind rather than jumping to conclusions – pupils will soon sense an adult's displeasure;
- looking directly at the pupil with 'gentle' wide eyes – pupils gain a lot of information from adults' eyes, so they should be reassuring and affirming;
- making an oral response, such as 'I see' or 'uh-huh' to signal understanding – silence may be interpreted as disapproval;
- repeating a key phrase from time to time in a tone that conveys interest, wonder or admiration – for example: *You got two medals? That's amazing!*
- observing the pupil's body language (non-verbal behaviour) – some pupils lose confidence when speaking directly to an adult, so it is essential to be alert to any signs that the pupil is faltering;
- concealing any inner doubts that may be entertained about what is said until the pupil has finished speaking – many adults find this strategy quite difficult, especially if the pupil is grappling with controversial subject matter or introducing prejudicial attitudes into the conversation;
- avoiding a tendency to contradict or argue with what the pupil says at the moment the pupil finishes speaking – a good rule is to thank the pupil and allow a few seconds' silence (count to three) before commenting;
- staying detached from contrary emotions – adults may be disappointed that a pupil is pursuing a false argument or frustrated about an unsatisfactory response; nevertheless, it is essential to continue listening closely;

- summarising the key points at the appropriate time and allowing the pupil to confirm, clarify or modify them – this approach reassures the pupil that the adult is still concentrating, as well as obliging the adult to synthesise what is being said;
- asking questions of clarification without sounding doubtful – a light touch is needed to encourage pupils to amplify what they are saying rather than being fearful that the adult has an alternative agenda;
- avoiding instant evaluations before properly understanding what the pupil is trying to say – in particular, eschewing a 'yes, but' response.

RESEARCH SUMMARY RESEARCH SUMMARY **RESEARCH SUMMARY** RESEARCH SUMMARY

Pupils' emotional needs

Fisher (2005) comments as follows:

All learners feel, at times, vulnerable and defensive. Time spent on building a sense of inclusion and trust is time well spent. Learning is not easy to achieve at times of emotional disturbance or social disruption. If emotional needs are ignored, the energy of the learner is deflected away from his or her capacity to accomplish learning tasks. In helping children to state their feelings clearly, or to discuss and reflect on situations of concern, we are helping them to learn about themselves and about other people. (p138)

- What indications will children give that they feel included?
- In what ways might the energy of the learner be deflected?

There are normally other pupils within earshot when a pupil is talking to an adult; they will often be listening closely to what is being said and may be bursting to contribute useful insights. Teachers have to maintain the balance between allowing these additional comments and embedding them into the warp and weave of the exchanges, or delaying them through a signal (raised palm, say) or verbal reminder of the rule ('please let Mark finish speaking').

Learning through listening and speaking
(Q17, 19, 23, 25d)

Every type of pupil learning involves them in some sort of immediate experience (experiential learning) and/or dialogue (learning by talking or 'oracy'). *Experiential learning* can be broadly divided in to 'observing others doing' and 'doing for oneself'. Observation is defined as any occasion that pupils watch or listen to someone else involved in an action or activity that is related to what they are learning, for example the teacher demonstrating a technique (e.g. in science), classmates explaining their work or a group presenting a drama performance. Furthermore, pupil observation may be direct (first hand) or vicarious (once removed). *Direct* observation means the pupils are seeing what is happening in the 'here and now'. A *vicarious* observation, on the other hand, involves a simulation of the real thing. For example, a direct observation of local decision-making would happen if the pupils were taken on a visit to a town council meeting. A vicarious or indirect observation of the same event would be to watch a recorded interview with councillors about a crucial meeting or read newspaper accounts about it. *Doing for oneself* refers to any activity where the learner is closely involved in constructing, sorting, creating, investigating, evaluating, presenting, role-playing or playing independently.

Dialogue can be classified into two types: dialogue with self and dialogue with others. To develop dialogue with self, pupils have to be taught how to reflect, ponder, cogitate and think deeply about issues, decisions and strategies. A teacher can, where appropriate, ask pupils to keep a journal or compile a project folder in which they register their own ideas and thoughts. Pupils can write or draw about what they are learning, how they are learning it and what difference the knowledge or learning has made to their understanding. Where emotive issues are involved, pupils can record their feelings or how their viewpoint has altered as a result of information received and discussed in class. Through dialoguing with the self in these and similar ways, pupils begin to think creatively rather than following a prescribed, objectives-driven curriculum path to knowledge, tightly controlled by a teacher. Dialogue with others is most dynamic and active when a series of small group discussions are organised on a given topic, loosely monitored (but not intrusively so) by an adult. In such circumstances, the adult acts as adviser rather than prescriber.

Teachers can also find creative ways for pupils to engage in dialogue with people that possess specialist knowledge or experience that have been invited into the classroom. For instance, local authors, sports personalities and older people can offer perceptions and insights from 'living history' and respond to pupils' queries. In organising such an event, teachers have to be alert to the fact that not all visiting personalities are used to handling pupils or answering their questions in child-friendly language.

Teachers who are committed to enhancing the level of interaction in the classroom by promoting active forms of learning are typified in the sections which follow.

They extend the range of pupil learning experiences (Q25d, 28, 30)

The most uninspiring forms of teaching consist of passive pupils listening to a teacher presenting a monologue or reading an extract that has been detached from its context. Drab teachers ask pupils questions to ensure that they are listening and have a grasp of the content but rarely invite comment or questions from them. Learning is sterile and does not penetrate beyond a superficial grasp of the basic facts or procedures for completing tasks. Excitement and enthusiasm are notably absent. By contrast, dynamic forms of dialogue that extend the range of pupil experience and thinking are generated by strategies such as the following.

- Dividing pupils into small groups and inviting them to make a decision, design a strategy, or answer a challenging question – such collaborative activity requires careful attention to group composition to ensure that the pupils are well-matched and the topic is relevant and interesting.
- Finding ways for pupils to engage in authentic dialogue with people other than classmates on the web or by e-mail – this approach is particularly powerful if links can be established with pupils in schools elsewhere (even overseas) but intra-school systems serve the same purpose.
- Making pupils keep a journal or build a learning portfolio (handwritten or computer-generated) about their own knowledge, thoughts, learning and feelings that are subsequently shared with a trusted friend.
- Offering pupils experiences to visit places of interest – any educational visit of this kind has to be carefully organised and each school has its own procedures to ensure that there is compliance with legal and health and safety requirements. The visit is designed in such a way that pupils have to collaborate in seeking out answers.
- Finding ways to extend learning across the curriculum – for example, there are numerous drama activities that help pupils to understand historical events, promote awareness of other beliefs or explore moral

dilemmas. Again, a thematic approach based on (say) the work of a local supermarket can incorporate many subject dimensions: food production, buying and selling, building plans, geographical locations of food sources, transport systems, all of which generate enthusiasm and meaningful talk.

They extend interaction by combining modes of learning (Q25d, 27, 28)

Each mode of learning (experiential or dialogic) makes its own particular contribution, so that using a mixture of them in the pursuit of understanding can serve to reinforce knowledge. For example, if pupils write their own thoughts on a topic (dialogue with self mode) prior to their engagement in small group discussion (dialogue with others mode), the quality of the group discussion is likely to be enhanced. The reverse is also true: if pupils are encouraged to discuss their ideas with others before they record them it serves to alert them to points of view and perspectives that would otherwise have been obscure. Similarly, observation of a situation or visual stimuli prior to involvement in an independent task (when pupils work alone) or activity (when pupils cooperate in learning) provides them with a better sense of what they are doing and, perhaps, its relevance. If, after completing the task or activity, pupils are given the opportunity to write or discuss the content with others, learning is cemented and reinforced. Ideally, the 'plenary' section of the lesson (everyone coming together to share ideas and review progress at the end of the session) provides an opportunity for high-level interaction. In fact, teachers that seek to enhance interaction use any suitable moment in a session for summarising and celebrating ideas.

They foster synergy between experience and dialogue (Q25b)

One variation of the interaction principles described above is to create a synergy between the two principal components of this model of active learning (experience and dialogue) when examining issues and dilemmas. New experiences have the potential to give learners a different perspective on what is true (beliefs) and/or what is good and right (values). Dialogue (whether with self or with others) has the potential to help learners construct many possible meanings from experience and to gain fresh perspectives. A teacher who can creatively set up a rhythm of activities in which pupils move back and forth between having rich new experiences and engaging in deep, meaningful dialogue about familiar ones promotes significant learning.

RESEARCH SUMMARY RESEARCH SUMMARY **RESEARCH SUMMARY** RESEARCH SUMMARY

Safety and trust

Hart and Kindle Hodson (2004) emphasise the importance of safety and trust if classrooms are to become places where effective communication takes place:

> *A relationship-based classroom uses guidelines for how to communicate with one another. In order for all voices to be heard, no matter how loud or soft, and for there to be a sharing without blame or criticism, teachers and [pupils] take the time to learn and practise a non-confrontational way of using language.* (p20)

Promoting pupil involvement (Q4, 10, 31)

Interactive teaching that involves extended forms of pupil–pupil or adult–pupil dialogue has become less evident in many primary schools over recent years because teachers like to inject 'pace' into the sessions, which in turn reduces the opportunities for thoughtful consideration and discussion of issues. Consequently, some teachers hesitate to allow pupils the chance to explore a problem, pursue an argument or express an opinion unless it can be done succinctly. Teachers also have to take account of practical factors; for instance, some younger pupils speak slowly, while other pupils need time to ponder, pause and rehearse their thinking. Accommodating these extended verbal exchanges has an impact on the time available for the remainder of the lesson and may restrict the number of pupils who have an opportunity to contribute.

When pupils initiate a conversation with an adult, they tend to do so by asking about work procedures to clarify what they are meant to be doing. However, less confident pupils sometimes prefer to struggle on uncertainly rather than risk a teacher's exasperation by asking about an aspect of the work they should already have grasped. Teachers find that there is less need to repeat what has been said if information and instructions are given precisely to pupils in the first place (see Chapter 3). As with all strategies it is important for teachers (especially novices) to keep matters in perspective and not to become upset if a teaching method does not work as smoothly as expected.

It is a commonly held view that boys are more reluctant than girls to talk constructively to other pupils about the work they are undertaking. While it is true that collaborative activities in groups can degenerate into mindless 'off-task' chatter, it tends to be *underachievers* who are less inclined to become involved, regardless of gender. Such pupils are often reluctant participants (especially in whole-class discussions) and this may have had a direct and adverse effect on achievement. By contrast, high-achievers often dominate positive learning interactions by volunteering answers, responding to adults and contributing knowledge to a group venture. By contrast, the contribution made by underachievers is less productive; a small number of vulnerable pupils try to compensate for their limitations by making humorous or silly comments, which only serve to reinforce their inadequacy. Teachers can facilitate a positive involvement of verbally disadvantaged pupils during collaborative problem-solving, either by placing pupils of similar capability in the same group or by organising mixed groups and structuring the interactions in such a way that each person is offered a fair chance to contribute. The 'similar capability' groups provide stability; members of the 'mixed' groups have allocated roles (see later in this chapter under 'pupil communication skills'). To develop verbal competence across the whole group teachers sometimes use the strategy of 'tell a friend what you think before you say it publicly'.

To encourage pupils to think before they speak and promote less confident pupils' involvement, some teachers use the equivalent of a 'traffic light' system in which the pupil that offers a response has to preface his or her reply by saying red or amber or green. Red indicates that the pupil is very uncertain but willing to try; amber means cautiously certain; green means very certain. Teachers can also encourage involvement by asking for a hand signal response to indicate the pupil's level of confidence before answering. For example, the teacher makes a statement and tells the pupils to touch their noses if they agree or put their hands behind their backs if they do not or to cross their arms over their chests if they have no idea.

The 'think before you speak' policy also acts as a constraint on the tendency for enthusiastic pupils to call out spontaneous answers; thus pupils are not permitted to raise a hand until the teacher gives a specific signal (such as pausing before saying 'engage!' or counting quietly to three). These delaying tactics are only appropriate for questions that necessitate careful thought and are not suitable for quick-fire question-and-answer situations; nevertheless, they transmit the important message to pupils that while ill-considered incorrect answers are unacceptable, incorrect thoughtful ones are welcomed (see Chapter 4).

RESEARCH SUMMARY RESEARCH SUMMARY **RESEARCH SUMMARY** RESEARCH SUMMARY

The use of dialogic pedagogy

Drawing from the work of Jürgen Habermas, Morrison (2001) argues that it is important to support pupils as they engage in:

- cooperative and collaborative work;
- discussion-based work;
- autonomous, experiential and flexible learning;
- negotiated learning;
- community-related learning;
- problem-solving activities;
- increased opportunity to employ talk.

It is also important for teachers to play the role of 'transformative intellectuals' to support pupils as they talk and discuss issues, with the help of a framework in which the following pertains:

- freedom to enter a discourse, check questionable claims and evaluate explanations;
- striving to gain mutual understanding between participants;
- achieving consensus through discussion based on the force of argument alone;
- adherence to truth, legitimacy, sincerity and comprehensibility.

To what extent are you consciously guiding the pupils in your class towards these ends?

REFLECTIVE TASK

Balance of talk

Consider the following questions and their implications for practice.

- What proportion of the verbal interaction do you dominate?
- Are pupils encouraged to take some ownership of the learning process?
- When do they have an opportunity to talk for learning, other than in answering your questions?

When pupils are given a task to complete, teachers need to clarify for them whether they can or cannot discuss the work with one another. Younger pupils talk naturally to their neighbours about the things they are doing, so in practice it is rare for them to work wholly independently. Some older pupils may prefer to work alone and have to be encouraged to participate in a paired or group effort. The important thing is for teachers to ensure that they have considered their expectations beforehand and communicated them explicitly. Merely offering a vague indication of what is acceptable invites rule violations.

Pupil communication skills (Q1, 4, 10, 12, 23, 30)

Pupils need to communicate effectively with one another if they are to make the best use of opportunities to collaborate in problem-solving and investigative activities. To optimise the time available pupils need to become proficient in a variety of skills with reference to five key areas:

- conflict resolution;
- collaborating;
- discriminating;
- listening;
- reflecting.

A proportion of pupils in every class struggle to acquire and demonstrate these attributes and a very small number will probably have trouble doing so throughout their lives. Nevertheless, teachers can make a significant contribution to the process by modelling appropriate behaviour to pupils, explaining and showing why harmony is preferable to conflict and individualism, and why combined expertise benefits everyone.

Collaborating rather than acting independently is a skill that overlaps with but is different from straightforward cooperation. Collaboration is the process by which pupils work together in a team to reach a specified and predetermined learning objective. Cooperation, on the other hand, is a general term for courtesy and thoughtfulness. Consequently, pupils may be cooperative while not collaborating; effective collaboration, however, cannot take place without a high level of cooperation between pupils. Occasionally, primary age pupils take some persuading that finding solutions or 'agreeing to disagree' is preferable to conflict. A teacher's calm but decisive actions not only help to diffuse and resolve an immediate problem but set a standard of behaviour and mutual respect to which pupils can aspire.

Studies of primary classrooms suggest that work-related collaborative interaction between primary pupils accounts for only a small proportion of the total time they spend on learning, and tends to be in pairs rather than in groups. In a collaborative enterprise, a teacher may want to allocate a role to each member of the group; for example, one pupil may be leader and orchestrate the proceedings, another pupil makes notes, another pupil acts as 'fetcher and carrier' and yet another contributes practical skills. On other occasions, such as in creating a montage, all the pupils make similar contributions. A lot depends on the nature of the enterprise and the hoped-for outcome. For instance, if a group of older primary pupils are discussing an issue, there may be a 'chairperson' and someone to note key points on a sheet while the rest of the group offer suggestions. If a group of younger primary pupils are collaborating to produce a construction model then an adult may provide leadership and in effect become one of the group members. The extent of adult domination will depend upon the extent to which a teacher wants pupils to explore for themselves and, crucially, the time available for task completion.

REFLECTIVE TASK

Benefits of working in pairs

There are three benefits that accrue through pairing pupils for tasks.

1. They scaffold one another's learning through dialogue.
2. They motivate and encourage each other.
3. Two heads are better than one!

Write down three disadvantages of working in pairs; for each one decide how you can (a) prevent the problem occurring (b) recover the situation if it does occur.

It is important for teachers to make a distinction between a collaborative venture in which there is a *problem to be solved* (i.e. a single or narrow range of solutions) and *an investigation* in which there may be many possible solutions. In each case the focus of the enquiry-based learning will differ slightly.

- *Problem-solving* necessitates that members provide a pool of suggestions, conjecture about the outcome, trial the different propositions and experiment until the solution to the problem is found or agreed.
- *Investigation* follows a similar procedural pattern (suggestion/conjecture/trial/experiment) but results in a set of possibilities rather than a single solution. Some investigations begin as a group collaborative venture but end with individuals or pairs of pupils pursuing their favoured option.

Teachers cannot assume that pupils will work together effectively, other than in the case of older pupils who are used to doing so and are comfortable with the other members; even then there may be occasions when the group needs to be reorganised. One way or another, a small amount of time spent in explaining and rehearsing key aspects of the collaborative process pays dividends in the long term. As with any other endeavour requiring team effort, collaboration requires perseverance, tolerance and close adult guidance in the early stages until the process is firmly embedded and pupils can be self-governing.

Pupils can be taught to be *discriminating* in their judgements through being given regular opportunities to engage with challenges, where adults provide counsel and wisdom in guiding and responding to pupil choices. It can be difficult for pupils to separate the act of being discriminating (wise) from an attitude of *discrimination* (prejudice), the former referring to a properly informed and articulated position and the latter associated with hostility, misinformation and negative feelings. Prejudiced attitudes tend to be irrational and unjust; people demonstrate an intolerant attitude towards individuals or groups, often accompanied by stereotyping their supposed characteristics. Teachers face the challenging task of helping pupils to be open and reasonable in their dealings towards others, while taking account of the fact that differences in lifestyle and cultural priorities exist. Some pupils come from homes where there is little integrity with regard to attitudes towards others. In such circumstances it is important for teachers to understand that a pupil's prejudice and inappropriate speech often has its roots in family behaviour rather than personal disposition. Careful explanation and explicit but non-accusatory statements of principle are nevertheless essential if pupil attitudes are to be changed. Inexperienced teachers should be mindful of the fact that discussions about controversial issues that take place in school are likely to be continued at home, so tact is required.

As noted earlier in this chapter, careful listening is a key to success in learning for two main reasons: first, pupils who are perceived as failing to listen can find themselves being labelled with behavioural problems or seen as having an attention deficit; second, more confusion is created in classrooms through pupils not hearing (and therefore not grasping) what they are supposed to be doing than any other single issue. In addition, a substantial minority of pupils suffer from some hearing loss at one time or another; failing to listen may be due to an ailment rather than wilfulness or a psychological inability to engage with what is being said. Teachers of younger pupils in particular need to check with parents if they have concerns about the source of the problem.

Instead of constantly telling pupils to listen, wise teachers explain to pupils the benefits of being a listener, for example that good listeners know what is happening, learn many new and exciting things, make fewer mistakes and get better marks. Experience shows that good listeners also tend to have more and better friends because everyone likes someone who attends to what they are saying.

To teach listening skills, it is necessary for teachers to model them for pupils by listening respectfully to colleagues and parents in such a way that they do not interrupt them when they are speaking and use nods and affirmative murmurs to indicate that they are receiving what is said. However, it is not sufficient for adults to model behaviour and expect pupils to automatically understand what is happening and why. Teachers need to spend time explaining the nuances of social situations, with particular reference to aspects of their own or other pupils' behaviour, for instance, *Did you notice how I waited until Amy had finished speaking?* or *I liked the polite way that Shane opened the door for Mrs Watkins*. Fun activities can also be used to teach good listening skills.

- As the adult reads a passage of text, the pupils are asked to listen for a certain word/syllable and say it aloud or make a silent physical response (such as a nod) when they hear it.
- Each pupil in the group whispers a phrase or sentence to the next person in turn along the line and the final version is compared with the original one.
- Pupils act as an audience for a pupil as s/he reads aloud or talks about something of interest and a few pupils are selected subsequently to summarise the main points.
- A short passage is read correctly to the pupils and then re-read, making a specific number of deliberate mistakes during the second reading and asking pupils to keep a mental count of the mistakes they think have been made.
- Each pupil is given a piece of paper and pencil and asked to summarise in diagrammatic or pictorial form what the teacher has said. The results are later shared and the key issues discussed.
- The pupils are divided into pairs. One partner describes an unseen (simple) picture, while the other listens and tries to replicate it in a drawing. The pupils then switch roles using a different picture. Results are shared and discussed at the end.
- A story is narrated as it passes around the circle, with each pupil who wishes to do so contributing to the emerging story. At the end of the process, discussion takes place about the importance of listening.

Pupils benefit from receiving specific instruction and practising effective listening skills (see Figure 6.2).

1.	Look intently at the person who is speaking to you but do not stare.
2.	Do not interrupt the person.
3.	Nod or say something to show you understand what is being said.
4.	Ask questions to find out more about the subject or clarify points.
5.	Repeat what you heard in your own words.
6.	Thank the speaker and, where possible, say how useful and interesting it has been.

Figure 6.2 Six steps to productive listening

Careful listening facilitates thoughtful and well-informed reflection about information and issues. *Reflecting* in and on learning requires attention to what Pollard (2005, after Dewey, 1933) refers to as open-mindedness, responsibility and wholeheartedness. In particular, Pollard stresses that possessing an open mind is an essential attribute for rigorous reflection. However, he draws attention to the fact that having a quality of open-mindedness should not be confused with an absence of values on social and educational issues. Intellectual responsibility requires that a judgement can be made about what is worthwhile. Wholeheartedness, as the name implies, requires dedication, single-mindedness, energy and enthusiasm. Pollard concludes by saying *maintaining a constructive engagement, a willingness to imagine new futures and a self-critical spirit are thus all connected to reflective practice* (p19).

Pollard's analysis of reflective teaching is transferable to reflective *learning*, as the principles apply equally. Thus pupils are encouraged to grapple with open-mindedness, responsibility and wholeheartedness as they engage with their work. Teachers who are constantly looking for opportunities to help pupils to stand back and consider a variety of options, take account of other viewpoints and show a determined approach to task completion will have a classroom that is buzzing with purposeful talk (see Figure 6.3).

- Purposeful talking and listening.
- Child–adult and pupil–pupil affirmation.
- Striving towards clearly defined goals.
- Challenging but non-threatening activities.
- Willingness to risk failure to achieve goals.
- Unity of purpose.
- Clear and flexible limits for behaviour.
- Enjoyment in learning.
- Healthy, cheerful competition.
- Community celebration of individual attainment.

Figure 6.3 Characteristics of a communicative learning climate

Use of visual aids (Q17, 25a)

Experienced teachers find that the use of a small number of carefully selected aids to facilitate communication is preferable to struggling with an excess of them and spending more time dealing with the practicalities of handling the aids than with using them in teaching. Resources are always located within easy reach, especially if the teacher is seated and surrounded by pupils on the carpet, where movement may be limited. Efficient teachers also make sure that pupils can see a visual aid (or text) clearly by (a) placing it at an appropriate height and (b) checking that the pupils are sitting in a suitable position.

By contrast, inexperienced teachers may be tempted to employ visual aids as a substitute for active teaching when they are, as the name suggests, merely an 'aid' to learning. It is therefore essential to decide on its purpose, which may be to introduce a principle (e.g. using scientific apparatus), highlight a specific piece of knowledge (e.g. brush techniques used by an artist), reinforce a concept (e.g. use of mathematical equipment) or simply engage pupils' interest (e.g. using a puppet). Every aid should be exploited fully and not merely referred to 'in passing' because after working hard to produce or collate the resources for the lesson it is disappointing if the impact on learning is minimal. If visual aids are home-made it is better to make a simple stereotype and trial it before spending a lot of time and effort on the polished version.

Lesson pace (Q25c, 25d, 31)

The expression 'lesson pace' is used as a criterion to judge the effectiveness with which a teacher moves a lesson forward and has resulted in some novice teachers feeling under pressure to rush their teaching. In recent years, however, it has become increasingly obvious that the use of such terminology creates the impression that learning can be enhanced by doing everything at speed, thereby limiting the opportunities for pupils to think, reflect, cogitate and discuss the work content. The imposition of a structured literacy hour in the late 1990s added to the impression that the clock rather than depth of learning was the principal arbiter in determining progress. More recently, an emphasis on thinking skills and use of the imagination in creativity (see Chapter 7) has helped to moderate the unhelpful interpretation of pace in teaching.

Instead of equating it with speed, a more appropriate definition of pace is to denote a positive lesson rhythm, which is closer to *peaceful* (not to be confused with 'passive') than to *push*. Under such circumstances, the words of a persuasive teacher are controlled and precise, especially near the start of the lesson, but projected through an engaging tone of voice that captures the pupils' interest and sparks their imaginations, even when the subject content of the lesson is uninspiring. As the session unfolds, the teacher very gradually increases the tempo without leaving pupils stranded in the wake. Pupils are given opportunities to consider what they are being told, clarify points and offer suggestions. Skilled teachers introduce short pauses of suspended silence while they 'freeze the moment'. They introduce variations in the volume and speed of speech as they entice the pupils into the subject content, whet their appetite for learning and heighten their sense of anticipation. When a competent adult communicator finishes speaking, the pupils' eagerness to learn more is almost tangible.

Teachers that communicate a sense of peaceful purpose nod when pupils respond, let their eyes shine, smile gently and make it obvious that their fervour is earnest, not contrived. The expressions of passionate teachers originate in their hearts and are shown in their faces. They give hints, clues and guidance to assist less confident pupils, invariably followed by a firm *Well done, Conrad!* and *Excellent, Catrina!* and qualify their commendations by offering a reason, for example *Good answer, Igor. Your idea has helped us to see a different way of working it out*. These strategies are incorporated to inspire and provoke a comfortable urgency rather than manic coercion.

PRACTICAL TASK PRACTICAL TASK **PRACTICAL TASK** PRACTICAL TASK **PRACTICAL TASK**

Care of the voice

Here are eight tips to protect and take care of your voice:

1. Increase relaxation by easing the tension in your shoulders, standing erectly and gently 'shaking out' your limbs.
2. Exercise your voice daily by breathing deeply and steadily for one minute without raising your shoulders, followed by a further minute of humming to make your lips buzz.

3. Improve your intonation and loosen your facial muscles by reciting a tongue twister several times a day.

4. Drink plenty of room temperature water during the day.

5. Reduce your consumption of dairy products, caffeine and alcohol.

6. Form words in the chest, not in the throat.

7. Only raise your voice when absolutely necessary.

8. Swallow instead of clearing your throat.

Reading aloud in unison (Q10, 25a)

There are occasions when it is appropriate to encourage pupils to read in unison, most commonly with an adult (normally the teacher) as leader. Reading in unison is most likely to occur during English (literacy) lessons using a portion of text selected by the teacher for the purpose.

Teachers who employ reading aloud in unison as a teaching strategy should do so at no more than half the speed at which they would normally speak, as this pace allows the less competent readers and pupils who struggle to interpret the text to keep up with the rest of the class. Unfortunately, it is common for inexperienced teachers not only to speak too fast but also to increase the rate at which they speak until they leave behind all but the most efficient readers. As a result, some pupils appear to be reading in unison when, in fact, they are merely making 'goldfish' lip movements without actually speaking. As teachers have to concentrate on the text and may not be able to watch pupils closely throughout the reading, it is useful for a TA to monitor pupils' involvement and communicate to the teacher what is happening. In practice this strategy necessitates the assistant half-facing the class rather than sitting at the back where it is more difficult to observe pupil responses.

Reading in unison is primarily to familiarise pupils with the content of the passage, so it is essential to dwell on the text and 'savour' it, rather than dealing with it so rapidly that pupils are unable to absorb the detail. Depending on the text being used, it is helpful if teachers spend some time talking about the key words and pointing out significant phrases. For example, the teacher might indicate the position of apostrophes, refer to the punctuation and draw pupils' attention to stylistic features used by the author. It may be appropriate to demonstrate to younger pupils how letter shapes are formed when they are written. Perceptive teachers are on the alert for opportunities to point out spelling patterns in words, for example how many times the letter 's' appears in 'assassinations', the word 'wall' in 'wallet' or 'ear' in 'hear' – in fact, to use any strategy that strengthens learning and reinforces knowledge.

Reading in unison can be made more interesting by introducing variations on the conventional system, for example:

- whispering quieter parts of the passage;
- the teacher and the pupils alternately reading a sentence;
- the class divided into two groups, alternately reading a sentence;
- re-reading some or all of the passage, emphasising key words;
- using 'character' voices for direct speech parts to reflect the personality of the person speaking.

The last strategy (above) runs a small risk of pupils becoming over-excited, but it also demands that they concentrate hard to see where speech marks are employed in the text so that they can use the appropriate voice. One way or another it is essential that the text is chewed and digested rather than swallowed whole!

CASE STUDY

Selina was pleased with the progress she had made during her final school placement, teaching a combined Reception and Year 1 class. With just over two weeks to go and a job interview ahead of her she was starting to feel confident about her ability to complete the experience successfully. Most pleasing was the fact that all the tutors had commended her for diligence, good listening skills and a caring attitude. Selina was quietly proud of the fact that she communicated well with pupils and they reciprocated in kind. It therefore came as a considerable shock when the mentor expressed concern during a review of progress meeting about the fact that she did not always respond to advice provided by colleagues and seemed reluctant to incorporate their suggestions into her teaching. Selina was horrified and acutely anxious, but after talking at length about the situation with the mentor, it became clear that although she took advice from colleagues very seriously, she also evaluated its appropriateness before deciding whether to incorporate the suggestion into her classroom practice. In some instances she had decided *not* to follow the advice but had obviously failed to communicate the reasons behind her decision to the person who had offered it. Consequently, it appeared to the tutor that she was sometimes resistant to the guidance offered by more experienced practitioners. Once the issue had been aired, the mentor said that he was actually pleased and relieved to hear that Selina was taking professional responsibility for her actions. However, he urged her to make more effort to share the results of her thinking with the colleague concerned so as to avoid misunderstanding. The remaining few weeks of the placement passed smoothly and Selina was eventually appointed to a post teaching reception age pupils in her home town. She reflected ruefully that for all her well-honed communication skills with pupils, she would need to make a serious effort to be as open and transparent with adults!

MOVING *ON* > > > > > > MOVING *ON* > > > > > > MOVING *ON*

Based on the fact that children learn as much about teachers from their non-verbal actions and responses as they do from their words, make every effort to look smart and colourful, use a lot of bright facial expressions (especially smiles) and 'reach out' to children through listening carefully, showing amazement and delighting in their funny ways. Children instinctively know when adults like them, so even if you aren't impressed by certain pupils, it is worth making an effort to start speaking positively about them to other adults. By modifying your spoken language in this way, you will slowly change your attitude as well, which will gradually affect your non-verbal body language; these characteristics will, in turn, communicate to children that you are 'for' them.

REFERENCES REFERENCES **REFERENCES** REFERENCES **REFERENCES** REFERENCES

Fisher, R. (2005) *Teaching Children to Learn*. Cheltenham: Nelson Thornes.

Hart, S. and Kindle Hodson, V. (2004) *The Compassionate Classroom*. La Crescenta, CA: Center for Non-Violent Communication.

Morrison, K. (2001) Jürgen Habermas. In: J. A. Palmer (ed.), *Fifty Modern Thinkers on Education*. Abingdon: Routledge, 215–24.

Pollard, A. (2005) *Reflective Teaching*. London: Continuum.

FURTHER READING FURTHER READING **FURTHER READING** FURTHER READING

Cullingford, C. (2005) The ontological insecurity of childhood: a case study. *Education 3–13*, 33(3), 38–43.

Eke, R. and Lee, J. (2008) *Using Talk Effectively in the Primary Classroom*. Abingdon: Routledge.

Goodwin, P. (ed.) (2001) *The Articulate Classroom: Talking and Learning in the Primary School*. London: David Fulton.

Green, N. (2006) *Motivating Children in the Primary Classroom*. London: Sage.

Grugeon, E., Hubbard, L., Smith, C. and Dawes, L. (2006) *Teaching Speaking and Listening in the Primary School*. London: David Fulton.

Haynes, J. (2008) *Children as Philosophers: Learning Through Enquiry and Dialogue in the Classroom*. Abingdon: Routledge.

Latham, C. and Miles, A. (2001) *Communication, Curriculum and Classroom Practice*. London: David Fulton.

Myhill, D., Jones, S. and Hopper, R. (2006) *Talking, Listening, Learning: Effective Talk in the Primary Classroom*. Maidenhead: Open University Press/McGraw-Hill.

7
Creativity and imagination

Learning outcomes

To understand:

- **the meaning of creativity;**
- **the role of imagination;**
- **how teachers can be creative;**
- **how pupils can be creative;**
- **what a creative classroom looks like.**

Introduction

Despite its frequent use in the literature, creativity is a difficult term to define. The root of the word 'create' means 'to bring into being'. It encompasses *husbandry* terms such as germinate, grow, nurture and produce; *enquiry* terms such as create, experiment and devise; and even *transcendent* terms such as inspiration, spontaneity and revelation. Some authors argue that there is a synergy between teaching creatively and creative learning such that creative teachers aspire to give pupils the opportunity to extend their knowledge through pursuing their own interests and exploring their natural talents. Jones and Wyse (2004) suggest that creativity *should be a characteristic of an approach to the curriculum which values every child's interests and styles of learning and encourages them to use their skills in new contexts* (p34). Some scholars dislike using creativity as a noun ('the creativity'), preferring to use 'creative' as an adjective and applying it to specific contexts, thus the creative scientist, the creative writer and so forth.

The heart of creativity (Q8, 25a, 30, 31)

Creative teaching and learning cannot be reduced to a series of carefully crafted ideas and approaches, so that a list of lesson plans can be produced and followed through assiduously, though authors like Bowkett (2007) offer a useful framework for doing so. The essence of creativity is represented in part through instinctive behaviour and the sensitivity to grasp opportunities as they arise. These are qualities that defy neatly packaged units of learning and supersede the linear objectives–delivery–assessment model. On the other hand, creativity must not be confused with random, uncoordinated attempts to search for meaning through unbridled forms of expression.

Every teacher is acutely aware of the pressures exerted by time constraints and the demands of a society seemingly obsessed by formal examination results. However, as Jeffrey and Craft (2004) demonstrate so clearly through their in-depth case study of a primary school that seized and exploited creative opportunities, formal academic standards rise if creativity is viewed as an *attribute* rather than a technique. That is, teachers are constantly looking for ways in which the 'ordinary' can be transformed into the 'extraordinary' by creative means.

Creativity is distinguished by freedom of expression and being entrepreneurial; it is characterised by the generation of ideas and imaginings within a milieu of colour, spontaneity and laughter, all of which contribute towards greater productivity because pupils work much harder when they enjoy what they are doing. Creativity involves making a deliberate effort to see things from a different perspective, to break from constraining habits and stale beliefs to find new ways of thinking, doing and being. Consequently, far from being viewed as a useful addition to learning if time permits, creativity should be the norm, infiltrating and saturating every part of classroom life. The need for such a wholehearted approach is urgent, not least because if creativity is suppressed it can lead to frustration and a lacklustre learning climate.

Every child and adult is capable of being creative, so when pupils are forced to suppress their creativity its energy can be dissipated through wasteful means, such as inappropriate behaviour. This truth becomes all too obvious when teachers provide a strictly monitored curriculum, hesitate to deviate from the prescribed format and are unyielding in their insistence that the pupils must follow a rigid, predetermined pathway in learning. In such circumstances, passion for learning is replaced by passive compliance.

RESEARCH SUMMARY RESEARCH SUMMARY **RESEARCH SUMMARY** RESEARCH SUMMARY

Successful teachers and creativity

Success as a teacher depends in part on being situated in a school environment where innovation is promoted, for as Jeffrey and Woods (2003) maintain in their graphic description of a vibrant school situation:

> Teaching itself is creative, never formulaic. The aim is creative learning, with children coming to own their own knowledge and skills, being enthused and changed by the process, and having some control of the learning process, but under teacher guidance. (p3)

- What do you understand by 'formulaic teaching'?
- Are there occasions when it is necessary to be formulaic?

Creativity and the curriculum (Q8, 23)

Creativity is commonly associated with practical learning such as drama, dance and other dimensions of the arts, and a large number of publications focus specifically on these areas. However, every subject in the curriculum can be approached creatively, including the core subjects of mathematics, English and science.

Inspiring teachers use a variety of strategies and techniques in their teaching of arts subjects to foster a spirit of enterprise when pupils tackle the tasks and activities they are allocated and leave room for pupil initiative and imagination: the very essence of being creative. Most teachers consider that works of art produced by pupils should invariably be commended, providing they have made a sincere effort in making it. Thus pairs of reception age pupils work together to mirror one another's movements; a group of seven-year-old pupils collaborate to produce a collage; groups of nine-year-old pupils devise a game using small equipment; eleven-year-old pupils select a face from a magazine as the starting point for a poster. All these instances (and dozens of similar ones) provide opportunities for pupils to be creative and to be praised for their efforts, even if the final product is unexceptional. The creative enterprise in arts subjects relies on teacher and pupil to play their parts, thus:

- the teacher's ability to inspire, teach the necessary skills and organise for learning (Note: organise 'for' learning, not 'of' learning);
- the pupils' enthusiasm for the task/activity and willingness to take risks in learning.

By contrast with the 'dual creativity' (teacher and pupil both being creative) in the more practical areas of the curriculum, *core* subjects tend to be 'mono-creative', whereby teachers teach creatively but pupils use more conventional means in their learning. It is also generally true that in core areas, teachers tend to be rather less inclined to praise genuine effort, being more concerned with the product than the process.

The objectives-driven nature of English and mathematics teaching leaves little room for manoeuvre with regard to curriculum coverage and the rate at which it has to be achieved. If there are parallel classes, teachers and assistants plan jointly and try to keep 'in step' from week to week, further constraining the opportunities for exploring creative learning styles that, owing to the additional time absorbed by exploratory methods, might lead to a lack of synchronisation. As a consequence, some teachers are wary about organising too much collaborative work, problem-solving and investigative or play-orientated activities, as these approaches are time-consuming and the outcomes are less predictable than in strictly controlled learning situations where pupil tasks are tightly linked to learning objectives.

Many teachers conclude that as time constraints necessitate that they eventually have to provide part or all of the solution to a problem with which pupils are grappling, they may as well lead the pupils step by step towards the correct solution using a prescriptive approach, thereby streamlining the process. All teachers are faced with weighing time factors against the desire to exploit innovative practice.

Teachers strive to make their teaching of mathematics and English creative and inspiring, but the highly specified curriculum and national tests do not facilitate the same degree of flexibility in learning styles (though there are exceptions; see, for example, Franklin, 2006). Teachers may want pupils to employ more heuristic (problem-solving) approaches in (especially) mathematics and science, but fear that test results will be adversely affected if they deviate from the standard methods. Nevertheless, strategies such as using humorously written portions of text as the starting point for a discussion of verb use in English, visual effects to create a sense of wonder in science, magic number bonds in mathematics, chants, quiz times and opportunities for groups of pupils to present their findings imaginatively – all contribute to the sense of adventure in learning.

In defining and implementing creative ideas, teachers also have to take account of the purpose for which they are being employed. If creative thinking is equated with *enterprise and progress*, teachers can be innovative in their teaching as a means of advancing pupil learning. If, on the other hand, creative thinking is viewed as a means of *remedying* an unsatisfactory situation, then inexperienced teachers in particular need close guidance. Remedial work is traditionally associated with mastery through repetition, so the use of creative practice to reinforce knowledge and address misconceptions is more of a high-risk strategy, thus the need for advice from seasoned colleagues. In other words, while *enterprising* creative practice is practitioner-led and allows for considerable teacher autonomy, *remedial* creative practice necessitates a high degree of professional judgement. Nevertheless, creative practice has the potential both to accelerate achievement (enterprising practice) and correct learning difficulties (remedial practice).

Imagination (Q8, 28)

Creativity is frequently associated with imagination, which is broadly defined as the ability to form a mental image of something that it is not possible to perceive through the senses. Imagination involves the mind's capacity to build mental scenes, objects or events that do not really exist or have happened in the past, as memory is a manifestation of imagination. Even the simplest piece of learning requires that pupils envisage (imagine) a scenario. For example, when a teacher explains without the use of visual aids that one child has 10 marbles and another child has 12 marbles and asks questions about the total number of marbles or the difference between the numbers, pupils are obliged to use their mind's eye in helping to solve the problem. In fact it is arguable that the provision of visual aids may actually serve to suppress use of the imagination, though used with discretion they serve an important purpose in assisting pupils who struggle to think abstractly.

Every pupil possesses some ability to use imagination. The factors that affect the depth of a pupil's capacity are difficult to pinpoint but inspiring teachers promote speculation, 'just imagine' and alternative views of familiar situations to stir it in their pupils. Over time, the pupils respond to the teacher's prompting by offering more creative ideas, suggestions and solutions. Teachers can further assist the imaginative process and heighten pupil interest by raising stimulating questions during spare moments in the day, such as while pupils are waiting to leave the room, waiting on the carpet or lining up to leave the playground.

- What would dinner be like if all food were the same colour?
- What would be different about life if you bounced instead of walked?
- What would happen if people could see what we were thinking?

When teachers are reading a story, they can encourage the children to create a different ending or say what other decisions the central character might have made. Later on, they can link the story with artwork, drama or a construction activity.

Use of the imagination makes it possible for adults and children to experience alternative worlds inside their minds, to look at situations from different standpoints and explore mentally the past and the future. Imagination can be used to reproduce a sound, a taste or even a smell, to produce a physical sensation, to evoke a feeling or to stimulate an emotion. Pupils who possess a well-developed and strong imagination strengthen their creative potential. They have a 'thought tool' to use for remodelling existing concepts and deepening their capacity to find solutions that were previously elusive.

Teachers get irritated when pupils appear to be idle, but 'expansive daydreaming' that takes the pupil into new realms of thinking about the topic under consideration and 'escapist daydreaming' that provides some temporary calmness and relief from the tension of work, both have a place in learning. Properly channelled, pupils' imaginations carry them beyond the immediacy of the situation and into worlds where the impossible becomes possible and the unattainable is within reach. The imagination transports pupils into a situation of their choosing and offers unlimited opportunity for transformation. For the small number of unhappy pupils in school, their imaginations provide temporary security and release from the tensions of life and may be one of the few sources of emotional contentment.

Imagination therefore has great potential educational value. It is a creative power that provides the impetus for inventing a piece of equipment, designing a dress, painting a picture or writing a story. Teachers that promote the use of the imagination can transform a lethargic group of pupils into lively, thoughtful originators of ideas. Some of the ideas might initially be impractical or whimsical but with perseverance these 'brain-busters' yield positive results as they engage pupils' minds. By harnessing, freeing or stimulating pupil imaginations, adults in school can help pupils to fulfil some of their hopes and dreams and extend the conventional learning boundaries to incorporate new realms of achievement.

The creative classroom (Q8, 30, 31)

When visitors enter a creative teacher's classroom they are not only impressed with the colourfulness, vibrancy, attention to detail in things on display (clear labelling, crisp borders, thoughtful range of questions) and the quality of the work that the pupils have achieved, but also with the ability of pupils to stay focused on their work. The wallboards reflect a range of topics and art forms that are clearly the result of careful adult instruction and innovative practice. Each pupil's name is visible alongside one or more piece of work. Far from being characterised by random activity and vague aspiration, the creative classroom is brimming over with pupils enjoying the challenge of targeted (but not rigidly prescribed) activity.

In some classrooms a range of different activities occupies the pupils. Some have their heads down, immersed in completing a written task, while others are engaged in researching from books; a group is busy with an art project while a number of pupils are working in pairs on computers in the corner of the room, supported by an assistant. Yet others are quietly reading or completing work from earlier in the day. A small group of pupils are undertaking a science experiment with the teacher offering guidance and assistance. The atmosphere is businesslike but unhurried.

Visitors are especially impressed by the way that pupils persevere and show resourcefulness when they are left to work unaided, conveying the clear message that pupils are motivated and pursuing defined goals. As the session nears its end the teacher reminds the class about what needs to be completed and what can be finished on another occasion. Despite the variety of tasks and activities being undertaken, the atmosphere is orderly and cooperative; resources are tidied and stored correctly.

In the creative classroom, adults are industrious but relaxed and at ease with one another. There are smiles, occasional chuckles and supportive comments, as the teamwork ethic permeates every part of the room. The teaching assistant concentrates on her specific task but is unafraid to make suggestions about or intervening in the other activities that are taking place. From time to time she advises pupils to seek help from the teacher. There are no harsh words; instead, excitable pupils and those straying off-task are gently reminded about the priorities. During the session and after work is completed, the pupils are eager to share and show what they have done with an available adult or classmate. There is a powerful sense of expectation about high standards, yet understanding and assistance rather than criticism for any pupil who is struggling. Visiting teachers wish that their own classroom were like this one; visiting parents fervently hope that their children will be placed in it.

RESEARCH SUMMARY RESEARCH SUMMARY **RESEARCH SUMMARY** RESEARCH SUMMARY

Originality in teaching

Winkley (2002) argues that the best contemporary teaching consists of a mixture of individuality and corporate endeavour. He concludes:

Like good jazz, good teaching is both structured and improvised. It makes use of the finest instruments and themes available but deploys them in personal, original ways. (p329)

REFLECTIVE TASK

Creativity in cross-curricular teaching

Read the following five statements describing elements of creative teaching and learning. Use a cross-curricular topic that you have taught, or are considering teaching, and evaluate how you score on each of the statements (Strong feature/Partial feature/Weak feature). Consider how you might improve the level of creativity by selecting a strategy from one or more of the following options.

- Read stories to stimulate excitement.
- Use artefacts to generate discussion.
- Show a film extract to raise enthusiasm.
- Build in an aspect of drama to explore imagination.
- Incorporate investigative problem-solving to promote team work.
- Invite a guest speaker to inspire children.
- Plan a long-term project rooted in access to electronic information sources.
- Set up a science-based or D&T-based competition.

Practical ways to promote creativity
(Q8, 25a, 30, 31)

Creative classrooms do not offer pupils unbridled freedom because when things are in a state of flux and events are unpredictable it places considerable pressure on teachers and unsettles the pupils, thereby constraining rather than liberating innovative practice. In fact, the most creative environments in society are also the most stable ones. Thus the artist's studio, the research laboratory and the scholar's library are deliberately kept orderly to support the complexities of the work in progress. The parameters of creative classrooms are well defined so the unpredictable can more easily be accommodated.

Creativity does not occur in a vacuum. It relies upon a framework of understanding, skills and content knowledge that facilitates and supports experimentation, problem-solving and investigations. There is little point in letting pupils loose with equipment and resources when they have little idea about what they are to do, how they are to accomplish it and where the boundaries of behaviour lie. The most creative people already possess a repertoire of skills, gained by thorough initial teaching, regular rehearsal, observing others who have acquired mastery and getting advice from a more knowledgeable source.

For instance, if young pupils are given a range of musical instruments, they need to be shown how to use them correctly and practise a number of key skills and techniques before being allowed to experiment; otherwise, they are likely to make a cacophony of random sounds and may even damage equipment through carelessness. Once they have mastered these elementary skills, pupils can be given the opportunity to create new rhythms and sounds for a specific purpose: for instance, as an accompaniment to a popular piece of music. These sophisticated developments can only take place after the pupils have gained the basic mastery of techniques and been introduced to a range of strategies and practical forms of expression; otherwise, creativity can deteriorate into chaos. The establishment of a framework of competence also promotes creativity because it obviates the need for pupils to ask as many questions of clarification, prefaced by:

- Are we supposed to . . .? *(to clarify purpose)*;
- Does it matter if we . . .? *(to identify constraints)*;
- Do we have to . . .? *(to understand procedure)*;
- How long have we got to . . .? *(to improve time management)*;
- What will happen when . . .? *(to clarify outcome)*.

The tension that exists between being offered the opportunity to explore and gaining competence in mastery of skills through a structured programme and adult guidance can be summarised as follows:

COMPETENCE + GUIDANCE + OPPORTUNITY + STRUCTURE results in CREATIVE OUTCOMES

OPPORTUNITY minus COMPETENCE or STRUCTURE or GUIDANCE results in CHAOS

Of course there *are* occasions when pupils benefit from being given extensive freedom to explore and discover, especially during 'play' sessions. However, the spontaneous forms of play associated with life outside school are different from the structured play that so often characterises classroom situations, where adults impose health and safety, physical and curriculum boundaries. Klugman and Fasoli (1995) identify four broad categories of adult-monitored play as follows.

- *Functional play* – a common play type among young pupils that involves task repetition to gain motor skills and mastery; for example, dumping, filling, stacking, water play and outdoors play. Functional play can be either solitary or in parallel with another child.
- *Constructive play* – where a child creates or makes something and solves problems; for example, building with blocks, playing with arts, crafts and puppets and doing puzzles. This type of play develops thinking and reasoning skills and problem-solving.
- *Pretend play* – pupils transform themselves, others and objects from real into make-believe. Pretend play helps pupils to process emotions and events in their lives, practise social skills, learn values, develop language and create a rich imagination.
- *Games with rules play* – this type of play includes board games, ball games, chanting and skipping games, all of which involve the application of agreed rules. Pupils learn and practise cooperation, mutual understanding and logical thinking.

Creativity is often unlocked when pupils collaborate in problem-solving play sessions because the combination of their energy, initiative and ideas often leads to creative solutions. Play helps pupils to consciously realign their focus and look at situations in different ways; as a result, the insights they gain generate fresh understanding and give impetus to further achievement.

Creativity, values and spirituality (Q2, 18, 30, 31)

Values are variously defined in literature as everything from eternal ideas to behavioural actions and an integral part of every adult's role is to help pupils understand the key values that form the heart and spine of a civilised society. Consequently, teachers strive to inculcate new pupils with good working practices: cooperation rather than aggressive competition; partnership rather than selfishness; diversity rather than homogeneity; collaboration rather than isolation; participation rather than aloofness. To achieve such ambitious goals, teachers need first to ensure that they are clear about their own values so that they are better able to influence and shape young lives.

Adults in the classroom also grapple with issues of empowering pupils rather than forcing them to be dependent, managing the class without excessive coercion, motivating rather than threatening. Children face challenges when they wrestle with issues associated with basic values such as honesty, respect and accepting responsibility rather than blaming others. Indeed, every person in school is confronted by difficult decisions, whether to choose the easy road or the right one, and how much effort to put into promoting the self and how much to expend in assisting others.

Values in education have often been closely linked to moral and spiritual education. Parents, communities and government expect that staff in schools will help pupils to develop their character and attitudes to others in such a way that they are able to contribute positively to the society in which they live. Civilised behaviour impacts directly on the school environment where teachers and pupils work together, but it also filters beyond the school gate and into the home, local district and the wider world.

The development of 'character' in children begins by identifying core values that are acceptable to every proponent of civilised behaviour. For instance, the Resources for Character Education network (San Francisco) offer the following principles that underpin character education.

- Your character is defined by what you do, not what you say or believe.
- Every choice you make helps define the kind of person you are choosing to be.
- Good character requires doing the right thing, even when it is costly or risky.
- You do not have to take the worst behaviour of others as a standard for yourself.
- What you do matters and one person can make a big difference.
- The payoff for having good character is that it makes you a better person and makes the world a better place.

Creativity is not only associated with imagination and values, but also frequently linked with *spirituality*, though the term is subject to numerous interpretations and resists precise definition. Nevertheless, there appears to be a consensus about the fact that spirituality is integral to the subjective life, as contrasted with the objective domain of observable behaviour and material objects that are capable of direct measurement. Consequently, the spiritual domain relates to human consciousness, notably what we experience in our minds and the mysterious area of our spirits. Spirituality also involves our affective experiences (emotions, inclinations, sense of something that has a substance beyond a rational perspective) at least as much as it does our reasoning or logic. More specifically, spirituality has to do with the values that we cherish (see earlier), our sense of who we are, where we come from, our destiny (the meaning and purpose that we attach to our lives) and our interconnectedness with each other. Spirituality also has significance with regard to aspects of our experience that are not easy to define or analyse, such as intuition, inspiration, the mysterious and the mystical.

One form of education provision that places a lot of emphasis on 'spiritual creativity' is located in Waldorf–Steiner schools. Rudolf Steiner was an Austrian philosopher, scientist and artist. In 1919 he was invited to give a series of lectures to the workers of the Waldorf-Astoria cigarette factory in Stuttgart, Germany. As a result, the factory's owner asked Steiner to establish and lead a school for the children of the factory's employees. Steiner agreed to do so on four conditions.

- The school should be open to all children.
- It should be coeducational.
- It should be a unified twelve-year school.
- Those who would be working directly with the children should take the leading role in the running of the school, with a minimum of interference from governmental or economic concerns.

The owner agreed to the conditions and following a training period for the prospective teachers, the Free Waldorf School was opened on 7 September 1919.

Steiner designed a curriculum that was responsive to the developmental phases in childhood and the nurturing of children's imaginations. He believed that schools should cater for the needs of children rather than comply with the demands of external influences, and encouraged creativity and free-thinking. The aim of Waldorf schooling today is to educate the 'whole child': head, heart and hands, so that they are able, in and of themselves, to impart meaning to their lives. The curriculum is as broad as time permits and balances subjects deemed academic with artistic and practical activities. The intention is to foster a genuine love of learning within each child, thereby creating such intense internal motivation that competitive testing and grading is unnecessary. Nevertheless, the teacher writes a detailed evaluation of the child at the end of each school year.

There is no academic content in the Waldorf kindergarten (pre-school) classes though there is attention paid to pre-academic skills. There is minimal academic content for children in class 1. The letters are introduced artistically in class 2, with the children learning to read from their own writing in class 2 or 3. During the primary school years (classes 1–8) the pupils have a class (or 'main lesson') teacher who, ideally, remains with the same class for the first eight years of their schooling to provide continuity and stability. Other teachers contribute to the teaching programme.

Activities that are quite often considered peripheral in mainstream schools are central to Waldorf schools; subjects such as art, music, gardening and foreign languages are actively promoted. In the younger grades, all subjects are introduced through artistic mediums, in the belief that children respond better to this approach than to didactic teaching and rote learning. All pupils learn to play the recorder and to knit; they learn a stringed instrument from class 3 onwards. There are virtually no textbooks in the first five years of schooling, as the pupils essentially produce their own texts by recording their experiences and what they have learned. However, older pupils use textbooks to supplement their main lesson work. Access to electronic media by young pupils, particularly television, is discouraged.

Seasonal festivals and ceremonies are observed in school to raise children's awareness of the rhythms of nature and a sense of 'something beyond' to benefit the 'inner life of the soul'. Children are seen to revel in the anticipation and preparation for events, as well as in the celebration itself. Memories are deliberately cherished and nurtured. Spiritual guidance is thereby intended to awaken a child's natural reverence for the wonder and the beauty of life.

PRACTICAL TASK PRACTICAL TASK PRACTICAL TASK PRACTICAL TASK PRACTICAL TASK

Imagination in learning

Set aside learning targets, objectives, assessment criteria, levelling and marking for a time and let children's imaginations run riot by, for instance:

- writing new words to a familiar rhyme;
- bringing in their favourite photograph (with permission) and telling the class the story that lies behind it;
- drawing a self-portrait of what they would look like if they lived on another planet;
- acting out a favourite story using finger puppets;
- making up a game in PE using only three small items of equipment;
- writing and sending messages using a simple code.

CASE STUDY

James loved being at playgroup and enjoyed nursery school, especially the times when they were allowed to choose an activity. He particularly liked to draw and would scribble furiously, fusing a series of shapes and colours into a dense patchwork of interlocking patterns. James also loved to build towers and castles and would spend long periods of time erecting them out of anything he could find. He was less keen on sitting and listening; however, because of the enchanting stories and the love he had for his teacher and the other grown-ups, James tried hard to be good. His imagination transported him to regions far beyond the world of the classroom. One day after school he heard one of the assistants tell his mother that he was a bit restless in class and could be a bit of a fidget at times. On the way home James was told that he would have to settle down before he went to the 'big school'. James was happy about going to the big school because he thought that it would be like having an adventure in one of his imaginary towers or castles, but when he asked his mother several times *Why will I have to settle down?*, she became irritated, so he decided to keep quiet. The next term he began 'proper' school and found that it was similar to the nursery class except that he was more often expected to sit at a table and write, colour pictures and count. James did not mind doing these tasks but he wanted to create his own pictures and make up his own sums. He had great fun in the hall during PE, running around, dancing and singing as though he were in the park, but he was told off for being a 'silly boy' and made to sit at the side. After that, James stopped dancing, singing and running around and did what he was told, like the other pupils. When the teacher instructed them all to skip and dance, he skipped and danced. When she told them all to keep still, he stood like a statue. Back in class he sat with the other pupils to listen to a story, but did not enjoy it all that much because the teacher kept pausing and asking them a lot of questions. Why did she have to spoil the magic? Over the weeks and months James learned that if he wished to avoid trouble he must do what the other pupils did. He longed to break free and build a castle or create a kaleidoscope of colour like he used to do, but the teacher said that he must do those things at home because school was where you learned like a big boy. James did not want to be a big boy; he wanted to be James. At the end of the year he went to the school with his mother one evening to see the teacher and look at his work. James's mother examined his neat drawings of a cat; they were almost identical to the other pupils' drawings of cats. She studied his painting of a rainbow; the colours were the same as every other child's picture. She picked up his model of a 'shopping basket' made of card and glue; it was just like all the others. James heard the teacher telling his mother that he had done some good work once he had 'buckled down', but that he must work even harder to do well in the tests next year. James did not know what a test was, but did not like the sound of it much. His mother said, with a note of sadness, that he had once been such a creative child but seemed to have lost some of his sparkle. The teacher said that it was nothing to worry about and she was very pleased that James's writing was neat, he was learning his phonics and he could count in twos and threes, forwards and backwards. His mother nodded and said that she was also very pleased with his progress. James sighed. He was puzzled by all this grown-up talk. He just wanted to build a castle that reached to the sky and paint a different rainbow.

- In what ways can teachers unintentionally suppress pupils' creativity?
- How can a balance be found between conforming to external curriculum requirements and giving pupils freedom to explore?
- How much do you agree with the statement: School is for work; pupils can play at home?

MOVING *ON* > > > > > > MOVING *ON* > > > > > > MOVING *ON*

Don't think of creativity as a quality that some people possess and others do not. Being creative is as much about opportunity to experiment and investigate, supported by a helpful adult and the availability of good resources, as it is about natural talent. A sign that you are maturing as a teacher is a willingness to offer children the space and time to enquire, innovate, make mistakes and self-correct. Your role then becomes one of facilitator and guide, rather than instigator and corrector. Put another way, you become a shepherd that leads from the front rather than one who drives the flock from behind.

REFERENCES REFERENCES **REFERENCES** REFERENCES **REFERENCES** REFERENCES

Bowkett, S. (2007) *100 Ideas for Teaching Creativity*. London: Continuum.

Franklin, S. (2006) VAKing out learning styles: why the notion of learning styles is unhelpful to teachers. *Education 3–13*, 34(1), 81–7.

Jeffrey, B. and Craft, A. (2004) Teaching creatively and teaching for creativity: distinctions and relationships. *Educational Studies*, 30(1), 77–87.

Jeffrey, B. and Woods, P. (2003) *The Creative School*. Abingdon: Routledge.

Jones, R. and Wyse, D. (2004) *Creativity in the Primary Curriculum*. London: David Fulton.

Klugman, E. and Fasoli, L. (1995) Taking the high road toward a definition of play. In: P. M. Mikelson (ed.), *The Importance of Play*. St Paul, MN: Red Leaf Press, 195–201.

Winkley, D. (2002) *Handsworth Revolution*. London: Giles de la Mare.

FURTHER READING FURTHER READING **FURTHER READING** FURTHER READING

Bowkett, S. (2008) *Countdown to Creative Writing*. Abingdon: Routledge.

Carter, J. (2002) *Just Imagine: Creative Ideas for Writing*. London: David Fulton.

Fisher, R. and Williams, M. (eds.) (2004) *Unlocking Creativity*. London: David Fulton.

Foale, J. and Pagett, L. (2008) *Creative Approaches to Poetry for the Primary Framework for Literacy*. Abingdon: Routledge.

8
Exploring the Standards: lexicon

Learning outcomes

To understand:

- **the significance of key words used in the Standards;**
- **the context in which key words are employed in the Standards;**
- **how different Standards can be grouped around key words.**

The purpose of the Q-Standards

Imagine starting a journey through relatively unknown terrain without much idea about what equipment you need, the best route to take or the challenges that are likely to face you. Imagine orientating in the general direction of your destination, hoping for the best and relying on instinct to guide your decisions, while ignoring the advice of experienced walkers who have trod the route many times over. You would, of course, consider someone that behaved in such a way to be foolish, arrogant or deluded.

The process of becoming an effective teacher is also a journey in which you need a compass to successfully negotiate the way ahead – advice offered in the previous chapters of this book is intended to provide such expert guidance. By contrast, the Standards for QTS (Q-Standards) do not offer specific advice about the 'nuts and bolts' of effective practice or about negotiating the daily joys and hardships of being a teacher in a school. They do not speak directly to your particular situation or give you answers to some of the intractable dilemmas and decisions that teachers face. However, what the Standards do provide is a bird's-eye map of the territory that you, as a budding teacher, are hoping to successfully occupy and offer a framework for evaluating your progress.

It is important to remind yourself that the people who devised the Q-Standards have never been in your exact position, taught the children you teach or had to deal with the adults in the education setting in which you are placed. What the Standards offer is a description of the sorts of things that all new teachers should be aware of, and striving to demonstrate in their regular work; you have the responsibility to interpret the Standards' statements with respect to the context in which you are placed.

The Q-Standards have not been sent from heaven on tablets of stone; they don't express with total precision everything that you need to accomplish and achieve. Some of the statements are ambiguous; others are so complex that they take a considerable amount of unravelling. Even the majority of the clear statements require interpretation about their implications for practice. Nevertheless, despite all these reservations about the Standards, they are, for better or worse, the only authoritative set of requirements that exist. In short, if you want to succeed in gaining QTS, you have no choice but to engage with, draw from and become closely acquainted with the details contained in the descriptive statements.

Your tutors and mentors will give you expert guidance about satisfying the Q-Standards with regard to the educational setting in which you are placed but it is essential that you, also, have a thorough grasp of what they specify and their implications for your work as a teacher if you are to take command of your own learning. With these points in mind, the present chapter and the next chapter are written to assist you in three principal ways, namely:

1. to understand better what is expected of you as described in the Standards;
2. to have strategies for successful implementation of the Standards;
3. to find ways of achieving the Standards while remaining true to your moral and educational principles.

The composite nature of the Standards

Q-Standards vary considerably in their degree of complexity. For example, under the subheading 'Communicating and working with others', Standard Q4 states quite simply that trainee teachers should be able to: *Communicate effectively with children, young people, colleagues, parents and carers.* While the wording is plain, a moment's thought reveals that interpreting and implementing such a simple statement is far more demanding than merely understanding the description. Thus, communicating with children and a range of different adults necessitates using different voice tones, vocabulary and ways to reinforce meaning. In addition, there is also the matter of grappling with what is meant by 'effectively'. Meeting the Q-Standards therefore not only involves interpreting the printed word but also exploring ways to develop and demonstrate to an evaluator (mentor, tutor, host teacher, examiner) that you possess the relevant attributes attached to them. In the case of Q4, a complete list of these attributes might be something like the following:

- uses an appropriate medium for communicating (verbal, visual, written);
- uses an appropriate tone of voice for the age and maturity of the individual(s);
- speaks clearly and precisely;
- writes unambiguously;
- uses visual aids to reinforce ideas;
- maintains good eye contact;
- smiles and nods appreciatively;
- listens as much as speaks;
- provides accurate information;
- raises suitable questions to help the individual understand;
- responds to the individual's concerns;
- helps to clarify misunderstandings.

The list could easily be extended but the important point to grasp is that the mere assembling of words for each Standard description is only the beginning of the process.

Many Standards contain multiple expectations. For example, under the subheading of 'Planning', Q22 demands that trainees: *Plan for progression across the age and ability range for which they are trained, designing effective learning sequences within lessons and across series of lessons and demonstrating secure subject/curriculum knowledge.* This single Standard contains no fewer than four elements that relate to planning.

- Plan for progression across the age and ability range.
- Design effective learning sequences within lessons.

- Design effective learning sequences across series of lessons.
- Demonstrate secure subject and curriculum knowledge.

The position is complicated by the fact that it is quite possible for you to be successful in one element of the Standard ('planning for progression', say) and unsuccessful in others (e.g. 'secure subject knowledge'). If you are an inexperienced trainee it is also possible that you are able to plan for progression and design effective learning sequences within single lessons but not be at the point at which you can handle sequences across series of lessons. In other words, it is unlikely that you would meet the full demands of this Standard until you were more experienced and had opportunity to teach a continuous series of lessons on the same theme or topic.

Furthermore, each Q-Standard not only has to be interpreted but also understood in terms of the sort of evidence needed to convince the assessor that you have 'met' the requirements encapsulated within the Standard. In the example of Q22 noted above, it is one thing to design effective learning sequences on paper, but it is quite another to translate the plans into demonstrable classroom practice (as described in Q25). The Q22/25 link illustrates that although the Standards are listed separately, they are in fact interdependent. The practicalities of demonstrating and meeting the Standards are explored fully in the next chapter.

Using the lexicon

The lexicon consists of key words extracted from the Q-Standards, chosen on the basis of their frequency of use and their importance. Each word is accompanied by the appropriate Q-Standard references in which the word occurs and either the full Standard statement or, more often, the relevant portion of it. Although the Standards' statements use the overarching phrase, 'children and young people' in the descriptions, only the word 'children' is used throughout the lexicon. Similarly, the word 'learners' in the original descriptions has been replaced by 'children' to reflect the intimacy of relationship that should characterise teacher–pupil interaction in primary education. Occasionally, the original wording of the Standard has been slightly amended for ease of reading. For instance, Q25a, listed under 'Wellbeing', replaces *safeguarding and promotion of the wellbeing of children* with *safeguarding and promotion of children's wellbeing*.

Sometimes the exact wording of the Standard has been slightly altered to make it specific to the key word. For example, Q18 states: *Understand how children and young people develop and that the progress and wellbeing of learners are affected by a range of developmental, social, religious, ethnic, cultural and linguistic influences*. However, the influences involved – developmental, social, religious, ethnic, cultural, linguistic – are entered as single entries under each word, rather than in combination. Thus, under the key word 'Social', the accompanying phrase is: *Understand how children are affected by a range of social influences*. Similarly, under 'Cultural', the phrase used is: *Understand how children are affected by a range of cultural influences*, and so on. Many such variations are represented in the lexicon to aid explicitness; however, where a combination of factors must be considered together to make sense of the statement, there is no attempt to separate out the component parts. For example, Q31 states: *Establish a clear framework for classroom discipline to manage learners' behaviour constructively and promote their self-control and independence*. The description indicates that there are are three discernible but related elements to the establishment of a clear framework for discipline, namely: (a) to manage learners' behaviour constructively; (b) to promote their self-control; (c) to promote their independence.

In establishing classroom discipline, all three elements are equally important and separating them would distort the requirement; consequently, you will note in the lexicon that the entry for 'Discipline' contains the full wording of Q31.

Finally, the Standards descriptions have been made more personal by substituting 'your' for 'their' and 'you' for 'they'. Although the Standards are expressed impersonally, they have implications for every individual trainee's practice and, ultimately, success in gaining Qualified Teacher Status. In the end, therefore, the process of being evaluated against the Standards is unique to each trainee because every school placement situation is subtly different in kind and an interpretation of achieving them has to take account of circumstances. For instance, the first part of Q19 states: *Know how to make effective personalised provision for those they teach, including those for whom English is an additional language*, which is going to be far easier to demonstrate when teaching in a multilingual inner-city school than in a village setting where few if any children speak a language other than English. If you do not have much or any chance to work directly with children for whom English is an additional language, you may principally be judged on (say) your response to a written task or in one-to-one conversation with a tutor or teacher, who will act as a professional witness (PW).

To use the lexicon, simply look up the key word in which you have a particular interest and read the Standards statements that are listed. You are then advised to consider the extent to which you have fully met or partly met or not begun to meet the requirements, how you can provide evidence to confirm it and what action you intend to take to address the situation.

Overview of the Standards

The Standards are organised under three main headings, each of which begins with 'Professional'; thus: Professional attributes; Professional knowledge and understanding; Professional skills. The full list is set out below, with the relevant Q-numbers.

Professional attributes
- Relationships with children and young people (Q1–2)
- Frameworks (Q3)
- Communicating and working with others (Q4–6)
- Personal professional development (Q7–9)

Professional knowledge and understanding
- Teaching and learning (Q10)
- Assessment and monitoring (Q11–13)
- Subjects and curriculum (Q14–15)
- Literacy, numeracy and ICT (Q16–17)
- Achievement and diversity (Q18–20)
- Health and wellbeing (Q21)

Professional skills
- Planning (Q22–24)
- Teaching (Q25)
- Assessing, monitoring and giving feedback (Q26–28)
- Reviewing teaching and learning (Q29)
- Learning environment (Q30–31)
- Teamwork and collaboration (Q32–33)

Standards lexicon

Ability/ability range
Q14: Teach effectively across the age and ability range
Q15: Know curricula, frameworks and initiatives applicable to age and ability
Q22: Plan for progression across the age and ability range
Q25: Teach lessons and sequences of lessons across the age and ability range
Q25d: The ability to manage the learning of individuals, groups and classes

Accurate
Q27: Provide accurate and constructive feedback to pupils

Achieve
Q1: Ensure children achieve their potential
Q10: Provide opportunities for all children to achieve their potential

Achievement
Q18, 19, 20: Achievement and diversity

Activities
Q17: Wider professional activities

Additional language
Q19: Make effective personalised provision for pupils for whom English is an additional language

Advice
Q9: Act upon advice from tutors and colleagues

Age
Q14: Teach effectively across the age and ability range
Q15: Know curricula, frameworks and initiatives applicable to age and ability
Q22: Plan for progression across the age and ability range
Q25: Teach lessons and sequences of lessons across the age and ability range

Apply
Q25b: Enable children to apply new knowledge, understanding and skills

Approaches
Q12: Know a range of approaches to assessment

Assess
Q26b: Assess learning needs to set challenging learning objectives

Assessment
Q11: Know the assessment requirements and arrangements for the curriculum areas being taught
Q12: Know a range of approaches to assessment
Q26a: Make effective use of a range of assessment, monitoring and recording strategies

Attainment

Q5: Recognise and respect the contributions made by colleagues, parents and carers to raise levels of children's attainment
Q13: Use statistical information to raise levels of pupil attainment
Q27: Provide timely, accurate and constructive feedback on children's attainment

Attitudes

Q2: Demonstrate positive attitudes and behaviour

Behaviour

Q2: Demonstrate positive attitudes and behaviour
Q10: Have knowledge and understanding of behaviour management strategies
Q31: Establish a clear framework for discipline to manage children's behaviour constructively

Carers

Q4: Communicate effectively with carers
Q5: Recognise and respect the contributions made by carers to raise levels of pupil attainment

Changes

Q21b: Know how to identify and support children whose progress, development or well-being is affected by changes or difficulties in their personal circumstances

Children

Q1: Have high expectations of children
Q2: Demonstrate positive attitudes and behaviour to children
Q4: Communicate effectively with children
Q5: Recognise and respect the contributions made by colleagues, parents and carers to raise levels of children's attainment

Classroom

Q29: Evaluate the impact of your teaching on children's progress and modify your classroom practice where necessary

Coaching

Q9: Act upon advice and feedback and be open to coaching and mentoring

Collaboration

Q6: Have a commitment to collaboration and co-operative working
Q32: Working with colleagues and sharing effective practice
Q33: Ensuring that colleagues are involved in supporting pupil learning and understand their roles

Colleagues: see Q32, 33 under 'Collaboration'

Collective

Q3b: Be aware of the policies and practices of the workplace and share in collective responsibility for your implementation

Communicate
Q4: Communicate effectively with children, young people, colleagues, parents and carers

Concepts
Q25b: In teaching: build on prior knowledge, develop concepts and processes

Consolidate
Q24: Plan homework or other out-of-class work to sustain children's progress and to extend and consolidate learning

Constructive/constructively
Q1: Establish fair, respectful, trusting, supportive and constructive relationships with pupils
Q8: Have a creative and constructively critical approach towards innovation
Q27: Provide timely, accurate and constructive feedback on children's attainment
Q31: Manage children's behaviour constructively

Context
Q7b: Identify priorities for your early professional development in the context of induction
Q30: Identify opportunities for children to learn in out-of-school contexts

Creative
Q8: see under 'Constructive'

Critical
Q8. Have a creative and constructively critical approach towards innovation

Cultural
Q18: Understand how the progress and wellbeing of children are affected by cultural influences

Curriculum/curricula
Q11: Know the assessment requirements and arrangements for the subjects/curriculum areas you are trained to teach
Q14: Have a secure knowledge and understanding of your subjects/curriculum areas and related pedagogy
Q15: Know curricula, frameworks and initiatives applicable to age and ability
Q22: Demonstrate secure subject/curriculum knowledge

Demonstrate
Q2: Demonstrate positive attitudes and behaviour
Q22: Plan for progression and demonstrate secure subject/curriculum knowledge
Q25d: Demonstrate the ability to manage the learning of individuals, groups and whole classes

Design
Q22: Design effective learning sequences within lessons and across series of lessons
Q23: Design opportunities for children to develop their literacy, numeracy and ICT skills

Develop/developing/development

Q5: Recognise and respect the contribution that colleagues, parents and carers can make to children's development

Q7a: Take responsibility for identifying and meeting your developing professional needs

Q7b: Identify priorities for your early professional development in the context of induction

Q18: Understand how children and young people develop

Q21a: Know how to identify and support children and young people whose progress, development or wellbeing is affected by changes or difficulties in their personal circumstances

Q23: Design opportunities for children to develop literacy, numeracy and ICT skills

Q25b: In teaching: build on prior knowledge, develop concepts and processes

Q27: Provide timely, accurate and constructive feedback on children's areas for development

Q32: Share the development of effective practice with team members

Disabilities

Q19: Know how to make effective personalised provision for those who have disabilities

Q20: Know and understand the roles of colleagues with specific responsibility for children with disabilities

Discipline

Q31: Establish a clear framework for classroom discipline to manage learners' behaviour constructively and promote their self-control and independence

Discussion

Q25c: Adapt your language to suit the children you teach, introducing new ideas and concepts clearly, and using explanations, questions, discussions and plenaries effectively

Diversity

Q19: Know how to take practical account of diversity and promote equality and inclusion in your teaching

Q25a: Use a range of teaching strategies and resources, including e-learning, taking practical account of diversity and promoting equality and inclusion

EAL

Q19: Know how to make effective personalised provision for those they teach, including those for whom English is an additional language

Educational

Q1: Have high expectations of children and young people including a commitment to ensuring that they can achieve their full educational potential

Q19: Know how to make effective personalised provision for those who have special educational needs

Q20: Know and understand the roles of colleagues with responsibility for children with special educational needs

Effective/effectively/effectiveness

Q4: Communicate effectively with carers

Q13: Know how to use local and national statistical information to evaluate the effectiveness of your teaching

Q14: Have a secure knowledge and understanding of your subjects/curriculum areas and related pedagogy to enable you to teach effectively

Q19: Know how to make effective personalised provision for those you teach

Q22: Design effective learning sequences within lessons and across series of lessons

Q25c: Use explanations, questions, discussions and plenaries effectively

Q26a: Make effective use of a range of assessment, monitoring and recording strategies

Q32: Share the development of effective practice with colleagues

e-learning

Q25a: Use a range of teaching strategies and resources, including e-learning

Enable

Q14: Have a secure knowledge and understanding of your subjects/curriculum areas and related pedagogy to enable you to teach effectively across the age and ability range for which you are trained

Q25b: Enable children to apply new knowledge, understanding and skills and meet learning objectives

Equality

Q19: Know how to take practical account of diversity and promote equality and inclusion in your teaching

Q25a: Take practical account of diversity and promote equality and inclusion

Establish

Q1: Establish fair, respectful, trusting, supportive and constructive relationships with children

Q30: Establish a purposeful and safe learning environment conducive to learning

Q31: Establish a clear framework for classroom discipline to manage children's behaviour constructively and promote their self-control and independence

Ethnic

Q18: Understand how children are affected by ethnic influences

Evaluate

Q13: Know how to use local and national statistical information to evaluate the effectiveness of your teaching

Q29: Evaluate the impact of your teaching on the progress of all children

Examinations

Q11: Know the assessment requirements and arrangements for the subjects/curriculum areas you are trained to teach, including those relating to public examinations

Expectations

Q1: Have high expectations of children, including a commitment to ensuring that they can achieve their full educational potential

Explanations

Q25c: Use explanations, questions, discussions and plenaries effectively

Extend
Q24: Plan homework or other out-of-class work to extend and consolidate learning

Feedback
Q9: Act upon advice and feedback
Q26: Assessing, monitoring and giving feedback [main heading]
Q27: Provide timely, accurate and constructive feedback on children's areas for development

Formative
Q12: Know a range of approaches to assessment, including the importance of formative assessment

Framework
Q3a: Be aware of the professional duties of teachers and the statutory framework within which they work
Q15: Know and understand the relevant statutory and non-statutory curricula and frameworks
Q31: Establish a clear framework for classroom discipline

Groups
Q25d: Demonstrate the ability to manage the learning of groups

Guidance
Q21a: Be aware of the current legal requirements, national policies and guidance on the safeguarding and promotion of the wellbeing of children

Guide
Q28: Support and guide children to reflect on their learning

Health
Q21a, b: Health and wellbeing [main heading]

Homework
Q24: Plan homework or other out-of-class work to sustain children's' progress and to extend and consolidate learning

ICT
Q16: Pass the professional skills tests in numeracy, literacy and information and communications technology (ICT)
Q17: Know how to use skills in literacy, numeracy and ICT to support your teaching and wider professional activities
Q23: Design opportunities for children to develop their literacy, numeracy and ICT skills

Ideas
Q25c: Adapt your language to suit the children you teach, introducing new ideas and concepts clearly

Identify

Q7a: Reflect on and improve your practice, and take responsibility for identifying and meeting your developing professional needs

Q7b: Identify priorities for your early professional development in the context of induction

Q21b: Know how to identify and support children whose progress, development or wellbeing is affected by changes or difficulties in their personal circumstances

Q28: Support and guide children to reflect on their learning, identify the progress they have made and identify their emerging learning needs

Q30: Identify opportunities for children to learn in out-of-school contexts

Q32: Work as a team member and identify opportunities for working with colleagues

Impact

Q29: Evaluate the impact of your teaching on the progress of all children

Improve/improvements

Q7a: Reflect on and improve your practice

Q8: Be prepared to adapt your practice where benefits and improvements are identified

Inclusion

Q19: Know how to take practical account of diversity and promote equality and inclusion in your teaching

Q25a: Take practical account of diversity and promote equality and inclusion

Independence

Q31: Establish a clear framework for classroom discipline to promote pupil independence

Induction

Q7b: Identify priorities for your early professional development in the context of induction

Influences

Q18: Understand that children's progress and wellbeing are affected by a range of developmental, social, religious, ethnic, cultural and linguistic influences

Initiatives

Q15: Know and understand relevant initiatives applicable to the age and ability range for which they are trained

Innovation

Q8: Have a creative and constructively critical approach towards innovation

Involved

Q33: Ensure that colleagues working with you are appropriately involved in supporting learning

Knowledge

Q10: Have a knowledge and understanding of a range of teaching, learning and behaviour management strategies

Q14: Have a secure knowledge and understanding of your subjects/curriculum areas and related pedagogy

Q22: Demonstrate secure subject/curriculum knowledge

Q25b: When teaching: build on prior knowledge, develop concepts and processes and enable children to apply new knowledge

Language
Q19: Know how to make effective personalised provision for those for whom English is an additional language
Q25c: When teaching: adapt your language to suit the children you teach

Learners
Note: The word 'learners' in the original set of Standards has been replaced by 'children'. Owing to the frequency of the word 'children', it does not have an individual entry.

Learning
Q10: Have a knowledge and understanding of learning strategies and know how to use and adapt them, including how to personalise learning
Q20: Know and understand the roles of colleagues with specific responsibilities for individual learning needs
Q22: Design effective learning sequences within lessons and across series of lessons
Q24: Plan homework or other out-of-class work to sustain children's progress and to extend and consolidate their learning
Q25a: Use a range of teaching strategies and resources, including e-learning
Q25b: Enable children to meet learning objectives
Q25d: Demonstrate the ability to manage the learning of individuals, groups and whole classes
Q26b: Assess the learning needs of those you teach in order to set challenging learning objectives
Q28: Support and guide children to reflect on their learning, identify the progress they have made and identify their emerging learning needs
Q30: Establish a purposeful and safe learning environment conducive to learning
Q33: Ensure that colleagues working with you are appropriately involved in supporting learning

Legal
Q21a: Be aware of the current legal requirements, national policies and guidance on the safeguarding and promotion of the wellbeing of children and young people

Lesson
Q22: Design effective learning sequences within lessons and across series of lessons
Q25a–d: Teach lessons and sequences of lessons across the age and ability range for which you are being trained

Levels
Q5: Recognise and respect the contribution that colleagues, parents and carers can make in raising children's levels of attainment
Q13: Know how to use local and national statistical information to raise levels of attainment

Linguistic
Q18: Understand that the progress and wellbeing of children are affected by a range of linguistic influences

Literacy

Q16: Have passed the professional skills tests in literacy

Q17: Know how to use skills in literacy, numeracy and ICT to support your teaching and wider professional activities

Q23: Design opportunities for children to develop their literacy skills

Manage

Q10: Have a knowledge and understanding of a range of behaviour management strategies and know how to use and adapt them

Q25d: Demonstrate the ability to manage the learning of individuals, groups and whole classes

Q31: Establish a clear framework for classroom discipline to manage children's behaviour constructively and promote their self-control and independence

Meeting

Q7a: Take responsibility for identifying and meeting your developing professional needs

Mentoring

Q9: Act upon advice and feedback and be open to coaching and mentoring

Modify

Q25d: Modify your teaching to suit the stage of the lesson

Q29: Evaluate the impact of your teaching on the progress of all children and modify your planning and classroom practice where necessary

Monitor/monitoring

Q13: Know how to use local and national statistical information to monitor the progress of those you teach and to raise levels of attainment

Q26a: Make effective use of a range of assessment, monitoring and recording strategies

Needs

Q7a: Take responsibility for identifying and meeting your developing professional needs

Q19: Know how to make effective personalised provision for those who have special educational needs and disabilities and other individual learning needs

Q26b: Assess the learning needs of those you teach in order to set challenging learning objectives

Q28: Support and guide children to identify their emerging learning needs

Numeracy (maths)

Q16: Have passed the professional skills tests in numeracy

Q17: Know how to use skills in literacy, numeracy and ICT to support your teaching and wider professional activities

Q23: Design opportunities for children to develop their numeracy skills

Objectives

Q25b: Enable children to meet learning objectives

Q26b: Assess the learning needs of those you teach in order to set challenging learning objectives

Opportunities

Q10: Know how to provide opportunities for all children to achieve their potential
Q23: Design opportunities for children to develop their literacy, numeracy and ICT skills
Q30: Identify opportunities for children to learn in out-of-school contexts
Q32: Identify opportunities for working with colleagues, sharing the development of effective practice with them

Out-of-class

Q24: Plan homework or other out-of-class work to sustain children's progress and to extend and consolidate their learning

Parents

Q4: Communicate effectively with parents and carers
Q5: Recognise and respect the contribution that parents and carers can make to the development and wellbeing of children and to raising their levels of attainment

Pedagogy

Q14: Have a secure knowledge and understanding of your subjects/curriculum areas and related pedagogy

Personal (professional development) Q7–9

Personalise

Q10: Know how to personalise learning

Plan/planning

Q22: Plan for progression across the age and ability range for which you are trained
Q24: Plan homework or other out-of-class work to sustain children's progress and to extend and consolidate their learning
Q29: Evaluate the impact of your teaching on the progress of all children and modify your planning and classroom practice where necessary

Plenaries

Q25c: Use explanations, questions, discussions and plenaries effectively

Policies

Q3b: Be aware of the policies and practices of the workplace and share in collective responsibility for their implementation
Q21a: Be aware of the current legal requirements, national policies and guidance on the safeguarding and promotion of the wellbeing of children and young people

Potential

Q1: Have high expectations of children, including a commitment to ensuring that they can achieve their full educational potential
Q10: Provide opportunities for all children to achieve their potential

Practice/practices

Q3b: Be aware of the policies and practices of the workplace and share in collective responsibility for their implementation

Q7a: Reflect on and improve your practice, and take responsibility for identifying and meeting your developing professional needs

Q8: Be prepared to adapt your practice where benefits and improvements are identified

Q29: Evaluate the impact of your teaching on the progress of all children and modify your planning and classroom practice where necessary

Q32: Identify opportunities for working with colleagues, sharing the development of effective practice with them

Prior (knowledge)

Q25b: Build on prior knowledge, develop concepts and processes

Priorities

Q7b: Identify priorities for your early professional development in the context of induction

Professional/personal

- Q7–9 (Personal professional development)
- Q10–15 (Professional knowledge and understanding)
- Q22–26 (Professional skills)

Q3a: Be aware of the professional duties of teachers and the statutory framework within which they work

Q7a: Take responsibility for identifying and meeting your developing professional needs

Q7b: Identify priorities for your early professional development in the context of induction

Q16: Have passed the professional skills tests in numeracy, literacy and information and communications technology (ICT)

Q17: Know how to use skills in literacy, numeracy and ICT to support your teaching and wider professional activities

Progress/progression

Q13: Know how to use local and national statistical information to evaluate the effectiveness of your teaching, monitor the progress of those you teach and to raise levels of attainment

Q18: Understand that the progress and wellbeing of children are affected by a range of influences

Q21b: Know how to identify and support children and young people whose progress, development or wellbeing is affected by changes or difficulties in their personal circumstances

Q22: Plan for progression across the age and ability range for which you are trained

Q24: Plan homework or other out-of-class work to sustain children's progress

Q27: Provide timely, accurate and constructive feedback on children's attainment, progress and areas for development

Q28: Identify the progress children have made

Q29: Evaluate the impact of your teaching on the progress of all children

Promote

Q19: Promote equality and inclusion in your teaching

Q31: Promote children's self-control and independence

Promotion

Q21a: Be aware of the current legal requirements, national policies and guidance on the safeguarding and promotion of the wellbeing of children

Provision
Q19: Know how to make effective personalised provision for those you teach

Public examinations
Q11: Know the assessment requirements and arrangements for the subjects/curriculum areas you are trained to teach, including those relating to public examinations

Purposeful
Q30: Establish a purposeful and safe learning environment conducive to learning

Questions
Q25c: Use questions effectively

Raise/raising
Q5: Recognise and respect the contribution that colleagues, parents and carers can make to raising children's levels of attainment
Q13: Know how to use local and national statistical information to raise levels of attainment

Range
Q10: Have a knowledge and understanding of a range of teaching, learning and behaviour management strategies
Q12: Know a range of approaches to assessment, including the importance of formative assessment
Q14: Teach effectively across the age and ability range for which you are trained
Q15: Know and understand relevant initiatives applicable to the age and ability range for which you are trained
Q18: Understand how children are affected by a range of developmental, social, religious, ethnic, cultural and linguistic influences
Q22: Plan for progression across the age and ability range for which you are trained
Q25a: Use a range of teaching strategies and resources, including e-learning
Q26a: Make effective use of a range of assessment, monitoring and recording strategies

Recording
Q26a: Make effective use of a range of assessment, monitoring and recording strategies

Reflect
Q7a: Reflect on and improve your practice
Q28: Support and guide children to reflect on their learning

Relationships
Q1–2: Relationships with children and young people [main heading]
Q1: Establish fair, respectful, trusting, supportive and constructive relationships with children

Religious
Q18: Understand that the progress and wellbeing of children are affected by religious influences

Resources
Q25a: Teach lessons and sequences of lessons across the age and ability range for which you are trained in which you use a range of teaching strategies and resources

Responsibility
Q3b: Be aware of the policies and practices of the workplace and share in collective responsibility for their implementation
Q7a: Take responsibility for identifying and meeting your developing professional needs
Q20: Know and understand the roles of colleagues with specific responsibilities

Reviewing
Q29: (Subheading, 'Reviewing teaching and learning') Evaluate the impact of your teaching on the progress of all children and modify your planning and classroom practice where necessary

Roles
Q20: Know and understand the roles of colleagues with specific responsibilities
Q33: Ensure that colleagues working with you understand the roles they are expected to fulfil

Safe/safeguarding
Q30: Establish a purposeful and safe learning environment conducive to learning
Q21: Be aware of guidance on the safeguarding and promotion of the wellbeing of children

Secure
Q14: Have a secure knowledge and understanding of your subjects/curriculum areas and related pedagogy
Q22: When planning: demonstrate secure subject/curriculum knowledge

Self-control
Q31: Establish a clear framework for classroom discipline to promote children's self-control and independence

Sequences
Q22: When planning: design effective learning sequences within lessons and across series of lessons
Q25: Teach lessons and sequences of lessons across the age and ability range for which you are trained

Set
Q26b: Assess the learning needs of those you teach in order to set challenging learning objectives

Skills
Q22–33: Subheading, 'Professional skills'
Q16: Have passed the professional skills tests in numeracy, literacy and ICT
Q17: Know how to use skills in literacy, numeracy and ICT to support your teaching and wider professional activities
Q23: Design opportunities for children to develop their literacy, numeracy and ICT skills
Q25b: Enable children to apply new knowledge, understanding and skills

Social

Q18: Understand how children are affected by a range of social influences

Special educational needs

Q19: Know how to make effective personalised provision for who have special educational needs

Q20: Know and understand the roles of colleagues with specific responsibilities for children with special educational needs

Specialist

Q21b: Know when to refer children to colleagues for specialist support

Stage

Q25d: Demonstrate the ability to modify your teaching to suit the stage of the lesson

Statistical information

Q13: Know how to use local and national statistical information to evaluate the effectiveness of your teaching, to monitor the progress of those you teach and to raise levels of attainment

Statutory/non-statutory

Q15: Know and understand the relevant statutory and non-statutory curricula and frameworks

Strategies

Q10: Have a knowledge and understanding of a range of teaching, learning and behaviour management strategies

Q15: Know and understand the relevant statutory and non-statutory curricula and frameworks, including those provided through the National Strategies

Q25a: Use a range of teaching strategies and resources

Q26a: Make effective use of a range of assessment, monitoring and recording strategies

Subject/subjects

Q11: Know the assessment requirements and arrangements for the subjects/curriculum areas you are trained to teach

Q14: Have a secure knowledge and understanding of your subjects/curriculum areas

Q15: Know and understand the relevant statutory and non-statutory curricula and frameworks, including those provided through the National Strategies, for your subjects/curriculum areas

Q22: Demonstrate secure subject/curriculum knowledge

Support/supporting/supportive

Q1: Establish fair, respectful, trusting, supportive and constructive relationships with children

Q17: Know how to use skills in literacy, numeracy and ICT to support your teaching and wider professional activities

Q21b: Know how to identify and support children whose progress, development or well-being is affected by changes or difficulties in their personal circumstances and when to refer them to colleagues for specialist support

Q28: Support and guide children to reflect on their learning, identify the progress they have made and identify their emerging learning needs

Q33: Ensure that colleagues working with you are appropriately involved in supporting learning

Teach/teaching
Q10: Have a knowledge and understanding of a range of teaching strategies and know how to use and adapt them
Q11: Know the assessment requirements and arrangements for the subjects/curriculum areas you are trained to teach
Q13: Know how to use local and national statistical information to evaluate the effectiveness of your teaching and monitor the progress of those you teach
Q14: Have a secure knowledge and understanding of your subjects/curriculum areas and related pedagogy to enable you to teach effectively across the age and ability range for which you are (being) trained
Q25c: Adapt your language to suit the children you teach
Q26b: Assess the learning needs of those you teach in order to set challenging learning objectives

Teacher
Q3a: Be aware of the professional duties of teachers

Teaching
Q10–21: Sub-heading, 'Teaching and learning'
Q10: Have a knowledge and understanding of a range of teaching strategies
Q17: Know how to use skills in literacy, numeracy and ICT to support your teaching
Q19: Know how to make effective personalised provision for those you teach and to take practical account of diversity and promote equality and inclusion in your teaching
Q25a Use a range of teaching strategies and resources, including e-learning
Q25d: Modify your teaching to suit the stage of the lesson
Q29: Evaluate the impact of your teaching on the progress of all children

Team
Q32: Work as a team member and identify opportunities for working with colleagues

Understand/understanding
Q10: Have a knowledge and understanding of a range of teaching, learning and behaviour management strategies
Q14: Have a secure knowledge and understanding of your subjects/curriculum areas and related pedagogy
Q15: Know and understand the relevant statutory and non-statutory curricula and frameworks
Q18: Understand how children develop
Q20: Know and understand the roles of colleagues with specific responsibilities
Q25b: Enable children to apply new knowledge, understanding and skills and meet learning objectives
Q33: Understand the roles that colleagues are expected to fulfil

Values
Q2: Demonstrate the positive values you expect from children and young people

Wellbeing

Q5: Recognise and respect the contribution that colleagues, parents and carers can make to the development and wellbeing of children

Q18: Understand that the progress and wellbeing of children are affected by a range of developmental, social, religious, ethnic, cultural and linguistic influences

Q21a: Be aware of the current legal requirements, national policies and guidance on the safeguarding and promotion of children's wellbeing

Q21b: Know how to identify and support children whose progress, development or well-being is affected by changes or difficulties in their personal circumstances

Whole (classes)

Q25d: Demonstrate the ability to manage the learning of whole classes

Work/working

Q3a: Be aware of the professional duties of teachers and the statutory framework within which they work.

Q3b: Be aware of the policies and practices of the workplace and share in collective responsibility for their implementation

Q6: Have a commitment to collaboration and co-operative working

Q24: Plan homework or other out-of-class work to sustain children's progress and to extend and consolidate their learning

Q32: Work as a team member and identify opportunities for working with colleagues

Q33: Ensure that colleagues working with you are appropriately involved in supporting learning

MOVING *ON* > > > > > > MOVING *ON* > > > > > > MOVING *ON*

There is more to being a teacher than conforming to the Standards, as the previous chapters in this book attempt to make clear. In particular, it is noteworthy that the word 'education' does not feature anywhere in the Standards, either in the introduction or the descriptions. However, the absence of this key word does not mean that you have to disregard it. The reasons you became a teacher were to help fashion children's thinking; give each child memorable moments; and inculcate a sense of social responsibility and compassion. Education has a moral purpose – to know *why* – as well as a strictly academic one – to know *what* – so in the process of meeting the Standards you also need to keep ethical issues firmly at the heart of all you think and do.

FURTHER READING FURTHER READING **FURTHER READING** FURTHER READING

Denby, N. (2008) *How to Achieve your QTS*. London: Sage.

Overall, L. and Sangster, M. (2007) *Primary Teachers' Handbook*. London: Continuum.

9
Meeting the Standards

Learning outcomes

To understand:

- the component parts of Standards for which evidence has to be provided;
- forms of evidence to confirm that Standards have been achieved.

Demonstrating and confirming the Standards

Gaining evidence to meet the Q-Standards during school experience is a dual process: the trainee teacher demonstrating competence, together with a tutor or supervising teacher confirming that the evidence is valid. In this regard it should be noted that evidence is not the same as proof. Whereas *evidence* allows for professional judgement, *proof* is absolute and incontestable. The purpose of this chapter is to offer specific suggestions about ways you can provide evidence that you are 'meeting' the Standards.

We noted in Chapter 1 of this book that in seeking evidence for Standards compliance, it is rarely satisfactory to cite a single piece of confirmatory evidence that a particular standard has been dealt with. In fact, it is most unlikely that a single piece of evidence will suffice to demonstrate that you have fully complied with the requirements of a Standard. In practice, evidence of meeting the majority of Standards is a cumulative process, based on a number of instances of good practice, including (crucially) recent ones. You should also note that although all the Standards have to be met eventually, it is only during the final school placement that you are expected to achieve total compliance.

The principle of evidence being up to date and cumulative has implications for tutors when they have the responsibility for confirming it. The majority of 'hard' evidence is confirmed in one or more of three ways. The first and most common way is through lesson observation feedback (LOF), whereby key points are recorded by the observer and given to the trainee after the session to form the basis for discussion and advice about improving areas of practice. The second principal form of 'hard' evidence is by means of information in the trainee teacher's teaching file. We can refer to this form of evidence as ITF, which stands for information in teaching file. ITF confirmation will normally be concerned with planning and non-teaching Standards (e.g. working alongside a subject leader or observing someone teaching in a different key stage/foundation stage) rather than qualities of conduct and competence that are directly observable through classroom teaching. Thirdly, some actions are not confirmed by reference to classroom observation or teaching file entries but by a tutor or teacher who has been present and can act as a professional witness (PW). For example, you may spend time speaking to a mother about her child's behaviour or progress with the class teacher nearby, who can confirm the event and 'initial' against that particular area of competence – in this instance relating to an element of Q4 (*Communicate effectively with children, young people, colleagues, parents and carers*). Over time, you are able to garner all these different sources of evidence and link them to the appropriate Standards, as described below.

It is also worth noting that the verbs used in the statements give a firm indication about the kind of evidence that might be appropriate. For example, in Q3b (*Be aware of the policies and practices of the workplace*) the emphasis is upon 'awareness', whereas in Q13 the verb use is 'know how to'; thus: *Know how to monitor the progress of those you teach*. Many statements are unambiguous about what you need to do; for example, under 'Relationships', Q1 states that you must, *Establish fair, respectful, trusting, supportive and constructive relationships with children*. By contrast, under 'Reflect', Q7a requires that you: *Reflect on and improve your practice*, which is much more difficult to demonstrate and will require a combination of evidence, such as annotated lesson plans, being able to discuss the issues with a tutor, and teaching in such a way that it is clear to an observer that you have responded to advice about appropriate strategies. Consequently, evidence for each of the Standards listed below is allocated one or more of the following acronyms: LOF (lesson observation feedback); ITF (information in teaching file); PW (professional witness).

To facilitate ease of access to each Q-Standard, they are divided into their component parts and, as explained in the previous chapter, references to 'young people' have been omitted, the word 'learners' has been replaced by 'children' to emphasise the child-orientated nature of primary education and the statements have been personalised.

Warning!

The purpose of the present and the final chapter is to alert you to the requirements contained in the Q-Standards. Familiarisation with the content and a close consideration of the extent to which you are succeeding in meeting the requirements will empower you and help to ensure that you keep focused on key issues and aspects of classroom practice, liaison with parents and staff membership. However, you will not benefit from such scrutiny if you allow yourself to become obsessed by the process of providing evidence and demonstrating your worth to such an extent that you behave artificially and suppress your spontaneity and creativity. During active teaching there is a balance to be struck between making an effort to improve a weaker area of practice and enhancing what you are already good at doing. Similarly, time spent on planning, paperwork and creating resources should not lead to exhaustion and overshadow the priority need to stay fresh and alert in school. The rule of thumb is that you should master the Standards but never allow them to master you.

Professional attributes

Relationships with children and young people

Q1: Have high expectations of children, including a commitment to ensuring that they can achieve their full educational potential and to establishing fair, respectful, trusting, supportive and constructive relationships with them.

Component parts of Q1
- **Have high expectations of children**: achieved through being clear in your mind about what you expect children to learn and making it clear to them; helping individuals to set targets for learning; insisting on appropriate standards of presentation and application to the task (LOF/PW).
- **Ensure they can achieve their full potential**: achieved through offering practical support and reassurance; encouraging perseverance; removing the fear of failure; ensuring adequate time and resources to achieve goals (LOF/PW).

- **Establish fair, respectful, trusting, supportive and constructive relationships with them**: achieved through speaking courteously and directly; taking account of individual personality and disposition; explaining patiently; being fair-minded and reasonable; insisting on mutual respect; demonstrating that you like the children; celebrating their achievements (LOF/PW).

> Q2: Demonstrate the positive values, attitudes and behaviour you expect from children.

Component parts of Q2

- **Demonstrate positive values to children**: achieved through exercising patience; fairness and sympathetic treatment; politeness; willingness to see both sides of an argument (LOF/PW).
- **Demonstrate positive attitudes to children**: achieved through responding helpfully; tolerant of sincere mistakes; applauding effort and hard work; trusting; prepared to offer a second chance (LOF/PW).
- **Demonstrate positive behaviour to children**: achieved through being natural; willing to confront wrong; addressing the issue rather than the person; being decisive; enjoying learning; responding joyfully (LOF/PW).

Frameworks

> Q3:
> (a) Be aware of the professional duties of teachers and the statutory framework within which you work.
> (b) Be aware of the policies and practices of the workplace and share in collective responsibility for their implementation.

Component parts of Q3

- **Be aware of the professional duties of teachers**: achieved through gaining information from the General Teaching Council about expectations of teachers, familiarity with the *School Teachers' Pay and Conditions Document 2007* (sections 72.1–72.12) for qualified teachers (see Figure 9.1) (ITF).
- **Be aware of the statutory framework within which teachers work**: achieved through knowing about your own rights and responsibilities in areas of equality of opportunity, health and safety, special educational needs, child protection and teacher employment; familiarity with the five key outcomes for children identified in Every Child Matters (see Figure 9.2) and their implications; awareness of the six areas of the Common Core of Skills and Knowledge for the Children's Workforce (see Figure 9.3) (ITF/PW).
- **Be aware of the policies and practices of the workplace**: achieved through familiarity with school documentation; discussions with subject leaders, SENCO and other significant staff (ITF/PW).
- **Share in the collective responsibility for implementing the policies and practices**: achieved through demonstrating your awareness of the policies and practices in your classroom teaching; offering support for colleagues (LOF).

> Teaching; assessment and reporting duties; communicating and consulting with parents; providing guidance to pupils on educational and social matters; contributing to the preparation and development of teaching material and to pastoral arrangements; participating in national appraisal arrangements and in training and professional development schemes; helping to sustain the discipline and health and safety dimensions of school life; engaging in staff meetings; providing limited 'cover' for absent colleagues.

Figure 9.1 Professional duties of teachers

1. Be healthy.
2. Stay safe.
3. Enjoy and achieve through learning.
4. Make a positive contribution to society.
5. Achieve economic wellbeing.

Figure 9.2 Every Child Matters: key outcomes

The Core Skills and Knowledge relate to:
1. Effective communication and engagement with children, young people and their families and carers.
2. Child and young person development.
3. Safeguarding and promoting the welfare of the child.
4. Supporting transitions.
5. Multi-agency working.
6. Sharing information.

Figure 9.3 Common Core of Skills and Knowledge for the Children's Workforce

Communicating and working with others

Q4: Communicate effectively with children, colleagues, parents and carers.

Component parts of Q4

- **Communicate effectively with children**: achieved through speaking clearly; using appropriate spoken language and vocabulary; providing necessary information and guidance; repeating key messages for the purpose of clarification; using a variety of spoken, visual and kinaesthetic (hands-on) methods (LOF).
- **Communicate effectively with colleagues**: achieved through being adequately informed about the topic of conversation; asking appropriate questions at an appropriate time; finding out from them things that cannot be discovered by other means; offering your own perspectives (PW).
- **Communicate effectively with parents and carers**: achieved through being available for consultation; well-informed about their children's progress; responding helpfully; maintaining confidentiality; noting concerns; offering reassurance; being friendly, bright and personable (ITF/PW).

Q5: Recognise and respect the contribution that colleagues, parents and carers can make to the development and wellbeing of children, and to raising their levels of attainment.

Component parts of Q5

- **Recognise and respect the contribution of colleagues to children's development, wellbeing and attainment**: achieved through close observation of experienced teachers and assistants at work; knowledge of the contribution made by other professionals (such as social workers); liaising helpfully with colleagues; informing assistants of their role in lessons (ITF).
- **Recognise and respect the contribution of parents and carers to children's development, wellbeing and attainment**: achieved by setting sensible and appropriate forms of homework; discussing informally their children's work and progress; communicating by letter or electronic means to inform them of their

children's progress and particular needs; being available (alongside the regular teacher) for parent consultation meetings (ITF/PW).

> Q6: Have a commitment to collaboration and co-operative working.

Component parts of Q6
- **Commitment to co-operative working**: achieved through making yourself available to assist in organising, resourcing and managing the classroom; responding positively to colleagues' requests, advice and direction; respecting all colleagues, regardless of status; sharing expertise freely (e.g. knowledge of IT) (PW).
- **Commitment to collaborative working**: achieved through attendance at team planning meetings; contributing ideas and information at planning meetings; accepting team decisions; implementing decisions wholeheartedly (PW).

Personal professional development

> Q7:
> (a) Reflect on and improve your practice and take responsibility for identifying and meeting your developing professional needs.
> (b) Identify priorities for your early professional development in the context of induction.

Component parts of Q7 a and b
- **Reflect on and improve your practice**: achieved through listing strengths and weaknesses in practical teaching; setting targets for improving weaker features and enhancing stronger features, discussing strategies for improvement with experienced colleagues; monitoring subsequent progress (ITF/PW).
- **Take responsibility for your professional needs**: achieved through maintaining a check list of identified areas, as directed by tutors and mentors; creating an action plan for emerging needs in the short, medium and long term; consulting TDA supplementary information (ITF).
- **Identify induction priorities**: achieved through familiarisation with Induction Standards; completion of Career Entry and Development Profile (CEDP) (ITF).

> Q8: Have a creative and constructively critical approach towards innovation, being prepared to adapt your practice where benefits and improvements are identified.

Component parts of Q8
- **Have a creative and constructively critical approach to innovation**: achieved through a willingness to deviate from conventional lesson structures; incorporating problem-solving and investigative elements into the lesson; inviting children to contribute ideas, impressions and insights; including non-measurable outcomes (e.g. increase in team spirit, level of enthusiasm, etc.) in evaluating the quality of learning (LOF).
- **Adapt your practice appropriately**: achieved through taking account of previous experiences; modifying lesson plans accordingly; offering opportunities for children to benefit from a combination of visual, auditory and kinaesthetic (VAK) learning experiences; involving other adults imaginatively (ITF/LOF).

> Q9: Act upon advice and feedback and be open to coaching and mentoring.

Component parts of Q9

- **Act upon advice and feedback**: achieved through seeking advice from experienced teachers and tutors; entering an active dialogue with them, based on your own, as well as their evaluation of your achievements; identifying key areas for improvement; listing goals and strategies for reaching them; keeping teachers and tutors informed about progress and inviting further comment (ITF/PW/LOF).
- **Be open to coaching and mentoring**: identifying specific areas for improvement where expert guidance is needed (e.g. use of IT software); arranging and organising sessions with the appropriate subject or curriculum leader or teacher; focusing specifically on the skills, knowledge or implementation relating to that area of weakness; expressing gratitude for the support received; demonstrating a willingness to utilise the advice (ITF/PW).

Professional knowledge and understanding

Teaching and learning

Q10: Have a knowledge and understanding of a range of teaching, learning and behaviour management strategies and know how to use and adapt them, including how to personalise learning and provide opportunities for all children to achieve their potential.

Component parts of Q10

- **Have a knowledge and understanding of a range of teaching strategies and know how to use and adapt them**: achieved through using a repertoire of approaches, including didactic, group work, problem-solving and instruction (LOF).
- **Have a knowledge and understanding of a range of learning strategies and know how to use and adapt them**: achieved through taking account of children's preference for visual, auditory (spoken), written and kinaesthetic (hands-on) styles (LOF).
- **Have a knowledge and understanding of behaviour management strategies and know how to use and adapt them**: achieved through implementing the school's agreed policy; responding calmly and fairly; taking account of context; using extensive approval and praise (LOF).
- **Know how to personalise learning**: achieved through identifying children's specific learning needs; organising extra support, coaching or specialised assistance; monitoring progress closely (LOF).
- **Know how to provide opportunities for all children to achieve their potential**: achieved through motivating for learning; providing relevant and satisfying experiences; encouraging children to evaluate their own learning needs; ensuring equal opportunity (time, resources, spoken contributions) (LOF).

Assessment and monitoring

Q11: Know the assessment requirements and arrangements for the subjects/curriculum areas you are trained to teach, including those relating to public examinations.

Component parts of Q11

- **Know the assessment requirements and arrangements for the subjects/curriculum areas you are trained to teach**: achieved through knowledge of the school's assessment system; awareness of when and how children receive formal and informal testing (ITF).
- **Know the assessment requirements and arrangements relating to public examinations**: achieved through awareness of the school's approach in preparing for tests; knowledge of when national tests are held; procedures for receiving, administering and handling test papers (ITF).

> Q12: Know a range of approaches to assessment, including the importance of formative assessment.

Component parts of Q12

- **Know a range of approaches to assessment**: achieved through using questions; eliciting children's existing knowledge through discussion and written format; setting whole-class internal tests; marking work with constructive feedback; discussing progress one to one; encouraging peer and self-assessment where appropriate (LOF).
- **Know the importance of formative assessment**: achieved through giving regular feedback to children about their progress during sessions; clarifying misunderstandings ('wrong end of the stick' thinking) and misconceptions ('muddled thinking'); encouraging children to think by use of open-ended questions (LOF).

> Q13: Know how to use local and national statistical information to evaluate the effectiveness of your teaching, to monitor the progress of those you teach and to raise levels of attainment.

Component parts of Q13

- **Know how to use statistical information to evaluate the effectiveness of your teaching**: achieved through comparing the standard of children's work with other comparable measures over a reasonable period of time (e.g. minimum of half a term) (ITF).
- **Know how to use statistical information to monitor children's progress**: achieved through recording measurable progress over a given period of time (ITF).
- **Know how to use statistical information to raise levels of attainment**: achieved through using data to set targets for attainment (ITF/LOF).

Subjects and curriculum

> Q14: Have a secure knowledge and understanding of your subjects/curriculum areas and related pedagogy to enable you to teach effectively across the age and ability range for which you are trained.

Component parts of Q14

- **Have a secure knowledge and understanding of your subjects/curriculum areas to enable you to teach effectively**: achieved through informed planning; conveying accurate content during lessons; answering children's questions factually (LOF).
- **Have a secure knowledge and understanding of pedagogy to enable you to teach effectively**: achieved through planning lessons that build on previous knowledge and understanding; conveying information verbally and visually; allowing children to explore subject content through play, experimenting and investigation; drawing together threads of learning and reinforcing knowledge and understanding by repetition and use in other contexts (LOF).

> Q15: Know and understand the relevant statutory and non-statutory curricula and frameworks, including those provided through the National Strategies, for your subjects/ curriculum areas, and other relevant initiatives applicable to the age and ability range for which you are [being] trained.

Component parts of Q15

- **Know and understand the relevant statutory and non-statutory curricula and frameworks**: achieved through using the information in planning; able to discuss the implications with colleagues (ITF/PW).
- **Know and understand the National Strategies**: achieved through using the information in planning; able to discuss the implications with colleagues (ITF/PW).
- **Know and understand other relevant initiatives**: achieved through using the information in planning; able to discuss the implications with colleagues (ITF/PW).

Literacy, numeracy and ICT

Q16: Have passed the professional skills tests in numeracy, literacy and information and communications technology (ICT).

Component parts of Q16

- **Passed the professional skills tests in numeracy**
- **Passed the professional skills tests in literacy**
- **Passed the professional skills tests in ICT**

Q17: Know how to use skills in literacy, numeracy and ICT to support your teaching and wider professional activities.

Component parts of Q17

- **Know how to use skills in literacy, numeracy and ICT to support your teaching**: achieved through well-informed planning; explaining concepts clearly; using technology to support teaching and enhance children's learning (ITF/LOF).
- **Know how to use skills in literacy, numeracy and ICT to support your wider professional activities**: achieved through maintaining records of children's progress; keeping an accurate attendance register; summarising information for colleagues; writing notes and reports to parents that are grammatically precise and spelt correctly; conveying information to colleagues, written and spoken (ITF/PW).

Achievement and diversity

Q18: Understand how children develop and that the progress and wellbeing of children is affected by a range of developmental, social, religious, ethnic, cultural and linguistic influences.

Component parts of Q18

- **Understand how children develop and that children's progress is affected by developmental influences**: achieved by organising learning sequentially; taking account of age, maturity and competence when interacting formally and informally with children (ITF/LOF/PW).
- **Understand that children's progress is affected by social influences**: achieved by keeping child observation records; making opportunity to interact with parents and siblings; making allowance for behaviour that reflects home influence; promoting tolerance and respect through integration for activities (ITF/LOF).
- **Understand that children's progress is affected by religious influences**: achieved through becoming informed about significant religious practices, feasts, special events, etc.; making allowance for the impact of religious observance on children's learning (e.g. Ramadan); promoting tolerance and respect; acknowledging festival times (ITF/LOF).

- **Understand that children's progress is affected by ethnic and cultural influences**: achieved through encouraging children to talk about their background and share insights (LOF).
- **Understand that children's progress is affected by linguistic influences**: achieved through making allowance for English as an additional language (EAL) in planning lessons; taking special care over pronunciation and articulation of words; avoiding the use of colloquialisms; employing visual aids (diagrams, pictures, puppets) to reinforce meaning; making allowance for slower speeds of work in completing activities; ensuring that children still have opportunity to engage with creative and stimulating tasks (ITF/LOF).

> Q19: Know how to make effective personalised provision for those you teach, including those for whom English is an additional language or who have special educational needs or disabilities, and how to take practical account of diversity and promote equality and inclusion in your teaching.

Component parts of Q19

- **Know how to make effective personalised provision for those you teach**: achieved through an awareness of children's individual needs; organising for their support in lesson planning and during lessons; liaison with teaching assistants as appropriate; informing the regular teacher of pupil progress; communicating concerns over the welfare of any child with colleagues and maintaining a confidential diary record about such children as appropriate (LOF/PW/ITF).
- **Know how to make effective personalised provision for those for whom English is an additional language or who have special educational needs or disabilities**: achieved through liaising with the language co-ordinator and/or SENCO; organising lessons to include a 'buddy' system; using specialised resources where appropriate (PW/ITF).
- **How to take practical account of diversity and promote equality and inclusion in your teaching**: achieved through ensuring that classroom organisation facilitates clear visibility and hearing for all children; planning work appropriate to academic needs; ensuring fairness in use of equipment; drawing on children's interests; encouraging and welcoming spontaneous dialogue and suggestions (LOF).

> Q20: Know and understand the roles of colleagues with specific responsibilities, including those with responsibility for children with special educational needs and disabilities and other individual learning needs.

Component parts of Q20

- **Know and understand the roles of colleagues with specific responsibilities**: achieved through regular liaison with subject leaders and coordinators, and recording key points from conversations (PW/ITF).
- **Know and understand the roles of colleagues with specific responsibilities for individual learning needs**: achieved through discussions with learning support assistants and recording key points (PW/ITF).

Health and wellbeing

> Q21:
> (a) Be aware of the current legal requirements, national policies and guidance on the safeguarding and promotion of the wellbeing of children.
> (b) Know how to identify and support children whose progress, development or wellbeing is affected by changes or difficulties in their personal circumstances, and when to refer them to colleagues for specialist support.

Component parts of Q21

- **Be aware of the requirements on the safeguarding and promotion of the wellbeing of children**: achieved through noting and summarising key points from recent legislation (ITF).
- **Know how to identify and support struggling children**: achieved through seeking guidance from the SENCO; becoming a keen observer of children and recording instances of abnormal behaviour; reporting to colleagues comments by children indicating stress or abnormality or an abrupt decline in work quality (PW/ITF).

Professional skills

Planning

> Q22: Plan for progression across the age and ability range for which you are trained, designing effective learning sequences within lessons and across series of lessons and demonstrating secure subject/curriculum knowledge.

Component parts of Q22

- **Plan for progression across the age and ability range for which you are trained**: achieved through writing lesson plans that differentiate in terms of vocabulary used, questions asked, tasks allocated and homework set; showing awareness of principal and subsidiary learning objectives within specific lessons and over a period of time (ITF).
- **Design effective learning sequences within lessons and across series of lessons**: achieved through use of assessment criteria that monitor progress across specific lessons and over time; linking ideas and tasks across lessons to incorporate rehearsal of previous learning and introduce 'next steps' (ITF).
- **In planning, demonstrate secure subject/curriculum knowledge**: achieved through reference to key curriculum documents; identifying knowledge you will transmit and knowledge that children will acquire through tasks, electronic means and exploratory learning; fostering of cross-curricular links (e.g. using descriptive language in maths) (ITF).

> Q23: Design opportunities for children to develop their literacy, numeracy and ICT skills.

Component parts of Q23

- **Design opportunities for children to develop their literacy**: achieved through planning learning experiences based on the Literacy Framework; offering children experiences that enhance the scope and depth of their reading, writing, speaking and listening; organising tasks that locate literacy in everyday experiences (ITF).
- **Design opportunities for children to develop their numeracy**: achieved through planning learning experiences based on the Numeracy Framework; offering children experiences that enhance the scope and depth of their work in number; organising tasks that locate numeracy in everyday events (ITF).
- **Design opportunities for children to develop their ICT skills**: achieved through planning opportunities for children to learn operational skills by tuition, supervised experiences and task completion; incorporating ICT into single subject of topic sessions; using IT to discover information, communicate with others and produce summaries of findings (ITF).

> Q24: Plan homework or other out-of-class work to sustain children's progress and to extend and consolidate their learning.

Component parts of Q24

- **Plan homework or other out-of-class work to sustain children's progress**: achieved through setting tasks that relate to lesson contents; reinforcing existing knowledge and understanding; taking account of the fact that not all children come from advantaged home backgrounds; not assuming the availability of a computer; easily assessed and monitored (e.g. at the start of the day) (ITF).
- **Plan homework or other out-of-class work to extend and consolidate children's learning**: achieved through setting tasks that require active thought, using present knowledge creatively (e.g. to discover more about costs of household items) and problem-solving skills (e.g. finding words that rhyme with 'skipping' and putting each one in a sentence) (ITF).

Teaching

> Q25: Teach lessons and sequences of lessons across the age and ability range for which you are trained in which you:
> (a) Use a range of teaching strategies and resources, including e-learning, taking practical account of diversity and promoting equality and inclusion.

Component parts of Q25a

- **Teach, using a range of teaching strategies and resources**: achieved by combining direct instruction, interactive questioning and opportunities for children to talk; taking account of ways that children learn by explaining carefully, repetition, locating ideas in familiar contexts, use of visual aids and diagrammatic representations; employing IT where appropriate to clarify meaning, address misconceptions and modify draft versions (LOF).
- **Teach, taking practical account of diversity**: achieved by using carefully chosen language and vocabulary; ensuring that all children have opportunity to answer questions successfully, respecting and applauding children who try their best to do well; making allowance for children with weaker spoken and written English; providing tasks that facilitate success for all children, albeit at differing levels of attainment (LOF).
- **Teach, promoting equality and inclusion**: achieved by ensuring that all children are treated decently and receive a fair proportion of your time; being patient with slow learners; ensuring learning support provision is in place (LOF).

> Q25 (b) Build on prior knowledge, develop concepts and processes, enable children to apply new knowledge, understanding and skills and meet learning objectives.

Component parts of Q25b

- **Build on children's prior knowledge**: achieved through eliciting from children their existing knowledge and understanding at the start of the lesson and at other key points (LOF).
- **Develop concepts and processes**: achieved through asking questions that probe understanding; inviting children to contribute ideas and perspectives; encouraging play, investigation and problem-solving (LOF).
- **Enable children to apply new knowledge, understanding and skills**: achieved through setting up paired and small-group activities that allow children to explore, consider options, and make and challenge suggestions (LOF).
- **Meet learning objectives**: achieved through orientating your teaching towards key learning goals, while allowing for unanticipated learning opportunities (LOF).

> Q25 (c) Adapt your language to suit the children you teach, introducing new ideas and concepts clearly, and using explanations, questions, discussions and plenaries effectively.

Component parts of Q25c

- **Adapt your language to suit the children you teach**: achieved through speaking carefully, deliberately and using suitable vocabulary for the age range; expressing ideas in different ways; avoiding clichés and colloquialisms; allowing children opportunities to clarify meaning (LOF).
- **Introduce new ideas and concepts clearly**: achieved through gaining children's attention; sounding enthusiastic; linking information with previous learning; locating information in familiar settings (LOF).
- **Use explanations, questions, discussions and plenaries effectively**: achieved through high levels of interaction with children and between children; fostering openness, where mistakes and misunderstandings are treated seriously; inviting contributions; celebrating success (LOF).

> Q25 (d) Demonstrate the ability to manage the learning of individuals, groups and whole classes, modifying your teaching to suit the stage of the lesson.

Component parts of Q25d

- **Demonstrate the ability to manage the learning of individuals**: achieved through knowing and recording the learning history of each child; involving each child in interactive exchanges; making allowance for each child's learning capacity; encouraging each child to be involved in target-setting (ITF/LOF).
- **Demonstrate the ability to manage the learning of groups**: achieved through: organising groups that work together productively; setting tasks that allow for every child's involvement (e.g. collaborative problem-solving); encouraging tolerance, team-spirit and perseverance (LOF).
- **Demonstrate the ability to manage the learning of whole classes**: achieved through showing awareness of every child; using an incisive tone; insisting on attention and responsiveness; praising effort; explaining procedures; being active around the room; ensuring that tasks are appropriate to the age and ability of the children (LOF).

Assessing, monitoring and giving feedback

> Q26:
> (a) Make effective use of a range of assessment, monitoring and recording strategies.
> (b) Assess the learning needs of those you teach in order to set challenging learning objectives.

Component parts of Q26

- **Make effective use of a range of assessment, monitoring and recording strategies**: achieved through ensuring that learning outcomes are linked to assessment criteria; enlisting the help of a TA to note children's responses to questions and engagement with tasks; monitoring and recording measurable progress in regular class work (e.g. completion of set task/in reading/spelling tests, etc.) and homework; using formal tests and levelling of written output to rank progress (ITF/LOF).
- **Assess the learning needs of those you teach in order to set challenging learning objectives**: achieved through checking records of children's previous achievements; eliciting information from children about their present knowledge and understanding (e.g. by using questions); setting tests where appropriate to gain measurable results; setting specific pieces of work to evaluate children's ability to interpret and respond to the task (ITF/LOF).

> Q27: Provide timely, accurate and constructive feedback on children's attainment, progress and areas for development.

Component parts of Q27

- **Provide feedback on children's attainment, progress and areas for development**: achieved through evaluating progress by using children's responses to questions and task completion; discussing with the child areas of his/her learning that need addressing or would benefit from enhancement; offering suggestions or directing the child specifically; providing positive support, resources and reinforcement; commending effort and celebrating successes, large or small (LOF/ITF).

> **Q28:** Support and guide children to reflect on their learning, identify the progress they have made and identify their emerging learning needs.

Component parts of Q28

- **Support and guide children to reflect on their learning**: achieved through discussing individually and in groups how children evaluate their own progress; offering children a format (e.g. a sheet with options of the type, 'I felt very confident/a little unsure/very unsure with this task' and 'I think I succeeded well/ succeeded quite well/needed more help with the task') to complete; organising opportunities for children to share safely their perspectives (e.g. circle time) (ITF/LOF).
- **Identify children's progress and their emerging learning needs**: achieved through maintaining a written record of curriculum coverage; noting common misconceptions and misunderstandings that emerge during discussion and subsequently annotating lesson plans; analysing test results for repeated errors; discussing with individuals how to develop targets for learning (ITF).

Reviewing teaching and learning

> **Q29:** Evaluate the impact of your teaching on the progress of all children, and modify your planning and classroom practice where necessary.

Component parts of Q29

- **Evaluate the impact of your teaching on the progress of all children**: achieved through observing children's enthusiasm and motivation for learning and quality of behaviour; noting the impact of children's confidence to ask questions, persevere with tasks and work co-operatively; assessing the quality of children's spoken language (ability to express themselves clearly, listen carefully to other viewpoints, provide an explanation, hold a discussion, offer an opinion, defend a position, summarise opposing arguments); assess the quality of written work by use of assessment criteria (e.g. ability to convey ideas, accuracy, incorporation of researched information) (ITF/LOF).
- **Modify your planning and classroom practice where necessary**: achieved through discussing with relevant others (e.g. resident teacher, TA, subject leader) strategies for improvement; annotating lesson plans; modifying 'next steps'; adjusting the balance of visual, auditory and kinaesthetic experiences; spending time rehearsing, interpreting and reinforcing learning; writing lesson reviews that focus on (a) your teaching, (b) children's learning (PW/ITF/LOF).

Learning environment

> **Q30:** Establish a purposeful and safe learning environment conducive to learning and identify opportunities for children to learn in out-of-school contexts.

Component parts of Q30

- **Establish a purposeful and safe learning environment conducive to learning**: achieved through being clear about what you want to do during sessions and informing the children; highlighting and guarding against physical dangers; organising rooms to allow for easy access and good visibility; encouraging enterprise, questions, ideas and creativity; celebrating success and commiserating with a lack of it; being open, available, non-judgemental, pleasant, fair and helpful; valuing the child more than the achievement (LOF).

- **Identify opportunities for children to learn in out-of-school contexts**: achieved through liaising with the regular teacher about outdoor curriculum opportunities (including play); identifying locations that provide for extended learning experiences (particularly very local and easily accessible ones); being imaginative about how class-based work can be enhanced by educational visits; investigating the use of technology as a source of information (PW/ITF).

Q31: Establish a clear framework for classroom discipline to manage children's behaviour constructively and promote their self-control and independence.

Component parts of Q31

- **Establish a clear framework for classroom discipline to manage children's behaviour constructively**: achieved through being aware of classroom rules and school policy; organising routines carefully and being explicit about instructions; developing a friendly but no-nonsense approach to relationships with children; insisting on courtesy and good manners; applying sanctions sparingly and fairly (LOF).
- **Promote children's self-control and independence**: achieved through encouraging children to take responsibility for their own actions; teaching children specific strategies and approaches to handling disputes and moments of anger; allowing children to be involved in decisions that have a direct impact on their lives (e.g. taking turns for a popular activity); setting collaborative problem-solving tasks that require team effort and co-operation; allocating responsibilities for classroom duties (LOF).

Team working and collaboration

Q32: Work as a team member and identify opportunities for working with colleagues, sharing the development of effective practice with them.

Component parts of Q32

- **Work as a team member and identify opportunities for working with colleagues**: achieved through attending team and staff meetings; liaising with assistants about their role; offering insights about key issues; keeping a record of issues discussed and decisions made at meetings (PW/ITF).
- **Share the development of effective practice with them**: achieved through being well informed about an area of the curriculum; offering your expertise with humility and patience; making an effort to be helpful (PW).

Q33: Ensure that colleagues working with you are appropriately involved in supporting learning and understand the roles they are expected to fulfil.

Component parts of Q33

- **Ensure that colleagues working with you are appropriately involved in supporting learning**: achieved through finding out about the normal role assumed by teaching assistants; discussing with assistants the way that they perceive their role; making full use of their expertise in lessons; showing a willingness to learn from all colleagues (PW/ITF).

- **Ensure that colleagues understand the roles they are expected to fulfil**: achieved through having regular discussions with assistants and regular teachers; being sensitive to colleagues' priorities and time availability (PW).

MOVING *ON* > > > > > > MOVING *ON* > > > > > > MOVING *ON*

The concept of 'meeting each Standard' does not guarantee that you can teach well any more than being able to use the controls of a car means that you know how to drive. The real art of teaching, and of being a colleague in school, is to employ the skills and attributes demanded by the Standards but to do so with flair and ingenuity. To meet every Standard fully requires a lifetime of working in school, so remind yourself often – and get others to attest to the fact – that you are already doing very well and have the capacity to do even better.

FURTHER READING FURTHER READING FURTHER READING FURTHER READING

Jacques, K. and Hyland, R. (2007) *Professional Studies: Primary and Early Years* (Achieving QTS). Exeter: Learning Matters.

Sewell, K. (2008) *Doing your PGCE at M-level*. London: Sage.

10
The eternal teacher

Learning outcomes

To understand:

- **how the job of a teacher is worthwhile;**
- **what key educationists say about teaching and learning.**

Is it worth making the immense effort to train for teaching, followed by months and years of supreme effort, seemingly impossible demands and knowing that so many children, parents and members of the wider community are depending on you? Many educators have grappled with this question down the centuries and this final chapter consists of a selection of their thoughts. First, Jeffreys (1971) stressed the need for humility:

> If the teacher is ever tempted to mount a pedestal... he should remember that there is always a reciprocity between teacher and learner... Teaching is never all-giving, and learning all-receiving... The teaching–learning relation is one in which both partners are being changed. And the more alive and effective the relation, the more will be given and received on both sides. (p58)

Jackson (1992) argued that teaching enriches lives:

> Teaching, I have come to believe, has enriched my life in ways for which I shall always be grateful. It has caused me to be concerned about the wellbeing of others in much the same way as would a parent or a good friend, though with rather less emotional involvement of course. It has literally forced me to continue the pursuit of knowledge in a formal, scholastic way long past the time when most people leave school and lay their textbooks aside. It has allowed me the luxury of reflection and contemplation far beyond that afforded many who work at other jobs. (p76)

Noddings (1992) stresses the importance of care and mutual support in school:

> Relations with intimate others are the beginning and one of the significant ends of moral life. In supporting environments where children learn how to respond to dependable caring, they can begin to develop the capacity to care. Whether their caring will be directed to the people around them, however, depends in part on the expectations of their teachers; the adults who guide them and serve as models for them. (p52)

And Jesus in the Bible explained that adults have a major responsibility towards children:

> Jesus said, 'Be sure you do not hate one of these little children. I tell you, they have angels who are always looking into the face of My Father in heaven.' (Matthew 18: 3, 4, 10)

O'Quinn and Garrison (2004) use the evocative phrase 'models of love' to define the teacher's role:

By acknowledging the anger, pain, suffering, despair and grief, as well as the joy, wonder, pleasure, laughter and delight of our [pupils'] experiences, we can discard the illusion that we have the ability to force their growth and can instead focus on how we might help them realise their individual potential. Teachers who care in models of love rather than in roles of power accept the risks, allow the vulnerability and permit possibility in communion with their [pupils] without abandoning their obligation to make the classroom safe but not antiseptic. (p59)

And in his famous book about how children fail, Holt (1982) makes a telling comment about the need to see the potential in every child:

Nobody starts off stupid. (p273)

Day (2004) emphasises the fact that teachers can really make a difference to children's lives:

To be passionate about teaching is not only to express enthusiasm but also to enact it in a principled, values-led, intelligent way. All effective teachers have a passion for their subject, a passion for their pupils and a passionate belief that who they are and how they teach can make a difference in their pupils' lives, both in the moment of teaching and in the days, weeks, months and even years afterwards. (p12)

Finally, Manuel and Hughes (2006) have a message of hope for every aspiring teacher:

Teaching and learning, at its core, is about relationships and connections; between teachers and [pupils]; accomplished teachers and new teachers; schools and communities; hopes and their realisation; and aspirations and their fulfilment... In so doing, new teachers may indeed be sustained over the longer term in their dream to teach. (p22)

MOVING *ON* > > > > > > MOVING *ON* > > > > > > MOVING *ON*

The title of this book implies that you, the teacher, do the inspiring; in truth, the children are the *real* inspiration. Be that as it may, fifty years from now, when all else is a dim memory, the impact that you have had on children will live on in the hearts and minds of the pupils who once knew you as 'my teacher'. Now if *that* thought fails to motivate you, it is hard to imagine what will!

REFERENCES REFERENCES **REFERENCES** REFERENCES REFERENCES REFERENCES

Day, C. (2004) *A Passion for Teaching*. Abingdon: Routledge.

Holt, J. (1982) *How Children Fail*. London: Penguin.

Jackson, P. W. (1992) *Untaught Lessons*. New York: Teachers College Press.

Jeffreys, M. V. C. (1971) *Education: Its Nature and Purpose*. London: Allen & Unwin.

Manuel, J. and Hughes, J. (2006) Pre-service teachers' motivations for choosing to teach. *Teacher Development*, 10(1), 5–24.

Noddings, N. (1992) *The Challenge to Care in Schools*. New York: Teachers College Press.

O'Quinn, E. J. and Garrison, J. (2004) Creating loving relationships in the classroom. In: D. Liston and J. Garrison (eds), *Teaching, Learning and Loving*. Abingdon: Routledge.

FURTHER READING FURTHER READING FURTHER READING FURTHER READING

Hayes, D. (2005) A chip off the old block: whatever happened to passion in teaching? *Education 3–13*, 33(2), 31–6.

Holmes, E. (2008) *The Newly Qualified Teacher's Handbook*. Abingdon: Routledge.

McLaren, J. and Hiebert, M. E. (2008) *What's it Like to be a Teacher in an Elementary School?* New York: Edwin Mellen Press.

Richards, C. (ed.) (2001) *Changing English Primary Education*. Stoke on Trent: Trentham Books.

Wright, D. (2006) *Classroom Karma*. London: David Fulton.